Seeking a Newer World:

The
Fort Osage Journals
and
Letters
of
George Sibley
1808-1811

Edited with Introduction by
Jeffrey E. Smith

Lindenwood University Press
St. Charles, Missouri
2003

SEEKING A NEWER WORLD:

THE
FORT OSAGE JOURNALS AND LETTERS
OF
GEORGE SIBLEY
1808-1811.

Lindenwood University
209 S. Kingshighway
St. Charles, MO 63301.

FIRST EDITION

Hardcover ISBN: 0-9747864-0-3
Paperback ISBN: 0-9747864-1-1

Table of Contents

Forward

It is with great pleasure to present the first book published by the Lindenwood University Press. This manuscript covers a critical period in both the life of George Sibley and the national expansion of the trans-Mississippi West. Sibley arrived in St. Louis less than two years after the Louisiana Purchase, and was a key figure in advancing American commerce and ideas westward. He was one of this nation's early pioneers.

Sibley's early years at Fort Osage, as documented in his journals and letters, provide insights into his values-based philosophy. Sibley believed that people should have opportunities and be treated fairly, and that a man's word was his bond. He believed in providing educational opportunities which would enable people to help themselves. He believed in public service, and that one's work should ultimately benefit the people and community around him. Those values seen in the three years spanned by these journals and letters are the values upon which Lindenwood still stands.

Lindenwood University is an independent, public-serving institution founded by George and Mary Sibley in 1827. The importance of American culture and traditional ideals are important facets of a student's education. Lindenwood offers a values-centered education focusing on educating the whole person by combining professional issues with academic pursuits, the social with the intellectual, and the spiritual with the physical. This unique approach was started by the Sibleys and is still maintained by Lindenwood.

Dr. Dennis Spellmann

We hope this book will serve as a useful tool providing a glimpse of not only the dealings of Major George Sibley, but the story of westward expansion as well. Lindenwood stands as heir to a long and distinguished heritage of the frontier, with its founders dedicating their lives to service and education. Mary Sibley taught Native Americans at Fort Osage after moving there as a newlywed in 1815, and continued her work in education in St. Charles. Today, we continue their legacy of providing students with core knowledge and the values needed to be participating members of the American democracy.

Dennis Spellmann, President
Lindenwood University

Preface

When George Sibley left St. Louis in the summer of 1808 to head the new trade operations at Fort Osage, he was embarking on a fourteen-year journey to create a new kind of West. Men like Sibley envisioned the West as a place that would be inhabited by farmers and ranchers, miners and merchants living on farms and in towns. His job, as he and others envisioned it, was to bring order to what they saw as the chaos of the frontier.

Part of that process of imposing order was to "civilize" the people who already lived there: the Native American tribes. One prevalent strain of thinking at the time was that commerce and trade were essential in the process, because they would help the Native Americans develop a western concept of private property which, they figured, was a cornerstone of civilization. Thomas Jefferson saw this concept as the bedrock upon which democratic government stood, a nation of free men living on their own land. The United States government sought to bring this commercial activity—not to mention allying them with the Americans rather than the British—to the native peoples through a series of fortified trade sites called "factories," because they were run by "factors." The idea was that these factors would purchase an array of goods from the Indians, although furs constituted the largest and most lucrative group. They would provide tools, farm implements, consumer goods, ammunition, and other products in exchange. George Sibley was part of this process of taking the United States into the West. Sibley, like William Clark and others in the Missouri Territory, were then "seeking a newer world" that they thought would be fundamentally better.

Seeking a Newer World is a fitting choice to be the first publication released by the Lindenwood University Press. It is the earliest cohesive set of documents detailing the western experiences of George Sibley, who founded the university with his wife Mary. It was the factory system that brought him to the trans-Mississippi West in the first place, and his tenure at Fort Osage, St. Louis, and St. Charles that rooted him in this region. The journals and letters that follow are owned by Lindenwood University in their original form. The letters are written in Sibley's own hand. The journals are the small, leather-bound journalbooks provided by the Office of Indian Trade for factors to record their work.

In recent years, Lindenwood has more actively returned to its frontier roots. It acquired the home of Nathan Boone on the Femme Osage, where his famous father Daniel Boone lived and died. It offers programs, courses, and unique experiences for students in that setting as they gain a different kind of understanding of American values as they were expressed through the westering process. The Lindenwood University Press and this volume are part of that larger mandate of the University.

Acknowledgements

This project really started on the Great Plains, in many ways. After four years with the Great Plains Chautauqua I applied for another round of first-person interpretation on the Plains, and applied to portray William Clark. Even as a bit of a novice on the West, Everett Albers and the board accepted me, which led me west intellectually as well as physically. I owe Everett and the board a great debt of gratitude for pointing me westward. That's why I was reading *Westward with Dragoons*, Clark's journal from his 1808 trip to the future site of Fort Osage edited by former Lindenwood College professor Kate L. Gregg. Her references led me to a series of Sibley manuscripts that were in the "Lindenwood College Collection." Finding George Sibley's journals—the leather-bound ones provided by the United States Office of Indian Trade—that recounted his experiences in the first three years at Fort Osage were quite the thrill; they led to a compelling story of our University's founder before he was in the education business. And, they had never been published.

All this led to the office of Lindenwood University President Dennis Spellmann, who agreed that Lindenwood ought to publish such resources as this as part of our ongoing work to reach into our community in creative and educational ways. So here we are. My thanks to President Spellmann, Provost James Evans, and Dean of Humanities Jann Weitzel for supporting this endeavor.

I have noticed over the years that the people who probably suffered through the most when someone writes a book are the ones who are thanked last. This seems especially strange when considering that it is family who hold our entire lives together while we engage in this intellectual endeavor. Such has been the case with this volume. My wife Kris Runberg Smith and our daughter

Lucy have exhibited the proverbial patience of Job with my absence from family, household activities, sporting events, and leisure time, not to mention tolerating having to live with George Sibley and a host of others who became a bit like long-term house guests. It is at times like this that being married to a fellow historian has even greater benefit, providing help with research problems, sorting through ideas, considering interpretive concepts, and even typing. She has helped me immeasurably; without her help, I would be much older when I finished this project.

Many of my colleagues both at Lindenwood and beyond took time from busy schedules, their own writing, and teaching classes to read materials, offer corrections, and provide new perspectives. Mary Ellen Rowe gave invaluable insights and corrections throughout. Ray Scupin and Donald Heidenreich at Lindenwood and D. Jerome Tweton, professor emeritus at the University of North Dakota, offered valuable readings of parts of this. Colleagues Melissa Qualls, JoEllen Kerksiek, and Bret Wightman took on reading duties that were above and beyond their already-frantic schedules; St. Louis historian Mark Abbott has offered ideas, directions, and prodding when it was most needed. I came to rely on current and former students Leigh Hornbuckle, Amy Toti, and Virginia Ream to pour over typescripts to make sure we hadn't missed any of Sibley's words. One, Derek Herbert, even wrote the biographies herein. This book is a handsome volume, thanks to the time spent over and above the daily work of Larry Ruebling and Darren Collier.

There are many who helped with research along the way, pointing me to new resources, helping me make the climb toward understanding the period and the territory. They provided resources, research aids, ideas, and corrections along the way: Jason Stragman at the Missouri Historical Society; Steve Wilson and John Peterson at the Historic Fort Osage; Christine Montgomery at the State

Historical Society of Missouri; and of course Lindenwood's own John Bell for timely help with title design. Starting a university press is a daunting task, made far easier with the administrative help of Scott Queen and C. W. Stewart.

Having said all that, there remains the possibility that errors may have remained in this book. Of course, I take full responsibility for them.

Jeffrey Smith
St. Louis, Missouri
October, 2003

Notes on Editing

The process of editing historical manuscripts always involves a series of judgments. In the case of George Sibley's journals and letters, the spelling and capitalization are largely his, except in a rare instance where clarity requires a change. Like most people, Sibley had his set of abbreviations he used in his personal writing such as the journals, developed for personal ease and efficiency; however, they are neither to us as contemporary writers. Therefore, I have chosen to write out those abbreviations that might not be immediately apparent in the interest of making the documents easier to read. The dates appear as he wrote them as well, rather than being standardized.

The notes and annotations that accompany the journals and letters are designed to provide the reader with a wider context in which to see Sibley's experience. Like all diarists and writers, Sibley didn't write everything down—there was no need to, after all, if it was something he would remember. He knew the people, so felt no need to further identify them; he knew where places were, and saw no use in giving further details. However, modern readers may not. It is the place of the editor, then, to "fill in the blanks" of the work. In so doing, I have tried to place Sibley's experiences into a wider context as well, so readers gain a greater understanding of not only him but the place and time in which he lived. Some of the most interesting, compelling, and colorful people of territorial Missouri visited and used Fort Osage as part of their roles in "seeking a newer world." Sibley knew them, and probably knew their stories; now we can as well.

Introduction

"George Sibley and the Opening of the Trans-Mississippi West"

By Jeffrey E. Smith

George Sibley seemed a perfect choice to head a government Indian trading post when he arrived in Washington in early 1808. He had family links to both the West and the Jefferson Administration, held a high sense of ethics and moral integrity, kept meticulous bookkeeping records, and was unmarried, which left him free to move to the frontier. Both President Thomas Jefferson and Secretary of War Henry Dearborn, whose department oversaw the Indian Trade operations, knew his father John Sibley; his writings about the Red River Indians and region were among the first eyewitness accounts of the newly acquired Louisiana Territory that Jefferson read. Now, John's 25-year-old son George wanted to head the new government-run trade post—called a "factory" and managed by a "factor"— being established on the Missouri River, just upriver from Fort Belle Fontaine near St. Louis, where he was Assistant Trade Factor. It seemed a perfect fit. The prominence of the fur trade, a changing and evolving view of Indians and Indian treaties involving land cessions, an idealized view of Native Americans as "noble savages" who could and wished to be "civilized," and efforts to thwart the influence of Great Britain in the trans-Appalachian West, all came together in the Jefferson administration years to shape our understanding of Sibley and the Fort Osage[1] experience.

Relations between Euro-American settlers and the native peoples already living in North America were already a source of ongoing tensions when George Sibley arrived in St. Louis in 1805. The problem stemmed from a series of interrelated developments spanning back to earliest European contact. As Americans moved westward, they in turn pushed the Indians farther west. As the Indians moved farther westward, they lived in closer proximity to other tribes, so that more and more people drew sustenance from less and less land. This meant that more people were competing for the limited resources of that land — animals, timber, water, edible plants — for their survival. This problem was exacerbated by the growth of the fur trade, and became acute by the late eighteenth century in Missouri.

France owned the region including Missouri — dubbed Louisiana, for the patron saint of French kings — until the end of the French and Indian War in 1763, when it ceded the territory to Spain under a separate Treaty of Fontainebleu the previous year. But the French retained a prominent presence through its Francophone residents, merchants, and remaining French traders and trappers. Spain added Louisiana to its vast holdings in New Spain, which included present-day Mexico and much of the western United States. The Spaniards had never been as active in the fur trade as the British or French and spent most of their energies just trying to control and govern a territory that was far too big for it to manage. Britain controlled all of Canada and its Northern American coastal colonies all the way to the Mississippi.

When the United States gained its independence from Great Britain in 1783, the new nation spanned from the Atlantic to the Mississippi River, from the Great Lakes to roughly the 30th parallel. Americans poured westward beyond the Appalachian Mountains; George Sibley's father John was one of them, moving to the western commercial capital of New Orleans before the Louisiana Purchase. Others poured into regions such as the Northwest Territory,[2] Kentucky, and Tennessee. Problem was, there were already people living there — lots of them. This was the home of a host of other Native American tribes, some of whom were migrating west themselves as Americans inhabited their traditional homelands. When George Washington became president, the indigenous peoples in the trans-Appalachian West thought the region was already plenty full of people and frankly didn't need anyone moving in, clearing the forests, and killing the game.

Tensions came to a head in the Old Northwest. Indians were becoming increasingly restive due to heightened competition with white settlers for land and resources coupled with the continued presence of the British in the territory. Despite the terms of the Treaty of Paris of 1783, British military forts in the Old Northwest remained open and active, retaining and strengthening their alliances with the Indians there. The British went out of their way to ensure the friendship of the indigenous peoples and keep them from getting too cozy with the Americans. Many Americans in positions of authority in the army or territorial affairs felt—rightly, for the most part—that the British were constantly stirring up Indian animosity toward the Americans as well. Britain expanded its trade relations in both the Old Northwest and in the trans-Mississippi West with the tribes from the Great Lakes and Canada to northern Louisiana. From the perspective of westerners such as William Clark or George Sibley, it was these pro-British leanings of the Indians that dragged the United States into the War of 1812.

Participating in such commerce was nothing new to the Native Americans. Extensive and far-flung trade networks existed before the Europeans arrived, and continued to thrive after contact. Indians were as shrewd as any trader in a medieval market or bazaar. The Indians quickly figured out that they could play traders and fur companies off one another to gain more goods, tools, whiskey, or gunpowder for what they were offering. This led the British and American governments to use methods they already understood and used to better manage the Indian trade. When George Sibley became the Factor at Fort Osage in

When the United States acquired the Louisiana Territory from France, it more than doubled the size of the United States, and bro□□□□□□□□□□□□□□□□□□□ control. A year later, the Office of Indian Trade opened a trade factory in the new territory at Fort Belle Fontaine. (Courtesy, Larry Ruebling)

1808, he was heir to this tradition of using trade goods to gain cooperation from Native Americans.

One product the Native Americans offered held greatest interest for the Europeans—furs—which was essential to Indian relations because they were plentiful in North America and in high demand in northern Europe. It was the foundation of the relationship between the French and the Indians, and to some extent between Indians and England as well. Furs were value-added products in Europe. To the Europeans, it made the most sense to serve as jobbers for these wilderness producers who, as they saw it, worked cheaply for common goods, lackluster firearms, and rotgut whiskey. To the Indians, the Europeans were pipelines for all kinds of goods to improve their quality of life and were willing to take all the furs the Indians could trap and provide. Of course, this trade was a very mixed blessing for the Indians. On the one hand, European contact brought them tools, utensils, cookware, and such. However, it fundamentally changed their lives, culture, and geography.

Consider firearms. Guns, powder, and lead acquired from whites allowed the Indians to hunt more and larger game than before. When they hunted buffalo with the bow and arrow, for example, several hunters might stalk the huge beasts, and not all would return safely. With rifles, though, they could kill more of them without having to be quite so dangerously close to their prey. This gave the tribe much. The buffalo was a source of food, shelter, and materials for a variety of uses in addition to the skins for the fur trade. More efficient hunting produced more buffalo skins to trade to the whites for more goods, resulting in tribal expansion. But the Indians now had to travel farther and farther afield for more animals, so they needed more and more territory to fill the increasingly insatiable European appetite for furs. As these tribes expanded their reach, they were increasingly bumping up against other tribes in the same situation. Before long, these expanding tribes were competing for the same resources on the same territory. And, as with expanding powers on any other part of the globe, they tended to use warfare to settle issues of competition. These wars were now more deadly than before, since those same rifles that made hunting animals so much more efficient allowed them to kill more people in warfare with greater speed and efficiency as well.

This economic system was well entrenched when George Sibley was born in 1782, and it was this system of trade that the Americans sought to control themselves. However, it wasn't as easy as it sounded. Americans in frontier regions like Ohio and Indiana knew well the power of trade, commerce, and goods in forging relations with the Indians, and they had seen how those goods could become tools of domination over the indigenous peoples. Although George Washington, General (and Indiana Territory Governor) William Henry Harrison, Thomas Jefferson, and a young lieutenant under General Anthony Wayne in the Ohio Valley named William Clark all saw the same developments in the West, they came to different conclusions about the Native Americans. Harrison earned his national reputation not as a territorial governor but as conqueror of native peoples, earning him the moniker "Old Tippecanoe" for his destruction of a Shawnee village called Prophet's Town on the Tippecanoe River in 1811 — thus the 1840 campaign slogan "Tippecanoe and Tyler Too." Meantime, others — from George Washington to William Clark to George Sibley — saw the American Indian as part of a broader race of humanity, as someone who could become "civilized" — that is, more like white westerners — with the right kinds of encouragement and help. For them, the Indians had not forgone their hunter-and-gatherer ways because they didn't know better and hadn't been able to learn on their own, but because they hadn't learned a viable alternative (never mind that a number of tribes, including the Osage, had developed forms of agriculture already). With help from the United States, they would be able to give up the old "savage" ways and settle down to become prosperous land owners, farmers, cattlemen. They would learn English and become Christian, wear pants and coats and dresses instead of buckskins, breechcloths, and moccasins. What was needed was an infusion of goods, supplies, and protection from the benevolent Great White Father, they reasoned, to help the Indians along the road to progress.

Among the foremost thinkers along these lines was Thomas Jefferson, who held the view that the native peoples had not proceeded upward as quickly as westerners, and remained in their backward hunter-gatherer state. Jefferson, along with other Enlightenment thinkers, saw material goods as a key to accomplishing the dual goals of giving the Indians the tools to rise to his level of "civilization" by becoming farmers while at the same time opening more western lands to white settlement and expanding American commerce. "While they are learning to do better on less land, and our increasing numbers will be calling for more land," wrote Thomas Jefferson in 1803, "a coincidence of interests will be produced between those who have land to spare, and want other necessaries, and those who have such necessaries to spare, and want lands."[3] All this was rolled together in his expansion of the Indian trade factory system under his presidency. George Sibley was part of this expansion.

The federal government started regulating trade with Native Americans as early as 1786, and the Washington Administration began doing so more actively by 1790. The system of Indian trade factories came about in 1796, which established trading operations run by "factors" at forts, funded gifts and merchandise, and prescribed policies for procuring goods and auctioning the furs acquired from the Indians.

The factory system pursued the parallel goals of controlling the Native Americans through commercial rewards and punishments along with attempting to "civilize" them. The federal government was already pushing Indians westward, requiring more people to live on less land; clearly, the best way to facilitate this was to convince them to convert to a lifestyle that required less territory — which meant giving up hunting and gathering in favor of settling down on farms. Trade goods were both the proverbial carrot and stick for government officials in dealing with indigenous tribes. They would receive their own parts of the bounty the United States could offer in gifts and annuities so long as they refrained from intertribal warfare and ignominy against settlers, and generally played by the rules set down by the government in both its treaties and directives.

Meriwether Lewis was territorial governor when Fort Osage opened. His brother Reuben was a partner in the Missouri Fur Company and active in fur commerce in St. Louis and the West. (Used by permission, State Historical Society of Missouri, Columbia)

Breaking the rules or refusing to follow the wishes of the White Father of the eastern fires, and the Indians risked the wrathful withdrawal of support and goods upon which they had become so dependent. Those who had tried such a strategy felt that it worked most of the time. Upper Louisiana Governor Meriwether Lewis wrote long-time friend President Thomas Jefferson in 1808 of the successes realized by such a strategy with the Osage. In little time of withholding trade, the Osage "were reduced, in the course a few months, to a state of perfect submission, without bloodshed" wrote the Governor; "this has, in my opinion, fairly proven the superiority which the policy of withholding merchandise from the Indians has over the chastisement of the sword."[4] As Trade Factor at Fort Osage, George Sibley used the same tactics in dealing with restive Indians. After the Osage attacked and mutilated an Ioway warrior they caught spying at their camp near the fort, Sibley left no doubt in the minds of Osage Chief Sans Oreille and other leaders that if another such incident occurred, he would cut off all access to the factory and its cornucopia of goods.

The Office of Indian Trade in the War Department managed all this. The office decided on goods to provide and procured them, distributed merchandise through a central purchasing and warehousing system in Georgetown, ensured (albeit inconsistently) annuity payments, and tried (with limited success) to coordinate efforts with the Army. In many treaties in which the United States was gaining land from a particular tribe, the government compensated the tribe with an annuity — that is, a set amount of money paid regularly, usually for a set number of years. Since the government was helping push along this process of civilizing the Indians, officials such as William Clark figured that the most dangerous part of the process was the interim when they were trying to give up the hunter-gatherer life and settle into lives of land ownership and agriculture. It was then that government had the greatest obligation to ensure that the Indians, still progressing toward civilized life, neither starved, reverted to their old ways, nor fell in with the wrong crowd (that is, independent traders or British representatives).[5] Clark counseled the government to set the annuities for a set period of years—long enough for them to make the transition but sufficiently limited to keep them from becoming dependent on it.

Finances entered into the relationship between the United States and the Native Americans in other ways that proved more damaging to the Indians. Most treaties from the early nineteenth century included a clause stating that the United States government would pay Americans for any property or possessions lost or destroyed by the Indians; the one Clark drafted for the Osage in 1808, for example, stated that the United States would compensate Americans "with a view to quiet the animosities which at present exist between the inhabitants of the territory of Louisiana, and the Osage Nations."[6] Of course, the implication was that the government would get the payments back from the tribe committing the sin.

This is precisely what happened ten years later. Drafting a new treaty, Clark began by stating that "the Osage nations have been embarrassed by the frequent demands for property taken from the citizens of the United States, by war parties, and other thoughtless men of their several bands."[7] In fact, these "embarrassments" generally involved destroying property or stealing horses, cattle, and foodstuffs. The government even tried to alleviate this problem by providing horses to the tribes, both to cut down on the theft and hasten the transition to agriculture. It was not unusual for new treaties to include a clause stating that the tribe was unable to meet its financial obligations of paying for the sins of their tribesmen, so the benevolent United States was willing to wipe the slate clean with the cession of another large parcel of land, thus executing another "coincidence of interests."

Indian indebtedness also emanated from problems at the trade factory itself. To a large extent, debt was endemic to the system. When the Indians went on their semiannual hunting expeditions, they would need extra supplies, guns, lead, powder, traps, and such before going. The trade factory, where they acquired such necessities, always paid in merchandise rather than cash, so the tribes needed the factor — someone like Sibley — to allow them to purchase goods on credit. In fact, most of the factors allowed Indians to buy on credit regularly. Trouble came when the hunt didn't bring in enough to cover the debt, so it was rolled over. After a few years, Indians had no hope of paying the debt. The nature of the barter system in which they were engaged was part of the problem; it was exacerbated by the fact that the Indians produced raw materials (placing them at the bottom of the proverbial economic food chain), and that the government renegotiated the treaty with the tribe again, ceding more land to the United States in exchange for wiping its debt clean. The inherent problems are obvious: Indians were trapped in an endless cycle of debt, excluded from a cash economy, and living on less and less land. Government officials saw this as a positive, partly because it forced the Indians to resort to more "civilized" ways of living that required less land. Plus, it brought more and more Indian land under the government's control, which could then be homesteaded by Americans who would use it profitably. Besides, this land was essential to realizing the Jeffersonian ideal of a nation of landowners participating in a democracy. The harshest critics of the system suggest that it led Indians to come to see land as merely another commodity akin to furs, horses, or trade goods. Such was the case with the Osage, with whom Sibley worked so closely, who signed their first treaty with the United States just five years after the Louisiana Purchase. Explorer-turned-Indian Agent William Clark, by 1808 a Brigadier-General in the Missouri Territorial Militia, led a group of St. Charles Dragoons westward to meet with the Osage and negotiate a treaty in 1808. He took young Nathan Boone along as a guide to the prospective fort site, meeting up with the army contingent accompanying the trade goods and personnel (which included Sibley) for the new trade factory. The original treaty, dutifully copied by Sibley in his journal, promised paying the Great Osage $1,000 a year, and another $500 for the Little Osage.

William Clark was Indian Agent during the time spanned by these journals, although he went on to become territorial governor in 1813, but lost the election to become the state's first governor Alexander McNair. (Used by permission, State Historical Society of Missouri, Columbia)

However, financial problems plagued the Osage, especially after the War of 1812, compelling them to negotiate a new treaty with the United States at St. Louis in 1818, in which Clark wrote in Article I that thefts had "embarrassed" the Osage nations and that since "deductions from their annuities, in conformity to the said article [of the 1808 treaty] would deprive them of any for several years, and being destitute of funds to do that justice to the citizens of the United States which is calculated to promote a friendly intercourse," the government would accept a large parcel of land instead.[8]

Americans didn't want money in the hands of the Indians out of fear that the Indians would use money unwisely, be chiseled out of it by unscrupulous independent traders, drink it up, or spend it with British traders. This racial view was partly based on the belief that the Indians had not yet reached the same level as whites, so could not necessarily handle such tools of higher civilization. But another part of it was a desire to manage the Indian trade as much as possible. The factory system was an attempt to facilitate and manage this process in far-flung regions of an expanding America.

The number of Indian trade factories expanded significantly during Jefferson's presidency (1801-1809). The factory system grew out of a desire to control and "civilize" the Indians, which translated into gaining more Indian land without completely abandoning the old policy of paying Native Americans for it, while regulating the fur trade with the Indians.   As did the French and British, the Americans saw furs as central to Indian relations. The one product the Indians could produce en masse—and seemingly ad infinitum—was the skins of animals, and the demand for them in Europe and, to a lesser extent, eastern American cities, was great. Therefore, when seeking to control and manage the Indians through commerce, furs were the weapon of choice. Americans were moving westward into the trans-Appalachian West, a process accelerated by the

Louisiana Purchase. The tensions with people already living in those areas created a greater perceived need to manage the Indians on the part of the federal government. George Sibley came of age and was looking for a job in the West at just the right time for this.

Fort Belle Fontaine, where Sibley ended up as Assistant Factor, opened in 1805 just north of St. Louis on the Mississippi River in the new Louisiana Territory. The growing hamlet started as a base of operations for Maxent, Laclede and Company and had grown into a significant fur trade center dominated by the Chouteau brothers, Auguste and Pierre, along with challengers such as Manuel Lisa. By the time the United States acquired the territory in the Louisiana Purchase, St. Louis was already a thriving commercial center as a sort of hinge connecting several trade theaters: French fur traders upriver on the Missouri; the downriver commerce from the United States in the Ohio Valley coming west; the French and Spanish operations based in New Orleans at the mouth of the Mississippi; and the British traders based in Canada who continued their commercial relations with Indians and others in the Northwest Territory, the Great Lakes, and even the northern reaches of the Louisiana Purchase. When Fort Belle Fontaine opened, it was the American hinge for both commerce and the military in the region. Excepting the tiny village of St. Charles just a few miles upriver on the Missouri, it was on the edge of the American western frontier. St. Louis was a thriving trade center that was easily supplied and already had the foundations of a lively western merchant economy. Its location on the frontier combined with the goods and wealth centered there heightened the need for defense as well as supplying the Indian trade. If government intended to manage the Indians through trade, this was among the most active places for it.

War Secretary Henry Dearborn appointed Rudolph Tilliers as the factor at the new fort, where the operation was sufficiently busy to warrant an assistant. Sibley was, in fact, something of a known quantity in Washington. George's father, Dr. John Sibley had a good reputation in the capitol, serving as Indian Agent for the territory of Orleans. Surely John Sibley's boy, George, would be a good choice to work under Tilliers. Under the watchful eye of young George, Tilliers' shortcomings became apparent to higher-ups. He tended to be fast and loose with inventory, and his record keeping was sloppy at best, both qualities that drove the fastidious George to distraction. He and Tilliers never got on well, perhaps for many reasons: a personality mix that resembled the proverbial oil and water, Tillier's loose record-keeping versus Sibley's fastidiousness, age versus youth. All came to a head in 1807, when Tilliers fired Sibley. Not one to take such matters passively, Sibley demanded an inquiry to clear him. Governor Frederick Bates and Indian Agent William Clark both came to his defense in letters

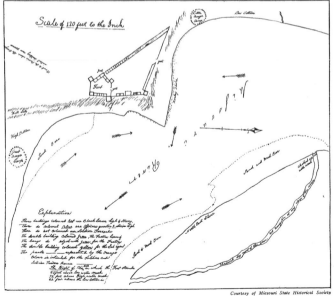

FORT OSAGE, DRAWN BY GENERAL WILLIAM CLARK

After choosing the site for Fort Osage, William Clark sketched the layout and design of the new fort in his journal. (from Clark, Westward with Dragoons)

to Washington, but Sibley decided to plead his own case and left St. Louis on horseback for Washington in early November, 1807. When he arrived more than three months later, change was already in the works. Accepting Clark's assessment of the situation, Indian Trade Superintendent John Mason decided to close the factory at Fort Belle Fontaine and open two farther west. The recently arrived George Sibley found himself the new factor at Fort Osage.[9]

In fact, the factory at Belle Fontaine was unsuccessful for a number of reasons apart from Tilliers' administrative shortcomings. The tribes disliked it, since it was inconvenient—just too far away to carry in all the furs to trade and to lug all the goods they received for them back upriver again. For white folks living in the region, the sight of contingents of Native Americans who they perceived as dangerous savages left them uneasy. After all, if the trade factory system was going to achieve its objectives of increased trade with the Native American peoples in order to bring them into the American social fold as farmers rather than wilderness folk, then the Indians had to use the factory. Experience had proved that with Indian trade factories, as with all real estate, three of the most important considerations were location, location, and location—and Fort Belle Fontaine didn't seem to meet any of them.

While at Fort Belle Fontaine, Sibley developed a strong reputation for sound business practices and integrity. His ongoing feud with Tilliers was apparently something of an open secret around the fort and fur-trade circles. Not only did his firing not turn into a liability, but his tenure at Fort Belle Fontaine was the key to future success. Sibley's time there placed him in the middle of a heady growth in St. Louis. At the fort, he dealt with all types of people, from traders just in from the western wilderness to prominent merchants in St. Louis. It was here that he would have met the movers and shakers in St. Louis and the western fur trade. It was here he met the great western explorers Meriwether Lewis and William Clark, who became territorial governor and Indian Agent respectively upon their return from the Pacific. He was probably among the first St. Louisans they met when they returned, too; the Corps stopped at the Fort, and allowed the Mandan Chief Sheheke and his family, traveling as guests of the captains, to go on a government-funded shopping spree.[10] In Sibley's two years in St. Louis, he learned of the inner workings of the factory system as well as the army assigned to protect it, the Indians it was to service and civilize, and the merchants that provided its conduit to the rest of the United States. By the time the federal government prepared to close the trade operations at Fort Belle Fontaine in 1808, George Sibley was a known quantity with practical experience.

Therefore, the Office of Indian Trade decided to close the trade operations at Belle Fontaine and open two new forts closer to the Indians at Fort Madison on the upper Mississippi near present-day Keokuk, Iowa, and near the mouth of the Osage River on the Missouri, just east of today's Kansas City. That spring, the government commissioned John Johnson as factor at Fort Madison and George Champlain Sibley at Fort Osage. The two left Washington in May to converge in St. Louis, where they were to divide up the remaining inventory at Belle Fontaine for their factories to augment the other goods they received as opening inventory. When Sibley left St. Louis August 12, his merchandise, valued at some $20,000, took a sizeable portion of the eight keelboats the army was floating upriver.

Meantime, a contingent of the Missouri territorial militia was traveling overland to meet them, under the command of Indian Agent General William Clark of the Missouri territorial militia. These Dragoons from St. Charles, just upriver from St. Louis, took along Nathan Boone as their guide. Boone was the youngest son of western legend Daniel Boone, now 74 years old and living with Nathan's family on a substantial parcel west of St. Louis on the Femme Osage River. Nathan and his older brother Daniel Morgan Boone owned a salt-making operation in present-day Howard County, so Nathan Boone knew the region well, making him a perfect choice to guide the group westward on the more direct overland route than along the winding river. These Dragoons were supposed to help with initial security for the group and to provide the labor for building the new trade fort. When they arrived at the site — a bluff overlooking the Missouri River not far from the mouth of the Osage — Clark sent Boone and an interpreter Paul Loise to the Osage village with the message that the Americans wished to hold a council with them and to open up friendlier relations. Clark remained back at camp, searching for an appropriate site to construct a fort.

This was a familiar routine for William Clark. Almost three years of sharing the command of the Corps of Discovery with Meriwether Lewis had put Clark in contact with tribes all along the Missouri and Columbia rivers. Here, Clark followed the tried-and-true format. He sent an interpreter with a message, met with the folks he figured to be the chiefs of the tribe, heard a speech or two from them, gave them some gifts, outlined the terms of the new arrangements between the tribe and its new American Father from the east, then smoked a pipe to seal the deal.[11] Many components of the treaty were pro forma: statements of mutual desire to live in peace, American promises to open a trade factory and to keep it well-stocked with "a well assorted store of goods, for the purpose of bartering with them on moderate terms," and commitments to protect and defend the Osage from restive neighbors coupled with Osage promises about decent behavior and avoiding inter-tribal warfare. Men continued to fell trees, dig ditches to insert the vertical logs, hew timber, and construct their new digs. Clark returned to St. Louis via keelboat later in September, too afflicted with his not-unusual digestive disorders to endure riding on horseback.[12]

When Clark returned, a glitch in the treaty arose almost immediately. As it turned out, there were some 74 Osage in St. Louis at the same time to meet with Meriwether

Lewis, who had now been actually on the job in St. Louis as Governor of Upper Louisiana for about a year and a half. When Clark returned and they heard of the treaty, this group was unwilling to agree to the terms, noting that the chiefs who signed it along the river weren't authorized to speak for them. What transpired next was and remains in some dispute. Pierre Chouteau was Indian agent to the Osage, since he and his older brother Auguste had a special relationship with the Osage for some years; the brothers traded with and supplied the Osage, spent time at their villages, may have even had Osage wives, and were considered their primary contact in the white world. Problem was, the boundary Clark drew left a parcel of land claimed by Pierre on the Osage side of the line. The question was complicated by a federal ban on individuals acquiring land directly from Native American tribes; Chouteau claimed that it was gift of long standing, and that the United States government could not seize property. So, Governor Lewis renegotiated the treaty with the Osage in St. Louis, which was exactly the same as the Clark version, except the boundary was drawn again to keep that Chouteau's claim on the American side of the line. Lewis sent Chouteau himself back to the Osage village in early November to present the new treaty to leadership out west.[13]

A dispute arose over Osage motives in St. Louis. Whispers and insinuations in St. Louis suggested that the Osage had not reached their conclusion about the Clark treaty entirely of their own volition, and that the whole thing had the Chouteaus' fingerprints on it. Apparently the brothers suggested that Clark had either misrepresented the original treaty or that the interpreter offered a less-than-accurate version to tribal leaders; in his report to Washington, Lewis noted that

> "I am fully persuaded that the Indians were urged to make those objections by some white person, or persons, in this place, [St. Louis] but, as I have not been able to collect any evidence of the fact, I shall avoid the mention of names. I well

know that General Clarke would not have deceived the Indians; and so fully am I impressed with the belief that Paul Louis, who was the interpreter on that occasion, had interpreted the treaty faithfully, that I have not thought it proper to dismiss him, which I should have done, could I for a moment believe that he had acted otherwise."[14]

Ill will resulted, at least for a time, though. Lewis noted that "the doubts and suspicions which overshadowed these transactions, conspired to create such sentiments in the minds of General Clark and Mr. Chouteau towards each other . . . . there still exists between those gentlemen a want of cordiality and confidence, which I fear may hereafter produce some irregularities in the Indian department, in not timely guarded against."[15] As it turned out, the final treaty ratified by Congress was the Chouteau version, although it took until 1810 for Congress to do so. Interestingly, Sibley didn't get the news of ratification and the final version of the agreement. He copied into his journal in March, 1811, the terms of the treaty which he borrowed from an Osage chief, then wrote a terse letter to headquarters suggesting that Washington keep men like him in the field at least as well-informed on such matters as the Indians themselves.

Assessments of the Osage in Missouri — the people with whom George Sibley was to work — vary, from violent and precarious to almost cowering under the thumb of the United States. It is true that the Osage had been expanding in the eighteenth century, which put them into conflict with their neighbors. Other tribes began moving westward as American expansion crowded them out of their older homelands, placing pressures on the region. The Osage had something of a reputation of being restive, contrary, and aggressive, and Sibley certainly knew something of them from his tenure at Fort Belle Fontaine. When Amos Stoddard raised the American flag at St. Louis in the spring of 1804, most of the tribes living anywhere near the Osage considered the tribe to be aggressive bullies who had left everyone in the region on the defensive; many of these tribes were growing in strength to stand up to what they saw as a menace. By the time Clark and Sibley arrived at the mouth of the Osage River, tribal leaders were beginning to feel encircled by hostile neighbors and willing to talk to the United States about help and protection. While the Americans promised both, they also extracted a high price—higher than Clark, Sibley, or the Osage realized at the time. It was the first of the treaties in which the United States gained more and more Osage territory in exchange for either debts or to pay for the indiscretions of some tribesmen. It began a process that ended up forcing the Osage to accept attacks from their neighbors and turning the other cheek, even against their inclinations and perhaps best interest. Within the next decade and a half, the Osage were reduced to the status of dependents on the United States. Reputation aside, Sibley appears to have worked well with the Osage, as well as the other tribes in the region. It was the Osage who accompanied him on his expedition in search of the great salt mountains in 1811, and an Osage chief to whom he refers as a friend. The record Sibley left behind leaves the impression of a good and cordial working relationship—certainly a better one that he had with his military protégés at the Fort.

British presence made relations with many of the tribes east of the Great Plains even dicier. In the Northwest, Britain held a series of military forts that used merchandise to gain and retain the loyalty of tribes opposed to continued American expansion; His Majesty's Government supplied a loose confederation under the leadership of Shawnee chiefs Tenskwatawa, known as The Prophet, and his brother Tecumseh, in the early years of the republic, designed to stop American encroachment. The War of 1812 finally settled the question of who would dominate the trans-Appalachian West; Tecumseh died in battle at the Thames in 1813, and The Prophet suffered defeat and ultimately relocation to Kansas after the war.

Those stationed and living on the western frontier knew the war was a distinct possibility within a year after Sibley began his tenure at Fort Osage as events on the frontier were being shaped by policies playing out far away. Jefferson and Madison both used commerce as a weapon in their relations with France and Great Britain as both presidents tried to compel them to stop seizing American ships and impressing their sailors. Jefferson's Non-Intercourse Act, seeking to sequester the United States, proved disastrous for the American economy—not to mention making it more difficult to acquire the British goods that Native Americans tended to favor at the factories. Macon's Bill No. 2, which tried to placate Great Britain or France by promising to enforce an embargo against the other if one stopped its depredations on the high seas, had only the effect of increasing the smuggling of merchandise in from Britain.

Small wonder, then, that Clark reported to the War Department (which, in turn, conveyed it to Congress) in 1809 that a recently received letter "confirms my suspicions of the British interference, with our Indian affairs in this country." Clark went on to report that the British "tell them [the Indians] that they pity them in their situation with the Americans, because the Americans had taken their lands and their game; that they must *join* and send them off from their lands; they told the savages that the Americans could not give them a blanket, nor anything good for their families."[16] By the time President James Madison delivered his request for a war declaration to Congress in June of 1812, a number of tribes were already lining up with their British allies, and many westerners felt little surprise.

Most Americans living in the West saw Great Britain as the key to most of the problems involving Native Americans. The British continued to offer more goods of greater variety at better prices than the Americans and that, naturally enough, tended to cement the British-Indian alliance.[17] Indian Trade Superintendent John Mason wrote to all the factors in August, 1811, to voice his concerns over the mounting tensions with Great Britain and the possible fall-out in Indian relations. Factors such as Sibley were to make sure the tribal leaders understood that the United States government's real problem was with Great Britain, and that the United States would protect and care for those tribes that remained loyal and friendly, punishing those who were not and who allied themselves with the European enemy.[18] The Osage remained in the American fold early in the war, but that came to change over time.

American diplomatic problems found their way to the Indian factories and to the likes of George Sibley. Many of the goods traded to the Native Americans for furs and such were imported, especially from Great Britain. The problem was exacerbated by both the fledgling American industry's inability to meet the demand as well as the connoisseurship of the customers at the factories. In short, the Indians were fussy buyers; they only traded for certain kinds of goods that had to meet certain specifications. Blankets, by far the most popular product at the factories, were imported from Great Britain because they were the only ones the Indians would accept. Even then, they would accept only certain kinds, colors, and patterns. Decisions being made in Washington and London meant that "the Indians were caught in the economic cross fire between the Americans and the British."[19]

Things remained pretty quiet at Fort Osage during that first summer of the war. Fort Commander Eli Clemson grew restless, itching to join the fight instead of hanging around in what he perceived as the middle of nowhere defending an operation run by the likes of George Sibley, with whom he hated working.[20] But the situation grew tense starting in the fall. Indian Trade Superintendent John Mason wrote Sibley in October to keep his eyes peeled for problems.[21] The warning and subsequent closing of the fort were not worries without cause; in the course of the war the British destroyed the factories at Michilimackinac near Lakes Michigan and Superior, Chicago at the southern tip of Lake Michigan, and Sandusky in northwestern Ohio, as well as threatening the people and property at Fort Madison on the upper Mississippi and Fort Wayne in northeastern Indiana.[22]

Heeding the warning, Sibley spent the winter packing everything for a move that would probably be a hasty one while not letting the Indians know he was doing so.[23] Governor Howard decided to close the fort and factory in early April, figuring that the Osage and other tribes in the region seemed well under control, and that those troops and resources could be better used elsewhere.[24] Sibley headed for St. Louis, waited for instructions, and lobbied new territorial governor William Clark to reopen the factory for the Osage in a different location.[25] Sibley argued that the reason relations with the Osage had remained peaceful was because the United States kept its factory open and stocked—in short, because it continued to abide by the terms of the 1808 treaty and took care of the Osage, so the tribe had no reason to cozy up to the British. Clark and Mason apparently agreed, and decided before summer's end to send Sibley to Arrow Rock, just downriver from the mouth of the Osage River, to set up shop for the winter.[26]

The winter went peacefully enough, but that spring more than just the frozen ground warmed up. A group of Osage murdered some settlers, and the Sauk and Fox renewed warfare with their traditional enemies the Osage. So precarious was the situation that Clark called Sibley back to St. Louis in April.[27] He tried to return to the region in late summer, but Mason was lukewarm; trade goods were scarce, and transportation dangerous, so he left Sibley's fate in the hands of Clark, who was closer to the situation. Threats of attacks by "an immense savage force" precluded Sibley's return West, so he took Clark's advice and traveled to Washington D.C., to convince Mason's office to allow him to return to Arrow Rock and pay the Osage' back annuities.[28] He was in Washington when news arrived that the two had signed a treaty to end what its critics called "Mr. Madison's War." He left in February, 1815, for St. Louis.[29]

At first, it looked as if the factory system would start again where it had left off. James Monroe (now heading both the War and State departments) wrote Governor Clark that he wanted to begin the system again, just as soon as treaties with the tribes were finalized. In early 1815, Madison appointed Clark, Illinois Territory Governor Ninian Edwards, and St. Louis fur baron Auguste Chouteau as a three-member commission to hold a council with over two dozen tribes at Portage des Sioux (north of present-day St. Charles, Missouri, on the Mississippi River) in order to dictate the terms of new treaties.

Meantime, Sibley was biding his time in St. Louis, waiting to hear about his future. While there, he met Rufus Easton's fifteen-year-old daughter Mary, whom he married August 19. Easton was a notable figure at the time: a former judge and postmaster, he became the territorial representative to Congress the year before.[30] Sibley wrote to his brother Samuel that Mary had "long ago expressed her perfect willingness to live any where with me and until I can withdraw from the Indian Service, she will willingly share with me the privations of a forest life. I mean to have a very comfortable establishment . . . in the howling wilderness."[31] Comfortable establishment, indeed: Sibley's quarters above the factory store were spacious, comfortable, and well-furnished, since the Indian Trade Office provided $200 for the initial expenses for furnishing the wilderness accommodations, and an additional $25 each year thereafter. When the barge *The Osage Factor*[32] left St. Louis October 1, its cargo included Mary's furniture, the Easton family organ, and her library.[33]

But the Fort Osage that greeted the newlyweds was not the one George had left. Neglect and time had taken a toll on it, and Sibley had to begin restoration. Mason's office authorized $600 for repairs to counter the ravages and deterioration of time.[34] Fort Osage was different in other ways too. It was true that it still retained something of its frontier atmosphere. Indians still came around and lived nearby; Mary, reported Sibley, enchanted them with her musical skills. Real frontier types still came through and visited as well, even if the dapper Sibley didn't look much

Thomas McKenney succeeded John Mason as Superintendent of Indian Trade, pursuing an enlightened policy toward the Native American tribes that was increasingly out of step with national policy by the end of the 1810s. (Courtesy, State Historical Society of Missouri, Columbia)

like he belonged there himself in stylish coats and black silk vests ordered from a Georgetown tailor.[35] Daniel Boone, already a legend among many Americans thanks to John Filson's 1784 biography, visited in the spring of 1816 on his way to the Platte River. At 82, Boone was undoubtedly the oldest visitor to the fort, although Sibley reported that he seemed "active for one of his years" and was "still vigorous of mind and is pretty well informed." He was, for Sibley, the quintessential frontiersman as well: "he might have accumulated riches as readily as any man in Kentucky; but he prefers the woods, where you see him in the dress of the roughest, poorest hunter."[36]

At the same time, though, the region was changing. Emigrants arrived in droves after the war — so many that the territorial legislature twice divided the region into smaller counties for easier governance and administration. It created a vast Howard County (of some 30,000 square miles) in 1816, then divided it two years later to create Cooper County south of the Missouri River. Folks in the know estimated that some 9,000 people lived in the region at the time; the population was up to some 12,000 by the time of Missouri statehood. Rather than small farmers, these new arrivals tended to be prosperous landowners from good families in Virginia, North Carolina, Kentucky, and Tennessee who moved westward with slaves to plant tobacco and hemp. Such growth also brought towns filled with merchants, craftsmen, distillers, and a host of other services required for a growing population.[37] The frontier was becoming tame, and quickly. Fort Osage even received its own post office in 1820; George Sibley was its first postmaster.

As more and more white settlers moved to the region, it put increasing pressure on the Osage living in the neighborhood. The Indians were trying to survive on a smaller portion of the land to support their growing population, and they had harvested too many furs for too many years, so the population of animals — both for food and furs — was shrinking. The temptation became too great for some of the Osage, who were making a habit of stealing horses and livestock from the settlers. The 1808 treaty held the United States government responsible for reimbursing Americans for such losses, which was becoming expensive. Governor William Clark saw the problem clearly; the thefts were on the increase, the chiefs were unable to bring the perpetrators under control, and the tribe could ill afford to compensate the government. So, in 1818, he orchestrated a new treaty with the Osage in which the United States would forgive all the debts and thefts in exchange for a substantial parcel of Osage land. The Osage even lost their factory when Congress abandoned the factory system in 1822, accepting a measly $2,329.43 to allow the government to close the factory for good.[38] The Osage had little choice and signed the subsequent treaties. By 1825, the Osage no longer had any choice but to acquiesce to American demands for land.

By the end of the 1810s, there was a growing clamor to close down the factory system. The debate centered on its success, and even the definition of success itself. Fur czar John Jacob Astor, whose American Fur Company was rapidly becoming the dominant force in the fur trade, wanted a free hand to trade with the Indians himself. All these regulations about licensing, auctions, what goods could or could not be sold to the Indians, and all the rest were simply impediments to business growth. When Thomas Hart Benton arrived in Washington as one of Missouri's first two senators, Astor wasted no time in convincing him that the factory system had to go. Others were already advancing similar arguments—the system hadn't civilized the Indians; it cost too much money and wasn't even profitable; the Indians preferred independent traders who had more goods, better prices, and alcohol; and private traders could better provide merchandise to the Indians. At Benton's urging, the Senate investigated the system to determine if institutional euthanasia was appropriate. Even William Clark, whose life was linked to the trans-Mississippi West and relations with Native Americans there since the Corps of Discovery, wrote a scathing report to the committee's questions calling for the end of the factory system. [39]

Congress and the Monroe Administration ended its experiment in Indian trade in 1822, and closed the remaining Indian trade factories. George Sibley closed up the factory, and purchased the remaining merchandise thinking he could continue a lucrative trade with the Osage. However, they had too little to offer, and the goods were too expensive now. The operation failed and, since Sibley was the only partner with actual property, he lost almost everything. The setback was temporary, though; more land acquisition, a contract to negotiate contracts with the tribes along the new Santa Fe Trail, and even opening a school for girls in St. Charles had Sibley moving back toward prosperity quickly.

Once at the vanguard of an advancing United States, George Sibley was, by 1822, in the midst of a booming region filling rapidly with people, farms, towns, and slaves. Steam-powered riverboats first chugged by Fort Osage in 1819, connecting the regions more effectively than ever before. When the Sibleys left Fort Osage, the end of era had arrived. "The paradoxical theme of Sibley's life between 1815 and 1822 was that of a man caught up in the life of a developing country while still wedded to a frontier institution which was passing away." [40]

NOTES:

[1] The site was sometimes called Fort Clark at the time as well, but Fort Osage was the most commonly used name in records and correspondence at the time, so I have chosen to use it. This "Fort Clark" should not be confused with the one established near the Mandan, Hidatsa, and Arikara peoples in 1830, just north of present-day Bismarck, North Dakota.

[2] The Northwest Territory was that region west of Pennsylvania, north of the Ohio River, east of the Mississippi, and south of the Great Lakes. It is today's Ohio, Indiana, Illinois, Michigan, Wisconsin, and part of Minnesota.

[3] Thomas Jefferson to Benjamin Hawkins, February 18, 1803, *Works of Thomas Jefferson,* vol. 9, 447.

[4] Meriwether Lewis to Thomas Jefferson, December 15, 1808, *American State Papers, Indian affairs,* vol. 1, 766.

[5] Steffen, *William Clark,* 133-134.

[6] "Treaty with the Osage, 1808," in Kappler, *Indian Treaties,* 95.

[7] "Treaty with the Osage, 1818," in Kappler, *Indian Treaties,* 167.

[8] *Ibid.*

[9] Jones, *Prairie Puritan,* 34-37.

[10] Clark, September 23, 1806, *The Definitive Journals of Lewis and Clark,* vol. 8, 370-371.

[11] Clark, *Westward with Dragoons,* 39-41.

[12] *Ibid.*

[13] In fact, Lewis instructed Chouteau to present the treaty only, and not engage in any other activities. See Lewis' instructions, enclosure with William Clark to William Eustis, February 20, 1810, *American State Papers, Indian Affairs,* vol. 1, 765-766.

[14] Meriwether Lewis to Thomas Jefferson, December 15, 1808,

American State Papers, Indian Affairs, vol. 1, 766.

[15] *Ibid.,* 767.

[16] William Clark to War Department, April 30, 1809, *American State Papers, Indian Affairs* 1, 799.

[17] Clark reported that "The marked difference between the American factors and the British Indian agents gave rise to comparisons but little favorable to the character of our country." See William Clark to Thomas Hart Benton, January 23, 1822, *American State Papers, Indian Affairs,* vol. 2, 331.

[18] John Mason, Circular Letter to Indian Factors, *Territorial Papers,* vol. 14, 450-451.

[19] Jones, *Prairie Puritan,* 95.

[20] *Ibid.,* 98.

[21] *Territorial Papers,* vol. 14, 613.

[22] Peake, *A History of the United States Indian Factory System,* 158-160.

[23] Daniel Bissell to John Armstrong, March 30, 1813, *Territorial Papers,* vol. 14, 646.

[24] Benjamin Howard to Daniel Bissell, April 4, 1813, *Territorial Papers,* vol. 14, 664-665.

[25] George C. Sibley to William Clark, July 9, 1813, quoted in Jones, *Prairie Puritan,* 101-102. Clark had succeeded Benjamin Howard as governor of the Missouri Territory in June 1813.

[26] George C. Sibley to Samuel Sibley, September 25, 1813, cited in Jones, *Prairie Puritan,* 104; George C. Sibley to William Clark, November 30, 1813, *Territorial Papers* 14, 711-714.

[27] George C. Sibley to William Clark, November 30, 1813, *Territorial Papers* 14, 711-714.

[28] John Mason to George C. Sibley, July 11, 1814, *Territorial Papers,* vol. 14, 773; Jones, *Prairie Puritan,* 109-110.

[29] Jones, *Prairie Puritan*, 110-111.

[30] Territories at this level sent one representative to Congress, although he did not vote there.

[31] George Sibley to Samuel Sibley, August 20, 1815, quoted in Jones, *Prairie Puritan*, 113.

[32] Fort Osage was one of only two or three trade factories that owned its own keelboat. The Office of Indian Trade authorized purchasing used ones twice for Natchitoches; however, it ordered new ones to be made in Pittsburgh for Forts Osage and Madison, because of the volume of business. It seemed like the best business decision, considering the quantity of furs being shipped east and trade goods coming west. No other factory received more goods than Osage during this 1808-1811 period ($25,539), and only one generated more revenue from furs (($20,272 at Osage). Peake, *A History of the United States Indian Factory System*, 187, 272, 276.

[33] Jones, *Prairie Puritan*, 114.

[34] *Ibid.*, 112.

[35] *Ibid.*, 117.

[36] *Niles Weekly Register*, June 15, 1816. Although an unsigned letter, Jones is certain that Sibley wrote the account of Boone's visit to Fort Osage.

[37] Hurt, "Seeking Fortune in the Promised Land: Settling the Boon's Lick Country, 1808-1825," *Gateway Heritage* 6-9. So prominent were these southern transplants that the counties along the Missouri River from Callaway County west were often called "Missouri's Little Dixie."

[38] "Treaty with the Osage, 1822," in Kappler, *Indian Treaties*, 201-202.

[39] William Clark to Thomas Hart Benton, January 23, 1822, *American State Papers, Indian Affairs* 1, 331.

[40] Jones, *Prairie Puritan*, 119.

Biographical Sketch of the George Chaplin Sibley

By Derek Herbert

Nestled amid the Berkshire Hills of Massachusetts, the town of Great Barrington was the childhood home of George Chaplin Sibley (1782-1863). Born on April 1, 1782 to Dr. John and Elizabeth Sibley, George entered a world filled with political and economic opportunity.

In the early 1800s, following the purchase of the Louisiana Territory from France, the United States, under the direction of President Thomas Jefferson, endeavored to fully record what exactly was in the Louisiana Territory. Indeed, in 1804, the United States government commissioned Meriwether Lewis and William Clark to survey the upper portion of the territory and its inhabitants in an attempt to investigate the possibility of any financial cooperation between the many Native American tribes and the United States government. What emerged from this early exploration and survey of the Native Americans was the government sponsored trading post – the factory system. It was this system of trade that Sibley was all too familiar with.

Prior to the purchase of the Louisiana Territory, Dr. John Sibley moved his family to Natchitoches (in the present-day state of Louisiana), where, upon his arrival, he was appointed U.S. Indian agent in charge of the region by Thomas Jefferson. It was in Natchitoches that John Sibley began grooming his son, George, for government service within the factory system.

Following the successful expeditions and commercial exchanges between western settlers and the various Indian tribes, the federal government sought to construct a compound on the frontier of the rapidly expanding republic to serve as a political, economic, and military bastion of American influence. The facility, completed in 1808, would serve as a vital staging area for American commercial and military needs; however, a skilled and knowledgeable administrator was needed in order to ensure the outpost's success. Seizing the opportunity, and likely a result of family influence, George Sibley was appointed chief factor of the proposed facility amid the Osage and placed in charge of its construction. While stationed at Fort Osage, Sibley was charged with a great many responsibilities; namely, he faced the burden of sustaining peace between the many Native American tribes, as well as between the local western settlers. In addition to sustaining the peace of the region, Sibley was responsible for documenting the domestic and inter-tribe characteristics of these Native American peoples. Though generally successful in his endeavors regarding the Native Americans, Sibley's duties at Fort Osage ended amid the onset of war. As the nation prepared itself for a military conflict against the strongest military power in the world, Great Britain, Fort Osage, along with its staff, was evacuated. For the time being, commerce and exchange ceased. Following the evacuation of Fort Osage, Sibley relocated his base of operations downriver, to a place called "Arrow Rock," and spent a good portion of his time in nearby Saint Louis. While in Saint Louis Sibley courted the daughter of Saint Louis socialite Rufus Easton, Mary Smith Easton; they wed in 1815. That same year, following the Battle of New Orleans, fighting ceased between the United States and Great Britain, ending the War of 1812.

Following the end of hostilities many Americans, none more than Sibley, yearned for the re-establishment of pre-war trade with the Native Americans. However, as the nation continued to grow many began to despise government control and competition in the economic arena of the country, specifically with regard to the factory system. Indeed, by 1827 Sibley not only negotiated a final treaty with the Osage, absolving the United States of any further obligations, but abandoned the fort entirely.

That same year Sibley and his wife moved to the family acreage in Saint Charles, nicknamed "Linden Wood," where they constructed a finishing school for young ladies. Sibley remained there until his death in 1863.

Lindenwood College 1847

Biographical Sketch of Manuel Lisa

By Derek Herbert

In the years following the purchase of the Louisiana Territory, few people were as pivotal to the development of the fur trade as Manuel Lisa (1772 – 1820). Indeed, it was Lisa that ultimately tapped the staggering wealth of the northern and western fur trade.

Born on September 8, 1772 to Cristobal de Lisa and his mother Ignacia Rodriguez, Manuel enjoyed a childhood in the vital trading port of New Orleans, along the Mississippi River. Though few details are known of his childhood, his proficiency at maritime trade and financial planning quickly placed him in good repute among the most wealthy of local business leaders. By the late 1700s, he had successfully petitioned the Spanish government for a grant of land along the Missouri River and by 1800, he had relocated to Saint Louis.

Upon his arrival in Saint Louis, he faced a daunting financial problem: the politically and financially powerful Chouteau brothers, Pierre and Auguste, dominated the local fur trade. To make matters worse, Lisa, though offered a small portion of the fur trade wealth, launched a full-scale attack against the Chouteaus in an attempt to destroy their monopoly. Beginning under the tenure of the Spanish government, Lisa argued time and again against the concept of a monopoly on Indian trade; moreover, he spouted and upheld the ideal of free trade with Native Americans and their tribes. Whether or not these virtues were heartfelt is quite a different matter. Though achieving moderate success under the Spanish government, true success came following the sale of the Louisiana Territory in the early 1800s.

Following the transfer of Louisiana from the Spanish and French authorities to the United States, Lisa aided in the supply of Meriwether Lewis and William Clark's journey to the Pacific. It was this action, perhaps more so than any other, that placed Lisa in the inner circle of the Saint Louis financial elite. Indeed, in 1809 Lisa formed the Saint Louis Missouri Fur Company and partnered with none other than his old rivals Pierre and Auguste Chouteau. With powerful financial allies and Lisa's personal knowledge of the numerous Indian tribes along the Missouri River, the Saint Louis Missouri Fur Company was primed for success. However, hostile Indian tribes, logistical problems of every sort, Lisa's personal debt, and the onset of the War of 1812 led to the company's ultimate collapse. The Saint Louis Missouri Fur Company collapsed in 1814. Though reeling from the disaster, his friend and financial ally, now governor, William Clark, appointed him subagent in charge of all the tribes along the Missouri River. His primary duty was to ensure peaceful Indian tribes while the United States concentrated on fighting British naval and land forces. As the War of 1812 drew to a close, Lisa once again attempted to tap the wealth of the fur trade, forming yet another fur trading company in 1819; however, Lisa's health began to falter and on August 12, 1820, Lisa died. Though his business ventures were not among the most successful and lucrative, it was the cooperation and trust he attained from the Indian tribes along the Missouri that speaks volumes to his merchant abilities – abilities that laid the groundwork for continued cooperation between the United States and the numerous Native American tribes.

Biographical Sketch of
Auguste and Jean Pierre Chouteau

By Derek Herbert

The history of the Mississippi River Valley, like all regional histories, is riddled with tales of legacy, prominence, and power. For some areas, these tales might reflect the community at large, that is to say, the community spirit; for others, these qualities might reflect a specific person or family. More often than not these stories take on lives of their own and morph into a kind of folktale or legend. At the confluence of the Mississippi and Missouri Rivers there is also such a tale: it is a story of family legacy – a legacy that embraced the qualities of social privilege, political power, ruthless commerce, unimaginable wealth, legendary vision, and keen commercial instinct. It is the story of a Saint Louis dynasty – it is the story of Auguste and Jean Pierre Chouteau.

Born in the parish of New Orleans to Rene Auguste and Marie Therese Chouteau, the intimate details of Auguste Chouteau's early years are rather sketchy to discern. What is known however, is that his Father, Rene, deserted Auguste and his mother in New Orleans, and relocated to his native home in France. Though disheartened by this betrayal, Marie Therese quickly enticed the passions of another French immigrant, Pierre de Laclede Liguest, a wealthy and prominent New Orleans merchant. It was this relationship and the position Laclede maintained in Auguste's life that would ultimately propel him to the heights of commercial and political power. Beginning in the 1760s, Auguste studied his stepfather's commercial technique and accompanied him on many an expedition. These travels culminated in 1763, when Laclede, accompanied by Auguste, surveyed the preliminary site for a commercial settlement on the western banks of the Mississippi River. By 1764, the construction of Saint Louis was well under way. In the years that followed,

Auguste Chouteau was head of the family that dominated the St. Louis fur trade under Spanish, French, and American control. (Used by permission, State Historical Society of Missouri, Columbia)

Auguste refined his commercial skills by overseeing and managing the tremendous amount of Native American trade in Saint Louis and the surrounding areas. Indeed, by 1770, Saint Louis was seemingly the crossroads – the epicenter – of trade with the Native American tribes. To this end, Auguste successfully negotiated numerous trade agreements between Spanish, French, and Native American officials. Perhaps the greatest of these economic triumphs was the six-year trading monopoly the Baron de Carondelet granted him with the Osage tribes; moreover, this arrangement resulted in the construction of a fort capable of supplying the needs of such activity, aptly named Fort Carondelet. Yet despite these successes under the oversight of the French and Spanish, a challenge loomed over Auguste and his family businesses – a challenge manifest in the territorial acquisition of Louisiana by the United States.

Following the purchase of the Louisiana Territory in 1803, the United States embarked upon a policy of government-sponsored trade with the Native American tribes – the factory system. It was this system that directly opposed the independent trade relations Chouteau secured between the various Native American tribes. Moreover, Auguste faced the competitive likes of Manuel Lisa and John Jacob Astor, not to mention the growing discontent between Native Americans and the incursions of European-American settlers. It was in this fluid atmosphere that Auguste began to court the political and economic elite of this new American republic, not least of whom were Meriwhether Lewis and William Clark. Indeed, these connections, political, economic, and social, were pivotal in preventing the decline of Chouteau prominence. During the first decade of the 1800s Auguste maintained his family's close hold over the fur trade; however, in 1812, war between the United States and the British Empire disrupted this trade and thrust Auguste into the direct service of his country. Shortly after the commencement of hostilities, Auguste was charged with the defense of Saint Louis and other diplomatic responsibilities. Following the war, Auguste focused his energies on other financial endeavors and retired from the fur trade. On February 24, 1829, he died at the age of seventy-nine. He was survived by his wife Therese Cerre and seven of his nine children.

Like his elder half brother Auguste, Jean Pierre Chouteau learned the basics of commercial trade and negotiation from Pierre de Laclede Linguest; the only difference however, was that Linguest was Jean Pierre's biological father. Born on October 10, 1758 in New Orleans, Jean Pierre was born into financial opportunity. Throughout his adolescence, Jean Pierre accompanied his father and elder half brother on many an expedition: from the founding of Saint Louis to various encounters with Native Americans, Jean Pierre quickly mastered the role of merchant. To this end, and as a result of his family connections, Jean Pierre attained the oversight of Indian trade with the various Native American tribes near Saint Louis during the Jefferson administration; moreover, his clever, and at times ruthless, business dealings gained him and his elder half brother a near monopoly on all of the Native American trade in the Louisiana Territory. Indeed, prior to the War of 1812, Jean Pierre allied himself with his longtime fur trade adversary Manuel Lisa, further consolidating his hold on commercial exchanges of fur and other goods in the nation. In conjunction with the economic power Jean Pierre attained, his political influence also increased in the years of and immediately after the War of 1812. Indeed, soon after the admittance of the Missouri Territory into the United States, Jean Pierre was elected to the state senate. Although his political career never developed into a completely successful venture, his economic power was unchallenged. Throughout his life Jean Pierre purchased numerous land holdings, consolidated industries, eliminated competitors, and secured a place in the annals of American history for his family name. Although greatly aided by his father's influence and social position, Jean Pierre furthered his family's power, both political and economic, via knowledgeable business transactions and the good fortune of having numerous heirs. Indeed, his heirs, along with the other Chouteau children, continued to advance and secure the House of Chouteau.

When one reflects upon the legend (and the facts) of Auguste and Jean Pierre Chouteau, one cannot help but be overwhelmed by the sheer magnitude of their influence on domestic and national matters. From the founding of Saint Louis to the control and oversight of the fur trade, the Chouteaus have played a pivotal role in the commercial expansion and successes of the nation; moreover, it was their pioneering spirit – their frontiersman mentality – that ensured their legendary status among the American people.

William Clark

By Jeffrey E. Smith

For most people, William Clark's *real* first name is
"Lewis and." The 29 months he and Meriwether Lewis
spent on their odyssey to the Pacific and back made them
national celebrities not unlike astronauts in the 1960s;
William Clark and Meriwether Lewis were, in a way, the
John Glenn and Neil Armstrong of their day.

They were perhaps the most famous explorers since
Columbus, heading westward from their homes with many
of the same motives. Thomas Jefferson wanted them to
find "the most direct and practicable water communication
across this continent for the purposes of commerce."
Missouri Senator Thomas Hart Benton summed it up best
when he thundered on the floor of the Senate that America
needed to go "to the East, to India." After an arduous
journey confirming that the fabled Northwest Passage did
not exist and, worse yet, "those tremendous mountains"
stood in the way, they tried to create a positive spin. Upon
their return, Clark wrote his brother Jonathan that they had,
indeed, reached the Pacific and were therefore "completely
successfull [sic] . . . Such as nature has permited [sic]."
Getting to the lucrative East Asian trade would be harder
than anticipated.

The trek to the west transformed Clark in ways neither
he nor any of the others could have imagined. He returned
as a man with a new respect for Native American peoples
that helped shape his vision of western development. He
became one of the great boosters for the West, and ranked
among the most respected authorities on United States-
American Indian relations — by both sides.

To William Clark, the West was a source of commercial
activity and national prosperity. It was a place where
government takes an active role in protecting and facilitating

expansion of trade, transportation, and culture. It was a place where Native Americans could evolve into "civilized" (i.e., agricultural, westernized) peoples under the protective eye of the United States. It is a source of scientific knowledge, commerce, and even a route to the lucrative Asian trade. And he planned to be part of it.

Part of his reward was appointment as chief Indian agent for the region, which necessitated moving to the frontier town of St. Louis. He spent the rest of his life there, seeing the former French and Spanish settlement grow into a thriving western city and staging point for western development. He became quite the booster for the area, too, telling his brother that it "presents flattering advantages at this time and I think it will increas [sic] as the population increases, which is beginning to be considerable." Yet alas, he never realized the level of personal wealth he envisioned. However, he did become a leading voice in the great national debate about the west—How should it develop? What role should government play? And what about all the people who already lived there when the United States acquired it?

As the son of a Virginia (and then Kentucky) planter, Clark held a somewhat patriarchal view of society; landowners had an obligation not only to govern and lead, but also to help care for those less able to function and thrive in "civilized" society. This is part of the foundation for his rationalizing owning slaves, for example. However, it also shaped his decisions about his political allies in St. Louis as well. When Clark arrived in the city before embarking up the Missouri River, he met with the most influential members of the community; the home of fur-trade czar Auguste Chouteau, for example, became a sort of unofficial headquarters that winter. When he returned and settled in St. Louis, Clark allied himself with those who he perceived to be like himself: men of property and prominence who, like himself, were the most qualified to govern simply by virtue of their position in society. These were the same men with whom he became partners in the Missouri Fur Company, and the ones who comprised the so-called "St. Louis Junta" in the political battles of the late 1810s. They were men of financial success and political influence who owned large tracts of the territory and held claims to even more real estate in large Spanish land grants (now under review since the Americans had taken over the region). When the public came to view this group as a self-serving political machine, Clark was tarred with the same brush; it kept him from being elected Missouri's first governor.

Clark's views on Native Americans didn't endear him to many expansionists, either. He saw different races as part of a large body of humanity, all of which can presumably rise to the level of "civilization" of the Euro-Americans. But they would all need help through trade, training, schools, land, and even annuities, and he told them so. Clark's home became the site of numerous negotiations between tribal leaders and himself, and Clark often offered the same message he had in 1805. "The object of my coming to see you," he told them, "is not to do you injury but to do you good. The Great Chief of all the white people . . . wishing that all his red children should be happy has sent me here to know your wants that he may supply them . . . . [He] intends to build a house and fill it with such things as you may want and exchange with you." It would be a "win-win" scenario in which both sides thrived, prospered, and advanced in this soon-to-be-tamed wilderness.

It shaped his views on slavery too. African-Americans would also need help that came through slavery and for some, eventually, mentored freedom. In Clark's mind, slavery protected African-Americans—including his manservant and fellow westward traveler York—from a society that they neither fully understood nor were fully capable of functioning alone within. He was, he no doubt figured, doing them a great favor by retaining them as slaves until they "ready" for freedom; in fact, Clark freed several of his slaves (possibly including York) in later years so they could pursue other lines of work.

Today, we still leave William Clark stuck on the Corps of Discovery. After all, it did shape the rest of his life, lead him to a life connecting east and west, white and native cultures, commercial realms. His gravestone in St. Louis' Bellefontaine Cemetery, constructed as part of the journey's centennial celebration, sports the heads of buffalo and bear, but it recognizes him as "statesman."

The Journals of George Sibley
1808 - 1811

The following are the journals and letters written by George Champlain Sibley during his first three years as factor at Fort Osage; all the hand-written journals are in the collections of Lindenwood University in St. Charles, Missouri.

Washington City Tuesday May 17th, 1808

This day received from the hands of the Secretary of War (Gen. Dearborn)[1] the Appointment of Agent to the U. States Factory or Trading House established at the Osage River in the Territory of Louisiana, accompanied by a Letter informing me that my Compensation as Agent aforesaid, will be $800[2] a year Salary & $365 annually in lieu of Subsistence, with an outfit for the purchase of domestic utensils &c. of $200 and $25 annually for the Same purpose after the first year.

[1]Although originally trained as a physician, Henry Dearborn (1751-1825) spent most of his life in government work. He served in the War of Independence, including spending the winter of 1777-1778 at Valley Forge, and later joined General Washington's staff. Many wrote to him as General Dearborn, his title

from service in the Massachusetts Militia in the 1790s. He was Secretary of War for both of Jefferson's terms (1801-1809).

[2] Sibley almost invariably underlines dollar amount. Most likely, he used his journal and letterbook as the partial documentation for his accounting to make it easier to locate all the expenditures—which was important to the government and its requirements, as well as reflecting Sibley's personal tendencies to accuracy and detail in record-keeping.

Thursday 19th

This day I Subscribed and Swore to an Oath of office before Doctor Thornton, agreeably to the form prescribed by law, & lodged it with Mr. Smith first Clerk in the War Office.

Friday 20th

Wrote this day by Mail (franked by the Secretary of War) to John Winslow Esquire Fayetteville No. Car. enclosing him my bond of Office for Signature also a Note to John Hay Esquire Requesting his name also to the bond. I desired Mr. Winslow to enclose the Bond after it is duly executed, to John Mason, Esquire, Superintendent of Indian Trade,[3] under the Same cover I enclosed Mr. Winslow $100 in a Note of the U. S. Bank on Acct. of a debt that I owe him. This evening about 4 P.M. 2 Boats Started for Cumberland Maryland. having on board 77 Packages of Goods, the Property of the U. States, John Johnson Esquire[4] & myself, all are destined for Wheeling and to be Sent on to that place by Mr. McMahon of Cumberland— Yesterday I Received from John Mason Esquire Supt. In. Trade the following Summes of Money Vizt.

In Advance of my Salary Acct	*$600*
In full of my Compensation to the 17th Inst.	
As Assistant Agent To the St. Louis Factory	*87.66*
For John Johnson Esquire to be accounted for by me	*131.00*
Pd. Ross & Getty's bill Agent Johnson	*105.96*
This day pd. Patrick McCarty's bill of Frt. Agent Mr. Johnson	*7.59*
Pd. Milligan's Bill	*20.82*
Pd, Hack to carry trunk up to Boat	*1.20*
Pd. Freight of the trunk	*0.75*
Pd. Cartage &c.	*0.37 1/2*
	137.00

Mr. Johnson owes me 6 Dollars

[3] When John Mason became Superintendent of Indian Trade October 1, 1807, he succeeded a list of no fewer than six men with assorted titles and limited effectiveness. As president of the Bank of Columbia, Mason was originally hesitant to take any position in which public service might get in the way of his private business interests. His combination of longevity in office, administrative skill, and business acumen made Mason an effective leader of the department. Former merchant Thomas McKenney succeeded Mason in 1816. (Peake, *A History of the United States Indian Factory System*, 38-39.)

[4] John Johnson and Sibley united again in St. Louis, since Johnson was the new factor at Fort Madison. Forts Madison on the Mississippi and Osage on the Missouri replaced the Indian trade factory at Belle Fontaine, just north of St. Louis. They divided the inventory from Fort Belle Fontaine's factory between the two forts.

Sunday 22nd
Wrote to John Sibley- Mary Sibley & Samuel H. Sibley

Wednesday May 25th
Received this day from General Dearborn & General Mason my final instructions &c. and I Shall Set off in the morning for Baltimore on my way to Pittsburgh- Received of General Mason $400 to hire Boat hands & pay other expences of transportation from Pittsburgh to St. Louis- for which sum I am to account.

Thursday 26th
Set off in the Stage for Baltimore this morning at 5 O'Clock:- Reached Baltimore by 5 P.M.

Friday 27th
Got a parcel of Silver ornaments from Thomas Warner amounting to $_____ for which Sum I drew on John Mason Esquire Superintendent of Indian Trade wrote to J. Mason this day.

Saturday 28th
Bought 50 pieces tincel lace[5] from Frederick Hammer for $70 & drew on Supt. Indian Trade in payment. Also bought Several articles for my own use, a Coat, Pantaloons, Flannel- Paper, a treatise on Mineralogy- Pistol, Flints, &c Flask- Spy Glass- Powder- Sword Cane- Cupping Instrument- Spring lancet- &c. &c.
Received of Mr. Horne a Small Bundle, & a little Japanned Box for Capt. House also a Set (2 Vols) Espriellas Letters- Wrote to General Mason.

[5] Lace with a shiny, metallic-looking thread woven into it.

Sunday May 29th, 1808
Went on Board the Philadelphia Packet (old line) at 5 A. M.13 passengers on board. Sailed at 10. Reached Frenchtown at 6 P. M. On board the Packet at New Castle at 11, after driving 17 Miles in the Stage from French Town.

Monday 30th
Arrived in Philadelphia at 7 A. M. Put up at the Mansion House Hotel. Met Major Pike, Lieut. Murray & Several other offices there. Also fell in with W. P. Hunt of St. Louis. Went to see Mr. Cushing & Miss McKee [McRee?]. Pike and Hunt talk of Setting off for St. Louis in 10 days.

Tuesday 31st
Set off at 4 this Morning in the Stage for Pittsburgh. Stage full. Went 12 Miles beyond Lancaster.

Wednesday 1st, June
Set off at 4. Breakfasted in Middletown. Stopped to change at Harrisburgh ditto at Carlisle. Halted at a house 10 miles from Carlisle.

Thursday 2d
Set off at 4. Breakfasted at Shippensburgh changed at Chambersburgh. Halted for the day at McConnelsburgh.

Friday 3d
Off at 4. 23 Miles to Breakfast, 15 to Bedford. Halted for the day. Bathed in Juniata.

Saturday 4th
Off at 4. Breakfasted at the foot of Allegany Mountain. Halted at Somerset for the day.

Sunday June 5th, 1808
Started at 4. Breakfasted on top of Laurel Hill. ---[blank] Miles to Greensburgh. Halted for the day.

Monday 6th
Off at 4. [blank] miles to Breakfast. [blank] Miles to Pittsburgh. Got there at 4 P. M. at 7 waited on Lt. Piatt. Find the Boat nearly Ready.

Tuesday 7th
Engaged Joseph Ogden as an Oarsman to go to St. Louis to give him 50

cents a day to St. Louis. $25 to bring him home again, & to find him during the Voyage.

Wednesday 8th

Hired Lee McMullin To day at the Same as Ogden. Took on board 30 Packages of Public Stores, Received of Lt. Piatt to be delivered at St. Louis to General Clark, Col. Hunt & P. Chouteau. Purchased the following Article for use of Boat & Crew—

2 Kettles - $1.25 – 12 Tin Cups $1---------------$3.50
10 lbs. Cordage $1.87 1/2 – 1 Axe helved & ground $2--------------3.87 1/2
25 Hooks and 4 lines 62 1/2 cents – 15 lbs. Chocolate $5.62 1/2 ----------
6.25
3 lbs. Candles 50 cents – 15 lbs. Sugar & Keg $2.37------------------2.87
Salt 40 cents - Bacon $2.37 – Potatoes 50 cents ------------------- 3.27 1/2
1 Barrel Whiskey & Barrel -----------------------------12.77
Raw Hide for tugs 3 lbs. Bread ---------------3.50
Pd. 5 Meals at tavern for Hands -------------------- 1.25
Spoons, knives, &c. $3

Wrote to General Mason

Thursday June 9th, 1808

This morning Hired 3 more hands at the Same Rates as those of yesterday & day before- Vizt. John Speer, Archibald Warden & Ebenezer Wilson. Mr. Johnson arrived in the Stage this evening from Baltimore. At 11 P.M. Mr. L. Valle & myself went on board the Boat & cast off into the Stream. We Rowed about an Hour & then came to for the Night.

Friday 10th

Morning cool & pleasant. Put off <u>at Sunrise</u>. Day excessively Hot. Men Rowed but badly. Came to before dark for them to cook. Made about ---- blank—Miles to day.

Saturday 11th

Morning clear & pleasant. Had the men at their oars before day, very foggy about day, had to Stop. Head Wind till 2 P.M.. Passed Steubenville at 12, Charlestown at about 1/2 past 1. Reached Wheeling just at dark. A Shower in the evening. River falling. Went to Major Spriggs & put up. Hear nothing of the Goods.

Sunday 12th

This morning indulged myself with the luxury of clean linen and a good Breakfast. Day very Hot the River falling a little.

Traffic on the Missouri River at the time included a wide range of crafts including flatboats, bateaux, and keelboats, seen here. (Jefferson National Expansion Museum/National ParkService, Courtesy, State Historical Society of Missouri, Columbia)

Wheeling Monday 13th

The morning clear & pleasant. Employed a Man to Build a Cabin on my Boat, but he got drunk, and neglected it. Hired another & he done the Same. Engaged a Smith to make me 4 Sockets and 2 Hooks for Boat poles. Bought 57 lbs. Bacon for the Hands.

Wheeling, Tuesday June 14th, 1808

Morning clear & Sultry. The Blacksmith completed the Sockets & Hooks for which I paid him $9.50. After a great deal of trouble I got the carpenter to go for the Boards for my boat's cabin, but he got drunk Soon after he conveyed them to his Shop. I paid $1.50 a Hundred feet for Seasoned white pine.

Wheeling Wednesday 15th

Heavy Rain last night which continued Still about 12 this day alternately Raining & Shining. About ten a wagon with part of the Goods arrived from Cumberland, the Rest to be here in a few days. Received a letter from Mr. Johnson by a Dutchman, also Some little things of his to be put in the Boat. River at a Stand. Got a letter out of the Post office from Mr. Johnson in which he tells me that he will be here tomorrow.

Wheeling Thursday 16th

Morning cool and Somewhat cloudy. Carpenter not yet done the Cabin. Bought a Rifle from a Mr. McClure for $18. Said to be a good one. Engaged a Painter to paint the Cabin, to commence early tomorrow if Clear. River at a Stand. Paid a tailor $5.47 1/2 for making a Flannel Coate, pair of drawers and a Morning Gown & finding Some linings, Buttons, &c. Frequent Showers of Rain during the day & at Night a heavy gust.

Wheeling Friday June 17th, 1808

Morning looks cloudy and is Sultry. River Rose a little to day. Wrote John Sibley.

Saturday 18th

Capt. Webster & Mr. Johnson arrived about 9 O'Clock from Pittsburgh in a Small Barge & 4 Men also a Flat, all loaded with Public Stores for St. Louis. I turned over 22 Packages of the Stores I received from Lt. Piatt at Pittsburgh on the 8th to Capt. Webster, being all that I received except 6 Kegs Nails and 2 Boxes hard Ware for Col. Hunt which I Still have in charge.

Sunday 19th

After dinner, Capt. Webster Set off. Mr. Valle went with him. Received a Letter from William McMahon of Cumberland, in which he tells me he has Sent on the 10th, in three other waggons all the Rest of the Goods except 5 Packages that the waggons would not hold, his letter is dated 13th Inst. Showery.

Monday 20th

Wrote Mr. McMahon directing him to Send the 5 Packages to Pittsburgh <u>immediately</u> to the care of Lt. Piatt Asst. Military Agent. Wrote also to Lt. Piatt. Hired 2 more Hands to day; to give them each $1 per day & find them to St. Louis. Commencing to day. The River has been Rising fast all day. Rainy.

Wheeling Tuesday 21st June 1808

Waggons not come yet. Carpenters yet pestering me with their indolence, impudence and villainy.

Wednesday 22nd

This day the Rest of the Goods arrived in a flat Boat from Brownsville. Took them on Board but found Some difficulty in Stowing them So as to use the Oars. Received a Letter by Mail this day from General Mason dated the 10ᵗʰ, Inst. in which he encloses me Invoice of Silver Ornaments & Tincel Lace and a duplicate of my Bill of Expenses while on public business in Baltimore, the last he desires me to Sign & Return to him.

Thursday 23ʳᵈ
Wrote to General Mason. Devoted the morning to Settling my Accounts with those Scoundrels that I was under the necessity of employing about my Boat. And after dinner at 3 O'Clock pushed off & proceeded on the Voyage. Went about 25 Miles before Sun down & after Supper put off and floated all Night. Found ourselves at the lower end of the long Reach at day Break.

Friday 24ᵗʰ
Reached Marietta this day at half past 3 P.M. went ashore for half an hour. Marietta is pleasantly Situated at the mouth of the Muskingum having about 90 Houses on the upper and 3 on the opposite bank where Fort Harmon formerly Stood. The inhabitants are principally New Englanders. It is the Seat of Justice for Washington County, Ohio. Lat: 30° 34' No. Lon. 82° 9' W. 146 Miles S. W. of Pittsburgh by land and about 170 by Water. Went 7 Miles farther before Supper. Floated past Blennerhasset's Island[6] at 9 O'Clock.

[6] This was an infamous landmark when Sibley floated by in 1808. It was the mansion home of Irish immigrant Harman Blennerhassett (1765-1831), one of the three alleged leaders in the Burr Conspiracy along with James Wilkinson and, of course, Aaron Burr. He was accused of providing substantial funding and support for Burr's alleged plot to separate the southwestern regions from the rest of the United States. In November 1806, Blennerhassett fled upon hearing news that Jefferson ordered his arrest, escaping just ahead of the Virginia militia. Burr was acquitted of high treason, but Blennerhassett landed in the Virginia State Penitentiary. After Burr's acquittal, Blennerhassett was released as well. When an ill-fated attempt at becoming a cotton plantation owner in Mississippi Territory failed, Harman Blennerhassett returned to Ireland.

River Ohio, Saturday June 25ᵗʰ, 1808
Last night passed little and Great Hockhocking River (about 7 Miles apart on the Ohio Side) Newbury Settlement & Bellville. Passed Shade River a little after Sunrise. Passed little & Big Sandy Creek after Breakfast. Letart's Rapids at 1/2 past 12. Point Pleasant & Great Kanhawa at 10 P.M., at 11, Gallipolis is 3 Miles below the Great Kanhawa & about 285 Miles (by Water) from Pittsburgh.

Sunday 26th
At 11 O'Clock: passed Great Sandy River the dividing line between the States of Virginia & Kentucky. This is about 340 Miles from Pitt.

Monday 27th
To day passed Big Kiota River, the towns of Alexandria & Portsmouth, and arrived at Limestone Kentucky at 5 in the evening (about 450 Miles from Pitt) went ashore here a few minutes to get Some Necessaries & then proceeded till night when we halted to Supper & again proceeded all night, at day light on.

Tuesday 28th
We found ourselves at Bullskin Creek. At 2 we got to Little Miami River. At 4 Reached Cincinnati. Here we laid by till after dark and then put off again. Cincinnati is handsomely Situated on a first & 2nd bank of the Ohio opposite Licking River. It is a flourishing town contains about 400 Houses besides Several elegant Public Buildings. It is 82 Miles N. by E. of Frankfort and about 380 by land S. S. W. of Pittsburgh & by Water about 525 Miles—39° 5' 54" N. Lat. & 85° 44' W. Lon. Opposite Cincinnati and just above the junction of the Ohio & Licking River Stands New Port at which place is an U. S. Arsenal or place of deposit, a magazine of arms ammunition &c.

River Ohio Wednesday June 29th, 1808
At 6 this morning passed Miami River. Floated past Kentucky River this Night at about 11 O'Clock.

Thursday 30th
Got to the Falls this evening at about 11 O'Clock. Halted at the Mouth of Beargrass Creek.

Louisville Friday July 1st, 1808
After Breakfast went up to Louisville to enquire for Capt. Webster (whose Boat is I find lying below the falls) & to get a Pilot. At Gwathmen's Tavern I met with Mr. John Nisbet from Statesville, No. Car. who is traveling through the Western Country for his health and amusement. Capt. Webster talks of Staying here for the 4th, if I will wait for him, which I could not think of promising. At about 12 the Pilot was Ready to put us over the falls and accordingly we done So & without any accident. Purchased Some

provisions &c. and made arrangements to Start day after tomorrow. Wrote to General Mason.

Louisville Saturday 2nd
Spent the day partly in laying in provisions &c. and in the company of my friend Nisbet. Bought some Sugar, crockery ware, a Straw Hat & some Bacon for the Men. Paid $ (?) 8 1/3 per Hundred. Took Tea at Mr. Fitzhughes. Capt. Webster very Suddenly got married this evening to a Young Woman of this place.

Louisville Sunday 3rd
Employed another Hand this morning by name Adam Payne, to give him a dollar a day and find him. After dinner we again Resumed our Voyage, but without the company of Capt. Webster, who in consequence of his recent marriage cannot make it convenient to leave Louisville So Soon.   A Boat worked (?) by Horses Set off from the Falls just before us bound for <u>St. Genevieve</u>. Soon after we Started there came on a Heavy Shower of Rain with high wind which obliged us to ly by a few minutes.

Note—It is about 705 Miles (by Water) from Pittsburgh to the Falls.

River Ohio Monday <u>July 4th</u>, 1808
Passed Blue River to day. Nothing material occurred.

Tuesday 5th
Passed Little Blue River (775 Miles from Pitt)

Wednesday 6th
Between Anderson's Ferry & the Hanging Rock (about 135 Miles below the falls) met Colonel Kingsbury & Family in a Public Boat with a Small detachment of Troops (about 4 O'Clock P.M.) from Fort Adams & bound for Marietta. The Col. is on Furlough & is going to visit his friends in New England. This morning I discharged Adam Payne for improper conduct & paid him $3 in full.

Thursday 7th
At 12 O'Clock passed Green River. At Sundown got to the Red Banks where is a Small Town called Henderson. After Supper Started again & floated all Night.

Friday 8th
Early this morning passed diamond Islands. Passed the mouth of Wabash River Early in the evening. Got to Shawanese Town (a kind of Ragged

Village where Salt is deposited from the works on the Saline River) at Sundown. Lay here all night.

Saturday 9th
Hired 3 more Hands here, to give them each $1 per day & find them. Had the Boat cleaned up, the tarpaulins better Spread, and Started again at 1/2 past 11 O'Clock. Reached the Cave in the Rock at 4 O'Clock; passed half an hour there. This Cave is about 125 miles above the Mouth of Ohio on the right Side or rather on the Indiana Shore. Went on till Sun Set when we Reached the head of Hurricane Island. Here we were detained Some time looking for the channel & at length were obliged to put to Shore & ly by for the Night.

River Ohio Sunday July 10th, 1808
Made Several attempts this morning to pass the Island before we found the Right channel which at last we effected & went on briskly. Passed Mile's ferry, where the road crosses from Kentucky to St. Louis. Arrived at the Mouth of the Cumberland River just at Sundown, Stopped to cook Supper & proceeded all night.

Monday 11th
At break of day we heard the Reveille beating at Fort Massac. Reached the Fort in time to Breakfast with the officers there, Lts. Whitlock & Johnson & Dr. Skinner. Remained at the Fort till after dinner and then put off again & went to the little Chain of Rocks where we lay all Night.

Tuesday 12th
Passed Wilkinsonville (an old deserted Village) in the early part of the morning. Got to the <u>Mouth of Ohio</u> at about 3 O'Clock; halted to make Some necessary preparations for entering the Mississippi and then entered that Noble Stream, which we found very difficult at first to stem, it being Remarkably low and Rapid. We got up about 2 Miles before Night & encamped on the West Shore.

River Mississippi July Wednesday 13th, 1808
Started early but could make but little head way, the current being very Strong, the hands unaccustomed to the River and many obstructions in the way. We made about 5 Miles however and encamped for the night on the West Shore.

Thursday 14th
Got pretty well into the Grand bend. Halted for the Night on the lower point of a large Sand bar on the East Side of the River just below Dog Tooth Island. Made about 8 Miles to day.

Friday 15th
Attempted to pass to the Right of Dog Tooth Island but found it impracticable & turned back. Got up to a Mr. Griffin's by Sundown where we lay all Night and got Some little Refreshment. Mr. Griffin calls it 25 Miles to the Mouth of Ohio from his House.

Saturday 16th
Breakfasted at Mr. Finley's (1 Mile above Griffin's) 10 Miles farther to the Widow Watter's where we halted for the Night.

Sunday 17th
Went 1 Mile and Struck a Rock on which we Stuck all day in Spite of every exertion to extricate ourselves, which could only be done at last by lighting the load. We lay this night within a Mile of our last Night's fire.

Monday 18th
To day we Reached Cape Girardeau which is called 50 Miles from the Mouth of Ohio. Laid in Some Sugar & Chocolate for the Men.

River Mississippi Tuesday July 19th, 1808
Went about 11 Miles to day being 2 Miles above the head of the Divel's [sic] Island.

Wednesday 20th
Got just above the Delaware & Shawnee Village making our Run about 11 miles to day.

Thursday 21st
Went about 10 Miles to Fenwick's.

Friday 22nd
About 5 Miles only to day.

Saturday 23rd
Went about 9 Miles to Patterson's.

Sunday 24th
Went about 10 Miles to day.

Monday 25th
Got within 3 Miles of St. Genevieve.

Tuesday 26th

Breakfasted at the Mouth of Gabaree Went about 7 Miles farther to day, being just below old Fort Chartres.

Wednesday 27th

Morning a little hazy—but cool—went about 2 1/2 miles & Stopped to Breakfast. While at breakfast a canoe came down from St. Louis the owner told me that the Troops were all Ready to Start up the River from Belle Fontaine & had fixed on this day week for their departure. A French Boat with Plank from St. Genevieve going to St. Louis passed us about 1 O'Clock. We got to within 2 miles of the Platter Rock to day, which is Said to be half way (30 miles) between St. Genevieve & St. Louis. Night Rainy.

River Mississippi Thursday July 28th, 1808

Started late this morning. Went 2 Miles to the Platter Rock & halted for Breakfast. The Rain continued till 11 O'Clock, & then cleared off cool & pleasant. Passed Lagle River (Indiana Shore) about 2 O'Clock. Swashing Creek is nearly opposite the Lagle & both are about 12 Miles below the Merrimak . Encamped about 4 Miles below the Merrimak.

Friday 29th

Head wind. Passed the Merrimak at 11 A.M. 15 Miles from here to St. Louis. At about 3 o'clock after having Cordell'd Round a Small Sand Bar near the middle of the River (which is just above Mr. Philip Fine's & about 2 Miles above the Merrimak) the men attempted to wade from the Point of the Bar to the main Shore thinking the water would not be too deep for them. But they all very Suddenly plunged from a Steep point of the Bar into water out of their depth, and they all made for the main Shore, which was about the Same distance from them the Bar was, & much the easiest to gain, there being an old tree lying between them and the Boat which was Rather above them. The wind heavy against them & current Swift. They had got within 30 or 40 yards of Shore, when John Speer the man who had the end of the Cordel & could not Swim a Stroke excited the attention of the Rest upon discovering Symptoms of drowning. Archibald Warren who was next to him Rendered every assistance in his power but was unable to Support him and called for more help, the person who held the Rope next in order was Bill Brooks (a free Negro). He Swam to their aid and Speer quit the hold he had on Warden with one hand and Seized Bill and for a considerable time (1/2 a Minute) Supported himself between the two drawing them both frequently under water which So much exhausted them that they were barely able to Support themselves and they would all three have been drowned but that Speer let Warden go, and laid hold of Bill with both hands. Warden with the greatest difficulty Reached the Shore but was unable to Stand for Several Minutes. Speer &

Bill after Struggling together about a minute (during which time they were alternately under & above water) disappeared and Rose no more.

The other Men who were out were John Scoggins, Asa Ledbetter & Nathan Taylor who held the Rope in the order they are named, Ledbetter Says he held Speer till he thought his own life was in danger & then left him. The Boat was far out of Reach & totally unmanageable with the few hands in her that it was not possible to give any assistance that way. I Sent a Man to acquaint Mr. Fine with the accident and to Request his assistance to find the Bodies. He came up & advised me to end to the Merrimak for a canoe that was there with which Search might be made with hooks I did So. We dragged Several times but without Success.

John Speer is I understand a Native of Pennsylvania. His Mother Resides near Pittsburgh on a place of General Ohara's. He was about 23 years of Age, tall & well made Hair neither light nor dark. His clothes & effects of but little value.

Bill Brooks was a Black Man about 23 or 24 years of Age thick Set & well proportioned. A native of New York State where he Said he had Some Relation on the Mohawk River near Albany. He has Resided Some time as a Servant in Pittsburgh with Mr. Williams [a] Tavern keeper who I am told has in trust or keeping His certificate of Freedom. His clothes & effects worth but little.

River Mississippi Saturday July 30th, 1808

Morning pleasant. Started from the unfortunate Spot at which we were so unexpectedly Stopped at about 9 O'Clock this morning. I hired another hand here to assist us to give him $1 a day. Got within 5 Miles of St. Louis Mississippi Rising fast.

Sunday 31st

Morning clear & cool. River Rose about 6 feet last night. Arrived at St. Louis at 11 O'Clock. Waited on General Clark to deliver Some Letters from the Secretary of War. Met Capt. House[7] & Mr. B. Wilkinson[8] there. The General Informs me that the Governor has considered it expedient to fix the Factory not on the Osage River as directed by the Secretary of War, but about ---blank--- Miles above at or near the Prairie de Feu or Fire Prairie. That Capt. Clemson is to take the whole of his company, and is nearly Ready to Set off, that it had been determined for Capt. C. to Start on next Wednesday leaving Lt. Lorimier[9] & 16 Men behind to take up the Goods when I Should arrive. I told General Clark I had not a word to Say with Regard to the location of the Factory, it having been I understood directed to be done by the Indian Agent. But that I Should feel much better

Satisfied if the Goods could go with the whole body of the Troops, that I expected be Ready by the 10th of August at farthest & hoped Capt. C. might be prevailed on to wait till then, this the General Thought to be Reasonable & Said he would write to Col. Hunt on the Subject. Dined with General Clark at table met Governor Lewis. After dinner paid off my Hands and discharged them. Hired a French crew to take the Boat up to Camp.

[7] Capt. James House was stationed at Fort Belle Fontaine when Col. Thomas Hunt died in August,1808; he and Sibley worked together at Fort Belle Fontaine. House thought enough of Sibley to write a letter of reference for him when Rudolph Tilliers tried to remove Sibley as Assistant factor at Belle Fontaine in 1807. (*Territorial Papers* 14, 208n.)

[8] Benjamin Wilkinson (d. 1810) operated a mercantile firm with Risdon H. Price (see below) in St. Louis. Like several of the men with whom Sibley dealt, Wilkinson was one of the founders of the Missouri Fur Company; he traveled to Louisville, Kentucky in 1809 to recruit men for the expedition upriver to return Sheheke, a Mandan chief who came to the United States with Lewis and Clark. However, he apparently didn't join the group, since he was serving on a grand jury in St. Louis that August. He was apparently on a buying trip to Baltimore in 1810 when he died at sea. Wilkinson was elected a captain in a Volunteer Company at a meeting in Mr. Yosti's tavern in St. Louis in 1808; Risdon Price was elected lieutenant.

His uncle James Wilkinson (1757-1825) was a somewhat notorious character. Although he was the highest ranking army officer starting in 1796 and governor of the Louisiana Territory in 1805-6, he had a dubious past: he served in the Revolutionary War under Benedict Arnold and was implicated in the so-called "Conway Cabal" to remove George Washington as commander during the War of Independence, resigning as the army's clothier-general in 1781 over questionable accounting. Later, he tried to persuade the western United States to form a pro-Spanish independent nation, even swearing an oath of allegiance to Spain in exchange for a $2,000 annual pension (which the Spanish government later increased to $4,000). He carried on extensive correspondence with Aaron Burr in 1805-6, but tipped off Jefferson of Burr's plot to facilitate breaking the union between the eastern states and western region. Not one to be bound by personal loyalties, Wilkinson later testified against Burr. Wilkinson himself survived an inquiry in 1811, then lost his command in the War of 1812 after a remarkable loss at Montreal. (Billon, *Annals of St. Louis in its Territorial Days*, 89; Holmberg, *Dear Brother: Letters of William Clark to Jonathan Clark*, 199; Douglas, "Manuel Lisa," *Missouri Historical Society Collections*, 257-260.)

[9] Lieut. Louis Lorimier (d. 1831) was the son and namesake of the famous trader in Ste. Genevieve, Louis (1748-1812). Young Louis attended the United States Military Academy at West Point only two years after its founding,

graduating in 1806. The Military Academy considers him its first Native American graduate, since his mother, Charolette Pemanpich Bougainville (d. 1812) was of Shawnee ancestry. He served his entire military career in the West until resigning from the Army at the end of 1809. This may be the same Lorimier who headed a trade expedition to the Crows for the newly reorganized Missouri Fur Company in 1812. Lorimier ended up owning a farm in Cape Girardeau. (Cullum, *Notices of the Biographical Register of Officers and Graduates of the U. S. Military Academy at West Point*, 103; Douglas, "Manuel Lisa," *Missouri Historical Society Collections*, 369.)

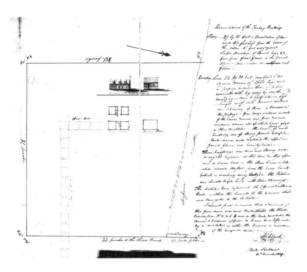

Sibley spent his first years as Assistant Factor at Fort Belle Fontaine, mapped here by William Clark in 1809. (National Archives, Courtesy, State Historical Society of Missouri, Columbia)

Camp Belle Fontaine August 1st, 1808

Started the Boat off at 8 O'Clock. After Breakfast left St. Louis with Mr. B. Wilkinson & Major Wilson,[10] got here to dinner. Waited on Col. Hunt, Mr. Tillier &c. Met Pierre Lorr[11] on the Road to St. Louis whither he was going to See me he said to know if I would want him for an Interpreter I told him Yes.

[10] Major George Wilson. Four years later, George Wilson was in St. Louis, appointed by Governor Benjamin Howard to purchase provisions in preparation for a spring campaign against Native Americans allied with the British and, therefore, hostile to the United States. Howard wrote William Clark in late November 1812, that he figured on needing 1,012 barrels of

pickled pork "which cannot be obtained hereafter in time," and assigned Wilson—a man "whose qualifications you well know," to oversee the provisioning. (*Territorial Papers* 14, 611.)

[11] Col. Thomas Hunt (d. 1808) was a career military officer who served in a company of Minute Men in the War of Independence. In only a few months after arriving in St. Louis, he rose through the ranks to become commander of the First Infantry and of the Cantonment Fort Belle Fontaine, succeeding Russell Bissell, who died in the post in 1807. Within just about two weeks of the dinner Sibley mentions here, Hunt died on August 17 or 18, 1808. Clark planned to have Hunt travel up the Mississippi to oversee the construction of Fort Madison, much as Clark was doing himself for Fort Osage, but Hunt died before leaving. (Billon, *Annals of St. Louis in its Territorial Days*, 225; Holmberg, *Dear Brother: Letters of William Clark to Jonathan Clark*, 143-146.)

Rudolph Tillier was factor at Fort Belle Fontaine the entire time the trade operations were open, from 1805 to the summer of 1808, but remained in St. Louis until at least November of 1809, since he had joined 38 others in signing a letter to James Madison recommending Judge John Coburn (Benjamin Farrar's brother-in-law, who convinced the physician to move to St. Louis in 1807; see below) to replace the late Governor Meriwether Lewis. Sibley's subsequent correspondence to him was most likely restricted to business, since mutual animosity marked their working relationship. Tillier tried to fire Sibley in late 1807; Sibley took Clark's advice and traveled to Washington, D.C., to defend himself before the Office of Indian Trade. He was on this errand when he received his commission to become the factor at the newly created Fort Osage. Tillier was apparently in his later years. In May, 1809, Superintendent of Indian Trade John Mason wrote to Lewis about events of the preceding fall, which presumably revolve around closing the factory at Fort Belle Fontaine and the resolution of his charges against Sibley. Mason asked that he and Clark "save the feelings of Mr. Tillier who from all accounts I consider a man of great honor and respectability and who has seen better times."(Recommendation from Citizens of the Territory to James Madison, November 3, 1809, *Territorial Papers* 14, 340; John Mason to Governor Meriwether Lewis, May 17, 1809, *Territorial Papers* 14, 275.)

Pierre Lorr was a full-time interpreter with the United States government, which was somewhat unusual in the trade-factory system. There wasn't really enough work to justify a full-time interpreter at most factories, so they were paid poorly, the government often getting about what it paid for. There was, however, enough activity and trade at St. Louis and Fort Osage to warrant a full-time interpreter.

Tuesday 2nd
The Boat arrived this evening & Mr. Johnson all safe.

Wednesday 3rd

Had the Boat unloaded & Mr. Johnson & myself Separated our things. This day we went to work in the Factory, dividing and packing up the Goods.

Thursday 4th

Continued very busily engaged in the Store.

Friday 5th

Ditto.

Saturday 6th

Ditto. This day drew a Draft on General Mason Supt. Indian Trade for $400 in favor Wilkinson & Price or order at ten days Sight and advised him of it by Letter.

Sunday 7th

Finished dividing the Goods packed my half of them up, and had them all Stowed on Board the Boats.

Camp Belle Fontaine Monday 8th August 1808

Capt. Clemson being now Ready to Set off, made his arrangements to do so having Received his orders from the Col. He embarked about 2 O'Clock, and began the Voyage. His command consists of His company of Infantry (of the 1st U. S. Regiment) in 4 Keel Boats containing Military Stores & Factory Goods, and 2 other Keel boats belonging one to Mr. Prince the Sutler the other to the Contractor.

Note: Major Pike[12] arrived Yesterday.

Wrote on the 6th to General Mason and Mr. Williams of Pittsburgh informing them of the death of John Speer & Bill Brooks & informing them how the friends of the deceased may get their things & the Money that I owe them for Wages. In these Letters I Shall enclose the Receipt of the person in whose hands I put the property (Mr. Alexander McNair of St. Louis) & forward them by Major Pike. On the 2nd, Inst. employed Pierre Lorr to be my Interpreter about the Factory. I am to give him $1 & 1 Ration per day. His time commences with this day. Wrote to my Father.

[12] Zebulon Montgomery Pike (1779-1813) was in and out of the St. Louis area during the period. Pike had a somewhat checkered career. Neither of his chief expeditions were successful—he never correctly identified the headwaters of the Mississippi River, and his trek to the southwest was riddled with misadventure. After returning some Osage leaders including Big

Soldier (see below) who were returning from a meeting with President Thomas Jefferson, Pike traveled on westward into present-day Colorado. He and his men were captured by the Spanish and taken to Santa Fe, then south to Chihuahua. The Spanish governor there decided to return Pike and his men to the American border at Natchitoches near the present-day Louisiana-Texas border. His name was often whispered in connection to the Burr Conspiracy, since Burr confidante James Wilkinson (who was also territorial governor and head of the army) had sent Pike on his trek to Santa Fe. There were winks and nods that Pike was part of Wilkinson's efforts to woo the Spanish into annexing part of the American West. His protests to Henry Dearborn compelled the war secretary to exonerate him, but the cloud of questionable character remained for some people; Sibley may have had his reservations about Pike, given the terse nature of his entry here. Pike was promoted to major in 1808; he died in 1813 during the War of 1812.

Camp Belle Fontaine Tuesday 9th August 1808

This day Receipted To R. Tillier Esquire for the public Property Received of him amounting to $14042.08. Wrote to General Mason & enclosed him 17 Vouchers for money expended in Public Account amounting to $697.43. Since my arrival here Capt. House put into my Hands Several Letters Vizt. from John Sibley, November 5th & December 25th 1807, Mary Sibley, Samuel H. Sibley, Secretary of War, and I Received on the 5th a Letter from S. H. Sibley dated June 7th, 1808.

Wednesday 10th

Busy all day writing.

Thursday 11th

Left Belle Fontaine this morning early for St. Louis got there a little after Breakfast. Settled up Accounts with Wilkinson & Price. Owe them a Balance of $94.59, for which I gave my Note or due bill. Left in their Hands a due bill of Ensign Immelles (?) for $41.50 to collect & apply to my Credit. Put into the hands of Alexander McNair the Money & effects of John Speer (Cash $45 & Some Clothing) and Bill Brooks (Cash $39.50 & Some Clothing) taking his Receipt for the Same in which he promises to deliver the above on demand to the legal Representatives of the Deceased. Enclosed the Receipt in my Letters of the 6th to General Ohara and Mr. Williams & left the letters with McNair to Send by Major Pike. After dinner Set off with Mr. Wilkinson for St. Charles. We arrived at the Ferry after dark in a heavy Shower of Rain which wet us both to the Skin lay all night at the ferry House. Capt. Clemson is lying just above St. Charles.

Friday 12th

Early got a Boat and joined Capt. Clemson. Took possession of my own

Boat and made the necessary arrangements &c. After taking Breakfast we proceeded on the Voyage.

Fire Prairie Friday September 2nd, 1808
Arrived here this day at 12 O'Clock and encamped about 2 Miles above at the first Bluff, examined the Situation and conclude it will not answer.

Saturday 3rd
Capt. Clemson, Mr. Lewis[13] & myself took two Men & a Canoe and went up the River about 3 miles to a Bluff, which on examination, we all think a fine Spot for the Fort, and Capt. Clemson determines to move the Boats here tomorrow.

> [13] Reuben Lewis (1777-1844) was Meriwether Lewis's younger brother. As a partner in the Missouri Fur Company, Reuben "brought his youthful vigor and considerable competence to the company" while also keeping his older brother, Territorial Governor Meriwether Lewis, apprised of all happenings. He was the first Indian Sub-Agent to the Osage in 1808, but didn't stay in the post long. Dr. John Robinson (see below) replaced him in March 1809. (Oglesby, *Manuel Lisa and the Opening of the Missouri Fur Trade*, 69; Jones, *Prairie Puritan*, 54, 58.)

Sunday 4th
After dinner moved the Boat up to the next point (commonly Called by Voyagers the "Big Eddy," & Sometimes the "Bad luck Hills") and encamped, just at dark General Clark joined us with a detachment of 80 mounted Militia. They left St. Charles the 25th Ulto. Night Rainy.

Monday 5th
The General dispatched Capt. Boon[14] & his Interpreter Paul,[15] to the Osage Towns, to know of them if they intend to come here to Settle. Recommending them very Strongly to do So, and avoid the fatal consequences of Refusing. Began to clear away a Spot for the Fort, and unloaded the Boats. I find all the Factory Goods in apparent good order except 2 Bales of Blankets and 2 Boxes Rifles which have got wet on the way from Belle Fontaine. Put as many of the Goods under cover of the Tarpaulin as could be Stowed, the Rest consisting of Tight Casks &c. not likely to be injured were piled up Separate and were obliged to be left uncovered.

> [14] Nathan Boone (1781-1856) was the youngest son of the famed frontiersman Daniel Boone. Nathan and his new bride Olive (nee Van Bibber) moved to Missouri soon after his father relocated there to live on land he received through a Spanish land grant. They built a cabin, then later a substantial

house on the Femme Osage River, northwest of brother Daniel Morgan Boone's settlement. Although a farmer and surveyor by occupation, Boone became known for his military career. William Clark convinced him to serve as a captain and guide of the militia for this expedition to establish Fort Osage, since he knew the territory well from his salt-making operations nearby (see below). He organized and commanded mounted rangers during the War of 1812; he was engaged in some battles, but most of his time was spent on patrols in northern and western Missouri. He was promoted to major in 1813, and discharged at the end of the war. As Superintendent for Indian Affairs Clark called his mounted rangers into service again in 1832 in the Black Hawk War. He served in a variety of capacities in the army in Missouri, Arkansas, Oklahoma, Texas, Minnesota, and Iowa, where he met or served under such distinguished figures as Stephen Watts Kearney, future President Zachary Taylor, and Republic of Texas President Sam Houston. He left the military in 1848 due to his health, finally resigning in 1853. (Hurt, *Nathan Boone and the American Frontier*; Hurt, "Nathan Boone," in *Dictionary of Missouri Biography*, 103-105.)

[15] Paul Loise (c. 1777-1832), sometimes referred to as Paul Louis or Paul Chouteau, was a full-time interpreter in government service, which was somewhat unusual for factories; often there wasn't enough work to keep an interpreter busy all year, so they were given shorter-termed contracts. Loise accompanied William Clark and the St. Charles Dragoons on this trek to Fire Prairie as Clark's interpreter. Later, when there was a controversy between Clark, Pierre Chouteau, and the Osages over the 1808 treaty, there was some suggestion that the Osage didn't understand the terms of the treaty because of faulty interpreting (either by malice or by accident) on the part of either Loise or Chouteau's interpreter Noel Magrain. In his letter to War Secretary Henry Dearborn reporting on the controversy, Clark defended Loise over Magrain because "as both the Osage interpreters are passionate and on bad terms with each other and frequently quarrel. Paul Lous [sic] professing to be in favour of the Government, and Noel Magra [sic] is devoted to the Agent of that nation [Chouteau]." Foley and Rice are reasonably certain that Loise was the son of either Auguste or Pierre Chouteau and an Osage wife; given Clark's comment, Auguste seems a stronger candidate for paternity. His link to the powerful Chouteau family might explain why both he and Lorr were interpreters at Fort Osage, St. Louis, or both. In 1827, Loise was one of the St. Louis promoters who convinced Big Soldier and five other Osages to travel to Europe as an exhibition of "wild Indians," where they were stranded for several years (see below). (*Letters of the Lewis and Clark Expedition with Related Documents*, 305n; Foley and Rice, *The First Chouteaus*, 45; William Clark to Henry Dearborn, Dec. 2, 1808, *Territorial Papers* 14, 243; "Missouriana: Mohongo's Story," *Missouri Historical Review*, 210.)

Tuesday 6th

General Clark had a talk with a Kansa Indian (who came up from St. Louis with us & is a Brother of the principal Chief of the Nation) and Sent him bound to his Village alone. He was directed to tell his Nation that if they do not make atonement for the outrages they have lately committed on Some Traders, that their Nation will be Cut off, that no traders will be Suffered to go to them this winter, or until they make Reparation, & that they Shall not come here to Trade

This home near the Femme Osage was still under construction when Nathan Boone served as a guide for William Clark's overland trek to Fire Prairie to negotiate the 1808 treaty with the Osage. (Courtesy, Larry Ruebling)

Tuesday 13th

From the 6th, to this day nothing material has taken place. The plan of the Fort has been fixed on and the work commenced & in Some Forwardness. Some of the Work-Houses nearly Raised, and 2 temporary Huts for the Factory commenced. After dinner Capt. Boon Returned from the Osage, there came with him about 80 of the principal Chiefs and Warriors of the 2 Villages to See General Clark, by whom they were Received in a friendly manner, and promised a hearing tomorrow in Council.

Camp near Fire Prairie Wednesday Sept. 14th, 1808

General Clark & the Military & Civil Officers present met the Osages this day in Council, where after the common Salutations &c. had passed, the General Read to them & had explained by the Interpreter, Articles of a Treaty that he had drawn up between himself in behalf of the U. States & them (the Osages) which having gone through, he desired them to consider of and determine whether or not they would Sign it. The two principal

Chiefs "White Hair"[16] of the Grand & "The Walking Rain" of the Little
Osage immediately declared their willingness to accept the Treaty. After
a number of other Chiefs & Warriors had expressed their approbation the
Council was adjourned till tomorrow morning.

[16] White Hair, or Pawhuska (?-c. 1809) was the first Great Osage chief by the same name, who was related to Clermont I, the peace chief of one of the major villages. The two disagreed markedly on cooperation with the Europeans, causing tension and competition for leadership. Clermont was skeptical and hesitant, while White Hair welcomed them—along with the goods and power they brought. White Hair was especially close to Auguste and Pierre Chouteau, who received a charter granting them a monopoly on Osage trade from the Spanish government and who used the rivalry to their economic advantage. When Clermont died in 1795 or 1796, his son Clermont II anticipated taking his father's post in the tribe, but the Chouteaus wanted nothing of him, so convinced the Spanish to confer the title of chief on the more cooperative and pliant White Hair instead. Clermont II left over the matter, and moved in with the Arkansas Osage (see below). Pierre Chouteau took White Hair to Washington in 1804 to meet Jefferson, who recognized him as head chief (regardless of tribal custom or consent). White Hair continued to be close to Chouteau interests—his daughter married Pierre's interpreter Noel Magrain—and was generally (and probably rightly) seen in St. Louis as a puppet of the Chouteau brothers. He died not long after signing this treaty, and was succeeded by his son Che-sho-Hung-ga, who took on his father's name and position as "government chief." This latter White Hair signed the 1822 treaty with the United States, which absolved the government of any responsibility for keeping a trade factory open stipulated in the 1808 agreement, and three years later granted the government right-of-way for the Santa Fe Trail. He later moved his tribe to southeastern Kansas, at Pierre Chouteau's encoragement. The town of Pawhuska, Kansas, is named for one of his descendants. (Rowe, "White Hair (Paw-Hiu-skah)," in *Dictionary of Missouri Biography*, 791-792; Clark, *Westward with Dragoons*, 59.)

Thursday 15th
Met the Osages again in Council, when the Treaty was Read & explained
to them again & they consented to Sign it on the Spot.

The foregoing Treaty was duly executed by the Respective Parties, and
after the General had made the Osages a Small present of Some Guns,
Ammunition, Tobacco, &c. which he drew from me, amounting to $317.74
the Council Rose. The Osages expect their Families here in the course
of 6 or 8 days. They have totally abandoned their old Villages and have
pitched on the Spots near this place (within 2 Miles) to Settle. The Little
Osage Seem perfectly well pleased with the exchange, but many of the

Great Osage do not express Such perfect Satisfaction as could be wished, however they firmly Resolve to move.

They all are highly pleased with the idea of having a permanent Trading House So near them, and on the whole I am inclined to think that these Indians may henceforth be kept peaceable and friendly with proper exertions on the part of the Agents, and a punctual fulfillment of every promise made them by the Government or its Agents, which I consider a matter of the first importance to be attended to in order to impress them with a high Sense of the Honor & good faith of the U. States without which no permanent arrangement can be expected to be formed. It ought to be observed as a maxim never to be departed from by the Government, to perform with the <u>most minute exactness</u> every promise made to Indians by any of its authorized Agents, and of course to use the greatest caution in making promises.

By General Clark I Received a Letter from Capt. House in which he mentions the death of Col. Hunt, who died on the 18th Ulto. I also Received a letter from Lt. Piatt of Pittsburgh enclosing me the Receipt of Samuel Perry for 5 packages of Factory Goods addressed to my care at St. Louis the Letter is dated July 10th. These 5 packages are the ones that were left behind at Cumberland by Mr. McMahon, 2 of them are for this post, the other 3 for the Le Moin Factory. I wrote this day to the Assistant Military Agent at Belle Fontaine to forward me those for this post by the first Boat (See Letter Book page 6). Wrote the following Letters to day—Capt. House, Samuel Sibley, John Sibley, Ensign Immell, & the Superintendent of Indian Trade. (For the last See letter Book page 6 & 7) My Letter to Capt House contains the one I wrote to Lt. Kimball Assistant Military Agent which I thought proper to Send open to the Captain, that in case Kimball's late Arrest interferes with his Agent's duty, the Captain may put it into the proper hands to have the business done which I have therein written him about. Those to Samuel H. Sibley & John Sibley are of a private nature altogether. The one to Ensign Immell is on the Subject of the Money he Owes me $41.50 pressing him to pay it to Wilkinson & Price either in Cash or by Returning the things he got from me.

Camp near Fire Prairie Friday Sept. 16th, 1808

This morning the Militia Set off on their Return home, and after dinner General Clark took his leave of us for St. Louis. The General goes by Water in the Boat I brought from Pittsburgh which I turned over to him as public property together with her Oars poles & flag.[17]

By him I Sent my Letters that I wrote Yesterday. I also wrote to day to Wilkinson & Price for the following Articles to be Sent me by the first opportunity

25 lbs Hard Soap
30 lbs. Butter
1/4 lb. White Thread about No. 20 or 25
3 P Wollen Stockings, not very fine
1 P. Warm Gloves
1 quart Clover Seed
12 or 15 Chickens

and Requested them to try to Send up Some Hogs by Major Wilson's drove if he Sends one, also 5 or 6 Head of Cattle belonging to Lorr by the Same opportunity.

[17] Clark was forced to return by boat rather than on horseback, so severe was his attack of dysentery. (Clark, *Westward with Dragoons*, 44.)

Saturday 17th
Morning cool and a little Cloudy. Nothing material happened to day. Some Rain.

Sunday 18th
Same as Yesterday.

Monday 19th
Day cloudy and the wind <u>high</u>, had a Shed built over the uncovered Households &c. a little Rain Night quite cool. Very Sudden change in the Weather.

Wednesday 21st
Last night <u>very cool</u>. This morning we found a large Fire pleasant wind high till in the evening when it died away.

At about 3 O'Clock Several of the Osages arrived with their families and Report that they left the Rest of the Nation within a few Miles of this place & that they will be here tomorrow or the day after. They offered a little Venison for Sale in order to procure Some ammunition of which they Seem to be much in need. To Serve them, I took their meat for the Troops & Supplied them with a little Powder and ball. Work going on to day with Spirit. Night cool.

Thursday 22nd
Morning clear and cool. This morning just before day light 3 Men deserted from the camp Vizt. Miller, Kincade, & John Williams, Soldiers of the U. S. they took with them a canoe belonging to a French hunter, 2 Rifles

belonging to 2 hired Sawyers and Several other things. Lieut. Lorimier with a command of Soldiers & Hunters Started off in pursuit of them in a Keel Boat about 7 O'Clock.

In the afternoon part of the Osages arrived with their families. Day Sultry & unpleasant.

Camp near Fire Prairie Friday 23rd Sept. 1808

Morning clear and Sultry. About 2 O'Clock a number of Kansa's arrived from their Nation, tomorrow they will make known their business. The Osages are Still falling in by Lodges & Families, as they find it convenient. The large Block House under cover to day. Capt. Clemson had the Ordnance put in firing order and posted in the most advantageous manner Round the Hill occupied by the guard, which commands the Bottom in which the Camp is. Our camp is now Surrounded by Indians who, though friendly, <u>might</u> notwithstanding be tempted by the prospect of getting possession of the Factory Goods & other Stores, to commit Some violent outrage. This I say is a thing by no means impossible though I do not consider it either as at all probable, but there is Strong Reasons for us to be on the alert and Ready at all times for an Alarm. The day, very warm and Sultry which is doubly disagreeable in consequence of the late Sudden transition from quite Cold to warm weather.

Note- I owe Mrs. Martinell for Washing 26 p. in this Month & 26 p. in the last Month & for making 4 Towels.

Fire Prairie Saturday September 24th, 1808

Last night at about 12, it Rained and the weather turned quite cool again. The morning cool enough to make a fire agreeable. Lt. Lorimier Returned about 12 O'Clock without the deserters he went in pursuit of. 3 of the Little Osages Chiefs dined to day with us. After dinner Capt. C. had the 3 Pounder & a Swivel fired with Shot, for the gratification of the Chiefs after which we were invited to eat in the Tent of a principal Warrior & we went accordingly. Rain alternately all day till Sun Set, when it cleared off very cool.

Sunday, 25th

Morning very cold and Windy. An old Osage came to me with Tears in his eyes, & begged for a little blue cloth to bury his Wife in. He brought a couple of Skins to pay in part for it and Said he would pay the Rest another time. Considering his age and distress as proper objects of favor I with Some trouble let him have 2 yards of Cloth and a Carrot of Tobacco and took the Skins he offered in part payment. Mr. Lewis had a talk with the Kansas this evening. Capt. Clemson has determined to Send off a Command to Belle Fontaine the day after tomorrow.

Fire Prairie Monday, September 26th, 1808

Morning cool and clear. This was a very busy day with me Removing the Factory Goods on the Hill & Storing them in Block House No. 1. I also had the Powder Removed into the Same House. I now have all the Factory Goods under Lock & Key & in good Strong Stores. Today I wrote the following Letters Vizt.

John Mason, Esquire, Supt. Indian Trade, Georgetown
General William Clark, Indian Agent, St. Louis
Capt. James House, Belle Fontaine
Wilkinson & Price, St. Louis
John Johnson, Esquire, River Le Moin

About noon the whole of the Big Osages arrived, and pitched their Camps about a Mile below us (the little Osage are about 1/2 a Mile above) they are about 4,000 in all.

Fire Prairie Tuesday Sept. 27th, 1808

Morning clear & cool. About 12 O'Clock we met the Chiefs & Warriors of the Big & Little Osages & the Kansas in Council and all Smoked the Pipe of Peace together. The Kansas Seemed very penitent for what they had done (Robbing & abusing their Traders &c.) & asked forgiveness and leave to come and Settle near us, which was granted them. I said a few words to them all on the Subject of Trade. Told them I Should give no credits. Should always expect them to offer me the Furs & Peltry that they killed and took with the Traps, Guns, &c. that I furnished them with. After the council Mr. Prince with the Boat Started for St. Louis, by him I dispatched the Letters I wrote yesterday.

Trade factories like this one at Fort Osage were imbedded in military forts for protection in frontier settings. Today, Fort Osage has been recreated and stands overlooking the Missouri River in Sibley, Missouri. (Courtesy, the author)

Fort Osage, Friday 1st Sept. 1809

Since the 27th Sept. 1808 I have entirely neglected my diary, but being now Somewhat Settled and more at leisure, I am determined to attend to it in future. The following are the most important occurrences that I can Recollect Since the 27th Sept. '08.

October 1st, 1808

This day I opened the Factory and began to Trade with the Osages. Find them very poor and very troublesome.

Oct. 10th

The whole of the Kansas arrived this day (to the number of about 1,000 Souls) their object is to Trade, and to Settle their differences with the Whites, about the 12th, they commenced Trading and about the 16th, I was ~~obliged~~ induced to Shut the Store against them on account of their insolent and violent conduct.

November 10th, '08

Ensign Immell arrived to day in a Public Boat from Bell Fontaine, by which I Received a Box of Beaver Traps and 1 Tierce Blankets That were left behind at Cumberland.

November 18th '08 [18]

To day the most of the Indians set out on the Winter hunt. I let the Kansas have a few Blankets, Some Powder &c. on the promise of their Chiefs that they would behave better in future, but more on account of the distressed Situation of their Women and Children.

[18] Sibley apparently wrote the November 7 entry later, since it appears after that for November 18 in the original diary.

November 7th, '08

Pierre Chouteau Esquire arrived here to day in a Public Boat on public business. His errand is to conclude another Treaty with the Osages, (the one made by General Clark on the 14th Sept. being Set aside on complaint of the Osages that they did not fully understand it) by order of His Excellency Governor Lewis. Mr. Chouteau held his council on November 11th, and the Same day the Indians Signed the Treaty. It is to be observed of this Treaty, that it does not differ very materially from the one made by General Clark. That Mr. Chouteau concluded it in great haste and made use of threats to make the Indians Sign it. He executed it in the presence of only one Witness (Mr. Lewis) whereas it appears on the face of it that Two other witnesses were present (Capt. Clemson & Lt. Lorimier) who in fact were not present at all, those Gentlemen Signing merely for form's Sake, which I was invited also to do, but peremptorily Refused.

Novr. 13th
This morning at 9 O'Clock, Capt. Clemson named the Fort. It was christened in the usual Military Style and called "Fort Osage." Mr. Chouteau departed for St. Louis about 12 O'Clock, by whom I wrote to General Mason, Gov. Lewis and General Clark.

Decr. 10th
The contractor's Boat arrived to day with Provisions[19] very Seasonably, for we were Seriously alarmed at the prospect of being obliged to march to St. Louis for want of Flour & Meat &c. Doctor Thomas came in the Boat to remain here Some months as Surgeon's Mate. The Ice began to run Several days ago.

[19] The most likely provisioners were James and Jesse Morrison, the Kaskaskia merchants who provided similar supplies for Sibley and the group leaving Fort Belle Fontaine to establish Fort Osage. (Gregg, "The History of Fort Osage," *Missouri Historical Review*, 440-441.)

Dec. 11th
The Boat returned to St. Louis. Could not prevail on the Pa------ to take a load of Peltry down, he was afraid to risk it.

Dec. 18th
The Missouri Froze over, and completely closed up.

Dec. 31st, 1808
On making up my public Accounts[20] to this day, I find that the Factory has cleared $ after paying all expenses, and has done business with Indians to the amount of about $ (blank again)[21] Since the 1st of October. The weather is excessively cold, frequent Snows.

[20] Factors were required by law to keep extensive and detailed notes; starting in 1806, federal regulations required factors such as Sibley to file quarterly reports which were audited by the Indian Trade Office in the District of Columbia, then forwarded to the Treasury Department. Later, Sibley's reports went to William Clark, his immediate superior, before being forwarded to Georgetown, where the Indian Trade Office was headquartered. (Peake, *A History of the United States Indian Factory System*, 2.)
[21] Under Sibley's management Fort Osage realized a net profit of $10,291.40

for its first three years of operation. (*American State Papers, Indian Affairs* 1, 784.)

March 13th, 1809

This day Dr. Robinson[22] arrived from St. Louis by land. He comes to take the place of Mr. Reuben Lewis as Deputy Indian Agent, by Gov. Lewis' Appointment.

[22] "Surely there has never lived on the soil of Jackson County" wrote historian Kate Gregg, "a more fascinating and mysterious gentleman than" Dr. John H. Robinson (1782-1819). Robinson already had a colorful and eventful past when he became Indian Agent to the Osage. He was part of Zebulon Montgomery Pike's expedition that left Fort Belle Fontaine in July 1806, traveling up the Missouri to escort home an Osage delegation who had visited Jefferson in Washington; it was standard procedure for the federal government to assume all costs and efforts to bring Native American leaders to places like St. Louis or to Washington, as well as paying for all their needs and accommodations while they were there as guests. They also escorted the return of some Osage women and children whom the Pottawatomies captured earlier, but had been reclaimed by the Americans.

After Pike completed a stockade and fort on the Rio Conejos in Spanish territory in present-day Colorado in February 1807, Robinson convinced him to allow him to travel to Santa Fe, a thriving Spanish trade hub. The doctor told Pike that he was supposed to collect a debt for a Kaskaskia merchant, William Morrison, should he arrive there. The Spanish governor became wary of Robinson's story that he was traveling with a group of hunters and sent a search party to find them. Pike and his men tried to pretend to be hunters, but failed to convince the posse who arrested them. Spanish escorts took Pike and his men beyond Santa Fe south through Albuquerque and El Paso to be imprisoned in Chihuahua. Rather than rile the Americans, the Spanish governor decided to have the party escorted to Natchitoches on the American border—where, incidentally, Robinson may have met Sibley's father John—in July 1807. Robinson tried to gain asylum and stay (despite having a wife and family in St. Louis), but the Spaniards wanted nothing to do with all this and sent him home with Pike. Spanish accusations of sending Pike as a spy and Secretary of State James Madison's denials led to a break in relations between Spain and the United States. Robinson returned to St. Louis, then moved to Fort Osage in March, 1809; after his family arrived, Sibley boarded with the Robinsons. Robinson remained there until 1810. His third child was born at Fort Osage in April 1810. He later moved to Ste. Genevieve and on to Natchez, where he died in a yellow fever epidemic. (*Early History of Greater Kansas City*, 143; "Zebulon Pike: Hard-Luck Explorer or Successful Spy?" The Lewis and Clark Journey of Discovery; Gregg, "The History of Fort Osage,"

Missouri Historical Review 446; Billon, *Annals of St. Louis in its Territorial Days*, 191-192, 382-383.)

March 16th

The Ice having broke up, Mr. R. Lewis and Dr. Thomas[23] departed for St. Louis in a Keel Boat. By this Boat I Sent 100 Packs of Deerskins to the address of General Clark at St. Louis. I also remitted $ (blank) to W. & Price[24] on private account, and Sent Several Letters to the Post office for different persons.

[23] Dr. William H. Thomas traveled with the Missouri Fur Company's expedition in 1809 as its surgeon. Sibley reports that a "Dr. Thomas" arrived December 10, 1808, from St. Louis to serve as a "surgeon's mate" who returned the following spring after the ice on the river broke up. It seems likely that the physician hired by the Missouri Fur Company would be one who already had some experience on the frontier, even if only as far west as Fort Osage. This was the expedition hired by Territorial Governor Meriwether Lewis to return the Mandan chief Sheheke and his family to the Mandan villages on the Missouri River, just above present-day Bismarck, North Dakota. Sheheke, his family, and that of interpreter Rene Jusseaume came to St. Louis and Washington, D.C., with Lewis and Clark on their return, with the understanding the United States would return them safely—which it had tried to do in the summer of 1807. The party, headed by Ensign Nathaniel Pryor, who was a member of the Corps of Discovery and therefore very familiar with the geopolitical landscape, was forced to scamper back to St. Louis after being attacked by the Arikaras in southern South Dakota; four of his men were killed and several wounded, including fellow Corps of Discovery veteran George Shannon. This time, the group heading upriver was far more substantial—and successful.

The first of two parties in this expedition left St. Louis May 17, then waited at the Cote sans Dessein settlement (not far from Fort Osage) near the mouth of the Osage River until the balance arrived on June 28. The whole crew set off westward, arriving July 8 at Fort Osage "which we saluted by a discharge of several guns from our ordinance barges, and were politely answered by an equal number from the fort," reported the doctor in his journal. "Here we experienced many civilities from the gentlemen of the garrison. This place appears to be the general rendezvous of all the Missouri Indians, whose continual jars keep the commandant on the alert. Osages, Ottas [Otoes], Mahas, Ponnis [Pawnees], Cansas [Kansas], Missouri, Souex [Sioux], Sac, Fox, Ioway, all mingle together here, and serve to render this quarter a most discordant portion of the continent."

After the group returned from its mission, Thomas wrote two articles about his journey for the *Missouri Gazette*, appearing in November and December 1809, and subsequently in the *Pittsburgh Gazette* the following summer. It was probably the first printed account of the famed and incredible escape of John Colter from the Blackfeet, since Thomas met the famous trader and explorer. (Jackson, "Journey to the Mandans, 1809: The Lost Narrative of Dr. Thomas," *Bulletn of the Missouri Historical Society* 179-183; "Introduction to Dr. Thomas' Journal," *Mountain Men and the Fur Trade: Sources of the History of the Fur Trade in the Rocky Mountain West*; Nathaniel Pryor to William Clark, October 16, 1807, *Letters of the Lewis and Clark Expedition with Related Documents*, 432-438.)

[24] Wilkinson and Price, St. Louis merchants.

March 31st

On making up my Factory accounts, to this day, I find, that the Factory has done business to the Amount of $ and cleared $ Since the 1st of October last.

July 3rd

Messrs. Miller[25] and Crook[26] Reached this place to day on their way up to the heads of the River. They Report that the Missouri Fur Company will be here in a few days.

[25] Joseph Miller became a partner with Wilson Price Hunt after the John Jacob Astor protégé arrived at St. Louis in the summer of 1810, then joined him on his ill-fated expedition to the Pacific. After Hunt took the advice of his crew and jettisoned the horses in October of 1811 at Fort Henry to travel by river, he lost Miller as a member of the group. Hunt sent a trapping crew out October 10, including Miller who "joined the party because, apparently, he was disgusted with the enterprise and had decided to throw up his share. The other partners were astonished and mortified at this strange resolution, but could not prevail upon him to alter it." (Chittenden *The American Fur Trade*, vol. 1, 183, 190.)

[26] Ramsay Crooks (1787-1859) came to America from Scotland at age sixteen and spent the rest of his days associated with the fur trade, which had taken him to St. Louis by 1806. He and Robert McClellan formed a fur-trading partnership the following year, which established a post near present-day Calhoun, Nebraska, after meeting Nathaniel Pryor's defeated party coming back down the Missouri. Pryor, a former member of the Lewis and Clark expedition, was hired by Governor Meriwether Lewis to lead a group to escort Mandan chief Sheheke and his family back to the Mandan villages in North Dakota, but they were repulsed by the Arikaras. At the time Sibley wrote this, Crooks was at Fort Osage and, according to Manuel Lisa (who mentioned running into Crooks there), was hurrying to leave to catch up with partner Robert McClellan at their camp upriver near the mouth of the Nodaway River (just north of present-day St. Joseph, Missouri). Lisa planned to take the fastest boat he had in hopes of overtaking the pair, even though Crooks had earlier promised Lisa that he would wait near Council Bluffs for Lisa's Missouri

In the 1808 treaty with the Osage, Clark and the United States government promised that the factory would always be well-stocked with varied and useful goods. As this recreated factory at Fort Osage suggests, Sibley offered a cornucopia of merchandise for both Native Americans and traders passing through. (Courtesy, the author)

Fur Company party. It turned out that Lisa was worrying unnecessarily; Crooks' party was at the prescribed place when Lisa's crew arrived. When he and McClellan parted ways the following year, Crooks went to Canada where he met Wilson Price Hunt, who was recruiting men for an overland expedition to the Pacific for the Pacific Fur Company. Crooks bought five shares of the company and became a traveling partner. Hunt left the exhausted Crooks and five others behind in the Blue Mountains of Oregon; Crooks finally reached the Columbia, caught up with Price, and promptly surrendered his share in the company. After a difficult return trip with Robert Stuart, Crooks arrived in St. Louis in April 1813. Crooks later rejoined the company and climbed the ranks until, by 1821, he was a member of the elite management of the fur company under Astor. A year later, Crooks received a one-fifth interest in the company and became its de facto head while Astor spent more and more time in Europe. Under his leadership, the Astor empire came to hold a monopoly on the fur trade from the Great Lakes to St. Louis and beyond the Rockies. When Astor left the business in 1834, Crooks purchased the Western Department and continued to operate it under the American Fur name. Although his health was never very good after his return from Astoria in 1813, Crooks continued to head the company actively until his death in New York in 1859. ("Ramsay Crooks" in *Dictionary of American Biography*, 565; Chittenden, *The American Fur Trade* 1, 182, 206, 365; Oglesby, *Manuel Lisa and the Opening of the Missouri Fur Trade*, 80.)

July 4th

To day being the anniversary of the Independence of the U. S. it was celebrated at Fort Osage (in a manner highly gratifying to us all) with firing of Guns, feasting &c. &c.

July 8th

In the afternoon the Boats of the Missouri Fur Company arrived to the number of _____ and _____ Men[27] (both blanks) under the command of Mr. Pierre Chouteau as they passed the Fort to the landing place they fired a Salute, which was Returned from the Fort.[28] This company is on its way up to the heads of the Missouri to catch Beaver &c. &c. Since they left St. Louis they have lost about 40 Men by desertion who carried off property to the Amount of about $7,000. They have the Mandan Chief and Family in charge, and are to convey them Safe to their Nation, for which Service the Governor is to pay them $7,000 dollars.[29] They Remained here making preparations, Repairs, &c. until the 10th, when they Recommenced the Voyage. On the Same day (the 8th) Doctor Robinson arrived from St. Louis with his Family.[30]

[27] Over the winter of 1808-1809, a group of St. Louis businessmen began meeting to figure out how they might reduce the risk—in terms of both danger

and competition—of the Missouri River fur trade, resulting in the creation of the St. Louis Missouri Fur Company. The list of founders included about all the major figures in the burgeoning fur town: Pierre Chouteau and his son Auguste Pierre, Manuel Lisa and his Kaskaskia merchant partners Pierre Menard and William Morrison, William Clark, Reuben Lewis (whose brother Meriwether was governor), Sylvestre Labbadie, merchant Benjamin Wilkinson (whose uncle James was the former governor), and Andrew Henry. The partnership grew as much as anything from a desire on the part of Jefferson and War Secretary Henry Dearborn to see Sheheke returned safely to the Mandan villages, consoling the dishonor of Pryor's party being prevented from doing so in 1807.

In a time when private enterprise and public service often became blurred, neither Lewis, Clark, nor the others perceived a problem in hiring this private firm for such a lucrative task as this. It was this errand to deliver the Mandan chief that brought the Fur Company representatives to Fort Osage at this time. The partnership was always a bit tense; no one fully trusted Lisa, and the company profits were distributed yearly instead of reinvested so the company lacked capital when it was needed. Clark was clearly invited to handle the assets, since he was the only person whom all of them trusted. The partners allowed the old company to expire in early 1812, after Charles Gratiot was unable to convince them that inviting Astor himself to the table would generate much-needed capital, and created a new company as a limited partnership (rather than the old co-partnership) with a board of directors. Just under $30,000 of the $50,000 in capital stock was to come from the funds and assets of the old Missouri Fur Company, the rest from public sale at $1,000 a share. The company was chronically under-capitalized, despite infusions of money from Lisa, Clark, and Morrison. (Foley, *A History of Missouri*, Vol. 1, 1763-1820, 144-145; Oglesby, *Manuel Lisa and the Opening of the Missouri Fur Trade*, 116-124.)

[28] According to Dr. Thomas's account (see above), the group stayed three days, until on July 11 "we got all ready for embarkation [sic], having laid on vegetables, &c. and bidding adieu to the face of civilized life pushed on our way." (Jackson, "Journey to the Mandans, 1809: The Lost Narrative of Dr. Thomas," *Bulletin of the Missouri Historical Society*, 183.)

[29] On instructions from Jefferson, Governor Lewis was taking no chances this time with the return of Sheheke (the Mandan chief) and his entourage, having been turned back two years previously. This time, he hired out the operation to the Missouri Fur Company with instructions to send 125 men—including forty skilled American riflemen—with a sizeable crew. Since this was an important and dangerous mission, the Company extracted a commitment for $7,000 from the governor, along with an exclusive (albeit short-term) license for the Indian trade above the Platte River. The War Department authorized

this advance, but denied the additional $500 to Chouteau for tobacco, powder, and gifts for the Indians, since the original sum was to cover all expenses. Secretary of War William Eustis later chastised Lewis for entering into such an expensive agreement without his knowledge, suggesting that "when an Agent of the Government appointed for other purposes [meaning Pierre Chouteau, who was also Indian Agent to the Osage] is selected for the command, it is thought the Government might, without injury to the public interests, have been consulted. As the object & destination of this Force is unknown, and more especially as it combines Commercial purposes, so it cannot be considered as having the sanction of the Government of the United States, or that they are responsible for consequences." Lewis fired back in August that he would come to Washington with his documentation and make his case, thundering that he had "been informed Representations have made been made against me," that the expedition was only to return Sheheke (although Sibley understood differently, and was right), and that "Be assured, Sir, that my Country can never make 'A Burr' of me." While on his way to Washington on this errand, Meriwether Lewis died in Tennessee, almost certainly by his own hand. (Potter, *Sheheke: Mandan Indian Diplomat*, 156-161; William Eustis to Meriwether Lewis, July 15, 1809, and Meriwether Lewis to William Eustis, August 18, 1809, *Letters of the Lewis and Clark Expedition with Related Documents*, 456-461.)

[30] At this time, Robinson's family included his Parisian-born wife Sophie (whom he married in 1805) and sons Edward (born October 6, 1806) and James (born August 17, 1808). Antoine Saugrain Robinson was born in April, 1810 at Fort Osage. (Billon, *Annals of St. Louis in its Territorial Days*, 192.)

July 10th

This day I hired an old Man (by name Colar) for the term of Six Months at the rate of $400 a year and 1 1/2 Rations per day. To be employed hewing Timber for the Factory,[31] *making Presses &c. and packing and managing Peltry &c. for which services he is well calculated.*

[31] Based on Sibley's comments on his experience at pressing and packing furs, Colar was probably one of the numerous fur traders and trappers who worked on and near the Missouri River. Since Sibley refers to him as "an Old Man," it seems likely that Colar may have become too old or enfeebled for the rigorous work in the wilderness and was now settling for a labor job. Theoretically, Sibley should have been able to use soldiers at the garrison for such jobs; that was the intent of the Office for Indian Trade. But relations between trade factors, who were civilians, and the military were generally strained, perhaps more so at Fort Osage than at many other forts. Enlisted men didn't really care to make a few extra cents a day for manual labor, and

commanding officers didn't feel compelled to force the work upon their men. Sibley often found himself at odds with local commanders, a situation not helped by his tendency to go over the commanders' heads and write directly to the War Department in Washington. (Gregg, "A History of Fort Osage," *Missouri Historical Review*, 444.)

August 10th, 1809

To day I wrote to John Winslow and enclosed him a Draft on John Mason, Esqr, Supt. Of Indian Trade for $100 drawn by myself this day in favor of John H. Robinson or order, payable at 10 days St. Out of the Draft, I directed him to discharge the balance I owe him, and to pay the rest to Robert H. Sibley and Ann E. Sibley. I Sent one Set of this Draft to my brother Samuel H. Sibley to deliver to Mr. Winslow immediately on Receipt. My Account with Mr. Winslow Stands thus.

Balance due him the 1st of March 1806	*$250.00*
Interest to the 1st of June 1808	*32.00*
	282.00
When I Remitted him $100 from the City of Washington	*$100.00*
	182.00
Interest to the 22nd Feby. 1809 (Say)	*8.00*
	190.00
When my brother paid him	*125.00*
	65.00
Interest	*4.00*
	69.00
last Remittance	*100.00*
Balance due me	*31.00*

The above is a Rough Statement and is I Suspect Rather against me.

Fort Osage Saturday 2nd Sept. 1809

The day cool and pleasant. The Factory Buildings are going on pretty well.

Sunday 3rd

The day cool and pleasant. River beginning to Rise to an unusual height for the Season.

Monday 4th

It is just a Year to day Since we arrived at this place. Dr. Robinson held a Council to day with the Osages at which I was present. The object was

When Fort Osage opened in 1808, it was the last stop for fur traders and others heading upriver to the Mandan and Hidatsa villages in present-day North Dakota. Most groups stopped there on the way to and from the region, and met George Sibley. (Courtesy, Larry Ruebling)

to enquire into the cause of Some complaints that Some of the Chiefs made Several days ago against the Doctor as they (the Chiefs) Said by the direction of the whole Tribe. It turned out on enquiry that the Chiefs had been over-officious and had made the complaints without the knowledge even of Some of the principal Men, and as they Said very much against their wishes.

Paul the Interpreter[32] left here very Suddenly to day for St. Louis it is Supposed. Dr. Robinson, under whose control he was placed by the Governor, did not know of his intention to go.

[32] Paul Loise.

Fort Osage Tuesday 5th, 1809
The morning cool and cloudy. A little Rain about Sunrise.

Note—Began to Mess[33] at Dr. Robinson's the 1st Inst. Furnished 15lbs. Rice, 2 Bottles Mustard and Some Vinegar.

Yesterday I wrote to General Clark for <u>165</u> Panes of Window Glass and

Putty enough to put it in with, to be Sent up by the very first opportunity. Size of the Glass 7 by 9 or 8 by 10. 7 by 9 preference if to be had. This Letter I Sent by a Frenchman in a Canoe who is on his way to St. Louis from the Mahas.[34] The day cool and clear. 6 or 8 Indians came in from the Villages to purchase Some trifles. The River falling a little.

The Factory going on well to day. The Logs nearly Raised. Paul the Interpreter has actually gone to St. Louis and taken 4 Indians with him. It Seems he has gone to lay in Some Complaints against Dr. Robinson the Sub-Indian Agent. This impudent Step will cost him very dear. His conduct generally has been improper.

[33] Military slang for taking meals.

[34] Independent traders were common on the Missouri River and had a long heritage there. Although the French, Spaniards, and Americans all granted special charters to companies or individuals giving them special commercial privileges, free-lance traders still operated with the tribes. This group was generally resented by United States government officials as well as the large fur trading companies like John Jacob Astor's Pacific Fur Company. They interrupted systematic trade, added competition thus forcing up prices, and shamelessly traded alcohol to the Native Americans. By the time Sibley arrived at Fort Osage, it was already illegal to provide alcohol to the Indians, although the ban was frequently broken (more by independent traders than anyone else). The major fur companies had a similar prohibition, since they wanted Native American hunters sober and capable of hunting or trapping as many animals as possible to generate as many furs as the market demanded. The Mahas referred to here are the Omaha tribe.

Fort Osage Wednesday 6th Sept, 1809
Morning clear and cool. Arose at Sunrise. The day clear and pleasant. Factory House Ready for the Roof.

Thursday 7th
The morning clear and cool. River falling. Rode out into the Prairie in the afternoon. The day fair and pleasant.

Friday 8th
Morning clear and pleasant. River Still falling a little. The day clear and pleasant. Two Osages belonging to the Arkansaw Band,[35] came here to day to complain of the Kansas having lately Stolen 30 Horses from them. Two Men of the Big Villages were dispatched by Dr. Robinson to the Kansas to demand the Horses. The Factory Building going on pretty well to day.

[35] Some scholars give the Chouteaus credit (or blame) for creating the Arkansas band of the Osage, claiming that they induced Big Track, a Great Osage chief, to break with the tribe and move to the Arkansas River after they lost their trade monopoly to Manuel Lisa in 1802. However, this branch of the Osage was living on the Verdigris River above the confluence of the Verdigris, Neosho, and Arkansas rivers since the 1760s. Once they drove the Wichita out of the area around mid-century, Osage hunters remained in the area to reap the benefits of both copious game and interaction with illegal traders from New Orleans. (Rollings, *The Osage*, 191-194.)

Fort Osage Saturday Sept. 9th, 1809

The Morning clear and pleasant. Arose at Sunrise. Nothing Strange occurred to day. The day fair and pleasant.

Sunday 10th

The morning clear and pleasant. Cloudy and a little Showery at 12 fair in the afternoon. Cool all day. Cloudy at Tattoo.

Monday 11th

Morning cool and fair. Day continued fair and pleasant. Rode to the Prairie[36] in the evening.

[36] Fire Prairie.

Tuesday 12th

The morning clear and cool. Day clear and pleasant.

Wednesday 13th

Morning cool and fair. Capt. Clemson,[37] Ensign Bissell[38] & Dr. Murry took a trip down the River to day in a Barge and Rowed by 12 Men, they Set off before Breakfast and Returned about 4 O'Clock in the evening.

[37]Ten years after Capt. Eli Clemson joined the army he was commander of the garrison at Fort Osage, where he served until Territorial Governor Benjamin Howard closed the fort and trade operations in 1813. In general, garrison commanders and career military officers seldom gave the civilian factors all the cooperation they might have, but the relationship between Clemson and Sibley was especially tenuous, for which there was plenty of fault on all sides. Clemson refused to provide help the factor needed in constructing buildings and warehouses, cleaning and packing furs, and moving merchandise. Unable to compel Clemson to other action by the end of the winter 1809, Sibley went over the Captain's head and wrote directly to Indian Trade Superintendent John Mason about the problem. Mason in

turn wrote to Secretary of War William Eustis in May of 1809, noting that "At some times the commanding officers and the factors draw pretty well together & labour [sic] is furnished when wanted at others misunderstandings exist and the public interest feels sensibly the effect." He went on to ask Eustis to order garrison commanders to provide as much help as needed, and that he "should be thankfull [sic] Sir if you would mention to Capt. Clemson the propriety of enableing [sic] Mr. Sibley to hasten the necessary work" since the factory buildings weren't finished. The men received the same extra pay as for "fatigue duty"; Mason mentioned to Eustis that this ran about ten cents a day in Chicago two years previously. Eustis provided just those orders to Clemson, which no doubt had a less than salutary effect on the working relationship. Still, Clemson apparently did the minimum required and reported to Washington in late June that the work on the buildings was largely completed with the aid of some 26 men forging iron parts, building structures, plastering walls and joints, laying masonry, and sawing logs. (Jones, *Prairie Puritan*, 57-58; John Mason to William Eustis, May 13, 1809, *Territorial Papers* 14, 273-274.)

[38]Lewis Bissell was stationed at Fort Osage by 1812 under the command of Eli Clemson. A month after the start of the War of 1812, Bissell signed a letter along with Lieut. John Brownson and Capt. Clemson to Daniel Bissell (Ensign Bissell's uncle), the commander at Fort Belle Fontaine, which he in turn forwarded to War Secretary William Eustis, saying they thought Clark and Sibley had selected a poor location for Fort Osage. Col. Thomas Hunt (see above) had been ill and unable to fulfill his duties, they said, which left Governor Lewis and his appointee William Clark to select the site for the fort that was ill-suited to the tribes in the region: "Having shown that there are no possible advantages accruing to the Indians from this situation as a place of trade, nor to the frontier as a Military Post, as in the case of an Indian War it can be no check (its own defence [sic] excepted) to their hostile acts. We may add that in our humble opinion it is a moth on the publick [sic] purse." (Eli B. Clemson to Daniel Bissell, July 22, 1812, *Territorial Papers* 14, 587-590.)

Fort Osage Thursday Sept. 14th, 1809

The morning clear and <u>cool.</u> Two Men arrived last evening from St. Louis by land, which place they left on the [blank] Inst. The Osages who went down on the 19th of August with Mr. McFarlane,[39] have also Returned to their Villages. As the 2 men above mentioned brought no Letters with them, Nothing of any consequence to be Relied on, can be gathered from them. In the afternoon the Arkansaw Chiefs came in and paid me a visit. They Say they have Settled all their differences with Governor Lewis and General Clark, who have promised them to open the Trade of the Arkansaw if they continue to behave well, they advise them to treat all

Traders with friendship, and if they ask too much for their Goods, to leave them and come here to the Factory to trade. These Chiefs appear to be about half pleased with the Result of their trip to St. Louis.

[39] Governor Meriwether Lewis appointed James McFarlane as an agent to the Arkansas Osage in an effort to placate their objections to the 1808 treaty, so he was in and out of the Osage villages and St. Louis in 1809. McFarlane's appointment, however, was caught in a political crossfire between the Chouteaus and Lewis. Pierre Chouteau, Jr. wrote to war secretary William Eustis that much had been negotiated with the Osage tribes without the advice and input of his father (whom he rightly figured had substantial influence with the tribe), and that in the spring of 1809 "the Governor thought proper to ingratiate himself with the Band of Osages established on the River Arkansas, but still without communicating his projects to my Father: he sent to them Mr. McFarlane, second Agent to the Osage Nations. Neither my Father nor myself have any knowledge of the Instructions that were given him. Mr. McFarlane, in the name of the Governor, made immense promises to the Osages, and arrived at St. Louis with the Chiefs of that Band: it was immediately proposed to them to proceed to Washington City with Mr. McFarlane; but the Savages refused to accede to it. The promises made to them upon the Borders of the Arkansas not having been fulfilled at St. Louis. Their Confidence is destroyed." (Rollings, *The Osage*, 228-230; Pierre Chouteau, Jr., to William Eustis, September 1, 1809, *Territorial Papers* 14, 317.)

Fort Osage Friday September 15th, 1809
The morning cool and clear. Wrote to Mr. Tillier[40] to day. The day continued clear and pleasant.

[40] Most likely, this letter regarded additional goods from Fort Belle Fontaine. Although the trade factory there closed in 1808, Tillier was still in St. Louis and apparently working in some capacity for Clark collecting funds and such through the end of 1809. (*American State Papers, Indian Affairs* 1, 771.)

Saturday 16th
Morning cool and threatening Rain a little.

In the evening or rather at night arrived Mr. Isaac Rawlings,[41] a young Gentleman Sent out by General Mason to be my assistant. He is the bearer of Sundry Letters from General Mason and General Clark and has in charge a large quantity of Indian Goods for me, which he has come in company with all the way from Georgetown.[42]

He left the Boat containing those Goods, a few Miles below here, and come up in a Small Barge with Capt. Clemson, who had gone down to meet the Boat, and to take an airing. They arrived about 12 O'Clock.

[41] Isaac Rawlings (d. 1839) joined Sibley in 1809 as assistant factor. After leaving Fort Osage, Rawlings moved to the young hamlet of Memphis, Tennessee, but retained ties to the Office of Indian Trade. In 1819, he received a contract to build an eighty-foot keelboat to carry goods to the Arkansas villages; only Prairie du Chien and Fort Osage had sufficient trade to own keelboats (Sibley's was christened The Osage Factor). In Memphis, Rawlings became a businessman and a leader in the growth of banking, early transportation, and insurance; he was elected the second mayor of Memphis in 1829 and again as its fourth in 1833. (Jones, *Prairie Puritan*, 59-60; Peake, *A History of the United States Indian Factory System*, 84.)

[42] Georgetown, District of Columbia, was the site of the Indian Trade Office's central warehouses.

Sunday 17th

The Boat arrived this morning with the Factory Goods, which were immediately unladen and Stored in the Garrison under lock and Key. Some of the packages appear to be Somewhat injured. Their contents must be examined without delay.

October 9th, 1810

Wrote to Mr. R. H. Price[43] of St. Louis this day by Mr. John Smith. Enclosed Mr. P $4 in Silver $3 to pay Dr. Farroe[44] for a pr. of Shoes that I got from him in St. Louis in August last and $1 for Ellen a Black Girl[45] who done my washing then.

Wrote to John Hancock at Boone's Saline[46] for 100 lbs. Butter, offer $15 per hundred to be delivered here before the Middle of November.

Wrote to General Clark on the Subject of Medals to Kansas and Pawnees[47] and Small presents to visiting Indians.

On the 21st of September I hired William Wells for the Term of One Year (if we can agree that long) at the Rate of $18 per Month and find him provisions. Same day Wells Started to St. Louis and the Settlements on Quiver in pursuit of my Horses. Furnished him with $5 to pay his expenses, and gave him $10 to be paid to Mr. Mossy[48] at Luther Lick, to whom I owe that Sum for hire of his Mare.

On the 1st of October hired a Frenchman Jo. La Revey[49] by name for One

Month or More at $18 per Month. This Man's time will the greatest part of it be employed about Mr. R. H. Price's affairs.[50]

[43] Risdon H. Price was a St. Louis merchant and businessman in partnership with Benjamin Wilkinson until the latter died in 1810. Price appears to have entered into a business arrangement with Sibley, raising crops and livestock around the fort after John Robinson left as Assistant Factor. Most likely, Price invested capital and Sibley provided land and labor to raise foodstuffs to sell to the government to supply the garrison. Price was a director of Territorial Bank of St. Louis, incorporated in 1813, along with such notable businessmen as Manuel Lisa, Auguste Chouteau, Moses Austin, and Rufus Easton; he became its president in 1818. (Billon, *Annals of St. Louis in its Territorial Days*, 85, 269-270.)

[44] Dr. Bernard Gaines Farrar (1784-1849) was a Virginian transplanted to Fayette County, Kentucky as an infant. After medical school he started a brief practice in Frankfort, Kentucky, before being convinced in 1807 to move to St. Louis by his brother-in-law John Coburn, a territorial judge there, making him the first American to establish a permanent medical practice west of the Mississippi River. One of his early surgeries was amputating the gangrenous leg of George Shannon (a member of the Corps of Discovery who was later hired by William Clark to help Nicholas Biddle compile and write the original published account of the Lewis and Clark Expedition) in October of 1807 after being wounded by the Arikaras; he operated his office in a room of William Clark's home in 1808-1809.

Later, he gained another connection to the explorer when he married Ann Clark Thruston, William Clark's niece (the daughter of Clark's sister Fanny) in 1820, a second marriage for both. He briefly operated a drug and medicine shop with Joseph Charless (publisher of the *Missouri Gazette*, the first newspaper in St. Louis), selling "spices, paints and stationery" according to their advertisement, but the business was dissolved in 1812 "by mutual consent." He moved his apothecary shop to "Mrs. Chouteau's house, opposite to Manuel Lisa's new brick house" in 1813, reported the *Missouri Gazette*, soon after being elected a member of the first territorial House of Representatives for the newly formed Missouri Territory in 1812. Farrar served as a surgeon in the War of 1812 as well.

Perhaps more surprising was his place in the history of St. Louis dueling. "In conflict with his dedication to the healing arts" writes historian James Holmberg, "was his active participation in dueling." He severely wounded James Graham in late 1810 in what was reported as the first duel on "Bloody Island" in the Mississippi River. Since dueling was illegal, "affairs of honor" were carried out on an island outside the jurisdiction of local authorities. Graham hobbled around St. Louis on crutches for about a year, then died on a trip back east. (Billon, *Annals of St. Louis in its Territorial Days*, 240-241,125, 128, 81-82; Houck, *A History of Missouri from the Earliest Explorations and*

Settlements, vol. 2, 3; Holmberg, *Dear Brother: Letters of William Clark to Jonathan Clark*, 162-163.)

[45] Renting slaves for a brief period or for certain functions was not particularly uncommon in more urban settings such as St. Louis. It was sometimes difficult to keep slaves busy all the time in town, so they could be available for occasional use (such as here) or for longer-term assistance.

[46]Boone's Saline was part of what was at the time called "Boon's Lick country." Nathan and Daniel Morgan Boone, sons of Daniel Boone, operated salt-making operations with James and Jesse Morrison along the Salt River (in present-day Howard County) starting in 1805 that only lasted a few years. Even though the business didn't last long, the famous Boone name remained attached to it. Governor Meriwether Lewis considered settlement in the region to be an infraction of the 1808 treaty with the Osage that expressly banned white settlement on tribal lands, but the small military presence in the region couldn't keep squatters out. By the time Sibley wrote this entry, settlers were coming to the region in today's Cooper, Howard, and Saline counties. A year later, when the botanist John Bradbury came through on his journey studying local flora, he commented that some 100 families lived in the region. (Hurt, "Seeking Fortune in the Promised Land: Settling the Boon's Lick Country, 1808-1825," *Gateway Heritage*, 4-5.)

[47] Medals were a crucial part of the practice of gift-giving with Native American chiefs. In general, American officials assumed that Native American political structures were akin to western ones, in that there were tribal leaders who had the authority to speak and make commitments for all. White officials such as Lewis and Clark—or George Sibley—identified those whom they thought were chiefs and designated them as such, disregarding the nuances of their status within the tribe. Both Europeans and Americans used medals to denote both peaceful relations and loyalty. The United States made them of gold or silver, and in three sizes to suggest status. The medals were designed and minted at no small expense (those made to start the Monroe administration in 1817, for example, cost $3,007 for 300 medals), each having the profile of the President. Each had a small hole above the president's head to which was tied a green or red ribbon. When a delegation of chiefs met a newly elected president (such as the group of Osage and others William Clark accompanied to Washington to meet James Madison in 1809), the guests received medals with the likeness of Thomas Jefferson (Madison's predecessor) with a promise that they could exchange them for some with Madison's profile when the medals were finished. (Peake, *A History of the United States Indian Factory System*, 127-128.)

[48] Probably one of the families living in a settlement not far from the fort.

[49] Probably a laborer who was also a trader; the Missouri River was still well populated with French fur traders and trappers. Since hiring men from the garrison was nearly impossible for Sibley, he would have needed someone to help with manual labor in his business concerns with Risdon Price (see above).

[50] Price's affairs included a partnership with Sibley to raise hogs and corn to sell to the army for supplying the garrison, which included planning fourteen-and-a-half acres of corn; Sibley oversaw the operation at Fort Osage. Ira Cottle started a similar business soon after, when he arrived with 110 head of cattle for the same purpose. However, the business didn't go well; over the winter the hogs were requisitioned by the Osage and troops alike and had a habit of escaping, so they lost almost half of them the first winter. (Gregg, "The History of Fort Osage," *Missouri Historical Review*, 447-449.)

Fort Osage Thursday November 1st, 1810

The Morning cool and cloudy. At an hour after Sunrise (after considerable unnecessary and very improper delay from the Garrison in detaining my canoe) I dispatched Pierre Lorr[51] to St. Louis in a light canoe with dispatches to the Supt. Of Indian Trade and Secretary of the Treasury enclosed to General Wm. Clark St. Louis, for him to forward them on by mail immediately. I wrote the General a long Letter on various Subjects relating to our affairs here, The Osage Treaty[52] &c. and Suggested to him a few advantages that would Result from the annuities being drawn from the Factory[53] if there is Such Stipulation in the Treaty. I Requested the favor of him to enquire of Governor Howard[54] the nature of the control (if any) which the Treaty will allow the Military to exercise here over the improvement made by Dr. Robinson, Stating to him the manner and under what authority and expectations that improvement was made and how it came into my hands. I gave him a description of the improvement, and enquired if it would not be wanted by the Government offering it for $500. I also wrote to Mr. John G. Comegys, Messrs. J. G. Comegys & Co.,[55] R. H. Price & Dr. Robinson.

[51] Lorr was the interpreter for Fort Osage.

[52] This is the treaty originally negotiated by William Clark in September of 1808, then renegotiated by Pierre Chouteau in November. It was ratified April 28, 1810.

[53] Advantages would include not giving Indians money, so they were required to deal with the factory rather than with British or with independent competing traders.

[54] Governor Benjamin Howard (1760-1814) has been described by historian

Mark Morasch as "a lawyer by vocation, a politician by obligation, and a soldier by preference." Like many early leaders in St. Louis, Howard was born in Virginia but moved to Kentucky during his boyhood, where he had his strongest family and political ties. And, like William Clark, Meriwether Lewis, Benjamin Wilkinson and others, he fought under General Anthony Wayne against Native Americans in the Ohio Valley in the 1790s. Howard always held his greatest affection for his native Kentucky, representing it in Congress starting in 1807.

Howard resigned his seat in April 1810, when James Madison appointed him the new Governor of the Louisiana Territory (the upper part of the Louisiana Purchase; the lower part was the Orleans Territory) after the death of Governor Meriwether Lewis in September 1809 (a position William Clark turned down at the time), which he probably saw as a stepping-stone to higher and more lucrative positions. Although immensely popular in St. Louis and the territory, Howard apparently missed his native state and regretted accepting the position. Threats from the British and their nearby Native American allies in 1811 compelled Howard to order the construction of additional defenses in outlying parts of the territory and the organization of a company of riflemen to patrol the northern reaches of the territory after William Henry Harrison defeated the Shawnee chief Tenskwatawa in a brutal encounter at Prophet's Town. His strong defensive stand helped make him popular with people living in the territory; he received a special commission from Madison as Brigadier General when the War of 1812 started in June. Howard resigned as Territorial Governor in March 1813, to accept command in the Illinois and Missouri territories. Madison appointed William Clark as his successor. So great was the outcry over the prospects of his transfer to Detroit in 1814 that the army ordered him to return to St. Louis, where he died in September of that year. The Territorial legislature named the newly created Howard County after him in 1816. (Morasch, "Benjamin Howard," in *Dictionary of Missouri Biography*, 406-407.)

[55] John Comegys was a partner in Falconer and Comegys, a merchant firm briefly located in St. Louis that apparently moved farther down the Mississippi River.

Thursday 1st November 1810

In my Letters to Comegys & Co. I enclosed 3 Bills of Exchange for $891.02 all made payable to them or order (See Copy of those Letters filed). I wrote very hastily to Mr. Price about his Hogs Crop &c. and Send him 75 cents In Cut Silver Money that I had just Received for a Bushel of his Potatoes. To Dr. Robinson I wrote merely a Short friendly Epistle. All of these Letters are dated 31st of October. This Morning Mr. Wilson P. Hunt and party consisting of 40 or 50 Men and Several Gentlemen in one Large Keel Boat and Two Batteaux,[56] left this place (after 2 days Stay) on their way up to the heads of the Missouri, and over to the Pacific Ocean.[57] Mr. Hunt is charged with this enterprise by the newly established New York Fur Company[58] of which the celebrated John Jacob Astor is at the head, as I understand. He has for object to open a new Trade. A Vessel has gone Round to meet them at the Mount of the Columbia River. I did not make any particular enquiry of Mr. Hunt Relative to the precise object of this expedition. It is well understood that the above is the object. The Party will not proceed farther than the Platt[e] this winter, a great portion of the Men will winter about _150_ miles above here. They appear to be well organized and every way prepared to carry fully into execution their object, & So far as it depends on human Skill and perseverance I have not a doubt of their Success.[59] Mr. Ramsay Crooks, Mr. Joseph Miller, Mr. Donald McKenzie[60] are of the party though I do not know if they are connected in any way with Mr. Hunt's enterprise except Mr. McKenzie. Capt. Robert McClellan now at the Platt[e][61] will join them there I am told. And in him the party will find a most valuable acquisition. A Mr. Airde[62] with a Small Barge and Some Indian Goods is also in this company; his destination I believe is to the Sioux where he expects to remain this winter for the purposes of Trade.

[56] A bateau is a long, narrow, flat-bottomed wood boat with a shallow draft and pointed at both ends—especially useful for navigating rivers like the Missouri with shallow areas and sandbars. It was a mainstay of river shipping in the eighteenth century. Bateaux were generally narrower than flatboats.

[57] Wilson Price Hunt was one of five partners whom John Jacob Astor invited to invest in his new Pacific Fur Company. In 1810, Astor commissioned two groups to travel to establish trading operations at the mouth of the Columbia. One, under Capt. Jonathan Thorn, arrived in the Pacific Northwest in March 1811, but the cantankerous Thorn managed to anger the Native Americans there to the point that they killed the entire crew. The other group was to travel overland from St. Louis, under the command of Hunt. This 59-member expedition, including fellow partner Ramsay Crooks, left in 1811; only 35 of the crew arrived at the mouth of the Columbia, thanks to starvation, hostile Native Americans, fatigue, illness, exposure and poor morale. They sold the fort to officials from the British Northwest Company in 1813 after finding out that their native country (Great Britain) was at war with the United States (where their company was chartered) and that a British warship was on its way.

[58] Sibley is referring to Astor's Pacific Fur Company.

[59] The reality facing the group was the exact opposite. It was as ill-fated as a trading group could have been. (Ronda, *Astoria and Empire*.)

[60] Along with Hunt, these were the four Pacific Fur Company partners on the voyage. Donald McKenzie arrived in Canada in 1801and worked for the Northwest Company; he joined Astor's Pacific Fur Company eight years later. Despite having more experience in crossing unknown regions, he was passed over to head the expedition.

[61] Fur trader Robert McClellan provided early news of the outside world to the Corps of Discovery in September 1806. As Lewis and Clark headed down the Missouri on their return, they met a number of traders and trappers as they approached St. Louis. They camped overnight with McClellan, who brought them up to date on events back in the United States. Lewis and Clark may have already known McClellan from their days in the Ohio Valley in the early 1790s, when all three served in the army under General Anthony Wayne in his campaigns against the Native Americans there. He later joined Wilson Price Hunt's 1811 expedition to the Pacific. (*The Definitive Journals of Lewis and Clark*, vol. 8, September 12, 1806, 357-358.)

[62] James Aird (d. 1819) also met Lewis and Clark between the Vermilion and Big Sioux rivers on the Missouri. "We landed and found a Mr. James Airs from Mackanaw by way of Prarie Dechien and St. Louis. This Gentleman has a license to trade for one year among the Sieoux [sic]" wrote William Clark on September 3, 1806. He also agreed to sell the captains enough tobacco for members of the crew to get them back to St. Louis, "an instance of Generossity for which every man of the party appears to acknowledge." Aird was a somewhat typical trader, always struggling to make a profit, drifting back and forth between frontier and town, between places such as Mackinac and the Missouri. He ended his fur-trading days with the American Fur Company, working for his former clerk Ramsay Crooks. ("Trade Goods, Biographies and Histories of Traders, Merchants, Chiefs, Officers, Voyageurs," http://www.usinternet.com/users/dfnels/aird; *The Definitive Journals of Lewis and Clark*, vol. 8, September 3 and 4, 1806, 346-349.)

Friday November 2nd, 1810

Morning clear and Cold. It froze Standing water to an ice 1/2 inch thick last night. I believe the first white frost we had was on the 2nd Ulto. Mr. Zadock Woods[63] arrived here late last Night with 33 head of Beef Cattle for the Contractor. Capt. Clemson departed from this place for St. Louis about the 26th Ult. At the Tabo he lost both his Horses, and they have not been found yet I believe. The day proved to be very Raw and cloudy, and in the evening it had every appearance of a Snow Storm.

[63] Zadock Woods (1773-1842) was the first white settler granted a land title in St. Charles County, Missouri, when he arrived from Vermont in 1801. He and fellow settler Joseph Cottle built Woods Fort around present-day Troy, Missouri, to enclose the cabins, spring, Universalist church, and tavern.

Benjamin Howard served as Territorial Governor during the period covered by these journals, although he probably spent more time in his adopted home state of Kentucky than in the Missouri Territory. (Used by permission, State Historical society of Missouri, Columbia)

Woods enlisted in Nathan Boone's Mounted Rangers in 1812, just before the war started, and ended up at the Battle of New Orleans under Andrew Jackson. In his absence, Lieut. (and future president) Zachary Taylor used Woods Fort as his headquarters for raids against pro-British tribes. Woods later moved to Texas as one of the families relocating with Moses Austin; he traveled between Texas and Missouri over the next decade and became active in the Texas independence movement. Woods was killed at a skirmish at Salado Creek, near San Antonio, on his 69th birthday.

Saturday 3rd

Very cool and Raw this morning, and cloudy. It hailed a little late last night.

Wrote this day to Mr. Jesse Morrison[64] about a Barrel of Salt I had of him, and an old Sorrel Mare of his that I had the use of for 2 days in pursuit of my Horses that got away from me on the Road from St. Louis to this place in Sept. last. Sent Mr. Morrison a Draft for $11 on Comegus & Co. St. Louis to pay for the Salt. (See Copy of my Letter filed)

[64] Jesse Morrison and his brother James were partners with another set of brothers, Nathan and Daniel Morgan Boone, in a salt-making operation in Missouri. The Morrisons and Boones started in their business in 1805, but Daniel Morgan Boone sold his interest to Morrison in 1810; Nathan left the salt business two years later, at the start of the War of 1812. Threats from Native Americans hostile to the United States compelled the Morrisons to abandon the operation until after the war. (Dickey, "Boone's Lick State Historic Site," http://www.dnr.state.mo.)

Sunday November 4th, 1810

Morning cool and drizzly. The day was drizzly throughout.

Monday 5th

Morning drizzly, weather moderate, turned fair and pleasant at 10, and So continued all day.

Tuesday 6th

Morning clear and cool. Yesterday I wrote a long Letter to my Father (5 Sheets Letter Paper) on a variety of Subjects. Sketch of my disputes and quarrels here, and of Dr. Robinson's &c. &c. &c. &c. &c.[65] the day changeable, Sometimes clear, Sometimes cloudy and like for Rain.

[65] Sibley had "disputes and quarrels" all right. By this time, Sibley was receiving letters from Indian Trade Superintendent John Mason about complaints lodged against him by his old nemesis Capt. Eli Clemson. In October of 1809, traders Joseph Robidoux and Francois Dorion (see below)

arrived at the fort on their way upriver. A group of "distempered Osages" met the two boats, which led to a commotion; Sibley and John Robinson went down to the landing "in the dark and rain" to investigate. After Robinson told the Osage chiefs to disperse and allow the traders to land without harm, they left. Later than evening, Sans Oreille, an Osage chief, came up saying that the group was on the verge of violence against the two traders. Sibley told him, apparently in no uncertain terms, that if anything happened to the boats or traders, everyone would be banned from all trade at the factory—period—and figured that was the end of it. The next morning, a group of Osage followed the traders upriver. Soon, the opportunity they were awaiting presented itself when Robidoux and Dorion ran the boats up on a sand bar; as the traders tried to release them back into the water, the Indians waded toward the boats. Pushing and shoving became more violent and one thing led to another, which included one of the traders hitting an Osage in the head with a boat pole. The Indians forced the boats back to the fort and ran to grab weapons for revenge. Robinson dispersed the Indians (again) and, according to Sibley, avoided bloodshed. The boats passed, the chiefs apologized to Sibley and Robinson, and later Sibley reinstated their trade rights.

Meantime, Robinson had spoken with Clemson and expressed his surprise (to put it mildly, no doubt) that Clemson hadn't ordered any troops to intervene. Clemson replied that "Such affairs are common and of no consequence." Strong words followed from both commander and factor. Clemson wrote to War Secretary Eustis charging that Sibley had actively incited the Indians to violence and warfare. It took two years for the charges to be made, letters sent back and forth, and for Sibley to travel to Washington in the winter of 1811-12 to answer the charges himself. (Gregg, "History of Fort Osage," *Missouri Historical Review*, 453-455; Jones, *Prairie Puritan*, 61-62.)

Wednesday 7th
Morning very cloudy and Raw. It Rained last night. Cloudy and disagreeable all day.

To day I Salted away 412 lbs. of very fine Beef which I purchased from Zadoc Woods at 5 1/2 cts. per lb. Also Salted down 13 Neats' Tongues.[66] *Paid Mr. Woods $22.66 for a very fine Barrett Cow, which yielded 412 lbs. Beef at 5 1/2cts. 45 lbs. Tallow at 10 cts. Hid $1—all $28.16.*

[66] Ox tongues; they were salted as part of the preservation process.

Thursday 8th November, 1810
The Morning very Cloudy and very chilly a little Snow about10 O'Clock.

This day I Settle accounts in full with Mr. Zadock Woods (See Account filed) and gave him a Draft on J. G. Comegys & Co. for $112 in full.

On the 3rd, I Settled an Account with Mr. J. H. Audrain.[67] Mr. A. held a Note on P. Lorr for $56.38 which I had promised Lorr to take up. I held a Note on Mr. A. (Sent me by J. G. Comegys to Collect) for $40.25. So I paid Mr. A. the difference ($16.13) in a Draft on J. G. Comegys & Co. dated the same day. I wrote to Mr. Comegys to day on the above Subject (See Copies of Letters and Drafts, filed) I Sent by Mr. Woods to General Clark an old Sorrel Horse belonging to the Indian Department and wrote the General a line to that effect . I also enclosed to General C. a Letter for The Supt. of Indian Trade covering merely, duplicates of the Salary Accounts & advices of Drafts drawn on account thereof on the 25th Ulto. A Letter to John Sibley dated 5th Inst. (5 Sheets) and Loose under Same wrapper my Letters to Comegys. Send this Packet by Mr. Zadock Woods.

[67] James H. Audrain (1782-1831) was one of the early settlers in the area. Audrain County was named for him five years after he died in St. Charles while serving as a member of the state legislature. It is unclear what business Audrain was in at this point, but a tavern was probably part of it. He opened the Grove Tavern in St. Louis in 1809, across the street from Pierre Chouteau's home. He advertised opening a "house of entertainment" in 1818 on the road between Boons Lick and the Salt River, some 14 miles west of St. Charles. Since his first establishment was so close to the Chouteau home, it is not beyond possibility that Chouteau enticed him to move west to settle on or near where he had a land claim. (Stevens, "The Missouri Tavern," *Missouri Historical Review*, 249; "Missouri History not Found in Textbooks," *Missouri Historical Review*, 503.)

Friday November 9th, 1810

Morning Cloudy. Day Cool and disagreeable till evening when it turned warm & pleasant. Mr. Wood Started this Morning about 10 O'Clock. To day I entered into a Written and formal agreement with William Wells, for his Services 12 Months to commence the 1st Inst. (See Agreement filed) Also had a Serious talk with Madame Lorr Relative to her Services in Kitchen &c. She promised to be more Regular attentive and managing, and from the wish I feel to assist her and her very Large Family I am induced to try her again, and I hope She will do better in the future.

Saturday 10th

Morning clear and pleasant. Somewhat Cloudy at times during the day. The greater part of the old Women and lads who have their winter camps here went out on a hunt to day to Stay 10 days. Blue Back is the leader.

Wells was Sick to day, he thinks it is occasioned by too free use of Whiskey for the few last days. Gave him a powerful dose of Salts[68] which done him much good he Says.

Standard medical practice at the time still relied on purging one's system as a medical treatment. It was based on the idea that health hinged upon balance in the body and that illness resulted from an imbalance of these fluids. As a result, bleeding (along with purgatives) was common practice. As Sergeant Charles Floyd lay dying just above Council Bluffs on the Lewis and Clark expedition in 1804, the captains treated his appendicitis with bleeding.

Sunday November 11th, 1810

The Sun Rose beautifully, while it was <u>Snowing</u>, but was quickly obscured by clouds. The day continued cloudy and for the most part <u>Snowy</u>, though warm. In the evening it changed to a warm fine Rain, and at Night we had a pretty hard Shower of Rain. I had my Stable fitted up to day, and now my Horses are comfortably Housed.

Monday 12th

Morning Cloudy and warm. A good deal of Rain fell last Night. To day I had 15 Bushels of <u>Turnips</u> gathered and put into my cellar for table use, for which I am to pay Mr. R. H. Price. Cloudy and disagreeable all day, about 12 it turned colder.

Morning very Cloudy and Raw. Ground frozen. To day I employed <u>10</u> or <u>15</u> Squaws to harvest Mr. Price's Corn. We got about <u>60</u> Bushels Snugly housed before night. It continued cloudy all day, and at night it Rained a little.

Wednesday November 14th, 1810

Morning cloudy and cold. It cleared off about 10 O'Clock, and continued fair & pleasant all day. I had about 120 Bushels of Corn gathered, Husked & Housed to day. The Osages who have taken up their winter Residence within Gunshot of the Factory consisting of from <u>30</u> to <u>50</u> old women, with a few Girls & a Number of Children, an Several men Young and old who are either too Sick or too aged or too badly provided with Guns &c. to accompany the Rest of the Tribe to the Hunt, were very much alarmed Yesterday and today by Some <u>Signs</u> which they Saw and heard of and which they believe to be certain indications of the near approach of Some Enemy. While I was at Supper 2 of the principal Men came to tell me of their apprehensions that they would be attacked to Night, which they had Scarcely finished, before I was informed that the whole of the Women were crowding Round the Factory, and were absolutely So much alarmed with their apprehensions that they could not be prevailed on to pass the night in their lodges. In order to quiet their fears and at the Same time to be Rid of the throng I put about <u>30</u> of the old women and a number of the Children in a vacant hut belonging to the Indian Department in my

*charge,[69] and Recommended to the Men to Patrole the Neighboring passes,
paths &c. during the Night.*

[69] By this time, the United States had the Osage somewhat under its thumb.
Part of the arrangements had included promises to protect the Osage from
their neighbors if they, the Osage, avoided violence or retaliation. Since the
village was largely defenseless during the hunt, Sibley most likely felt honor-
bound to help. In addition, part of his charge when commissioned was to set
an example of honesty and integrity, besides protecting the Indians.

Thursday 15th
*Morning Cool and Clear. Day continued fair and pleasant. Harvested and
housed about 80 Bushels of Corn to day.*

One of the Soldiers (King) died yesterday and was buried this afternoon.

Friday 16th
*Morning fair and Cool. The day continued fair and pleasant. Gathered and
Housed 25 Barrels of Corn in the ear to day.*

Saturday 17th
*The Morning fair and cool, could get none of the Squaws to gather Corn
to day. Wells got 3 1/2 Barrels of Ears Housed before dinner, and was
employed getting Fire Wood the Rest of the day.*

Day pleasant and fair.

Sunday November18th, 1810
*Morning cloudy and warm. Turned fair & very pleasant about 9 O'Clock,
and continued So all day. After Breakfast I Rode up the River Bottom as
far as the Blue River, accompanied by my Man Wells; we Returned by the
Ridge path. Our principal object was to look after Some Hogs belonging
to Mr. R. H. Price, but in this we were very unsuccessful, as by Some
chance or other we did not See a Single Hog.[70]*

[70] The hogs Sibley was helping to raise for a company headed by Risdon Price
were problematic; some escaped and turned wild, and others were never
found. The Osage procured some and the soldiers at the garrison occasionally
enjoyed pork before it had been sold by Risdon's concerns. (Gregg, "The
History of Fort Osage," *Missouri Historical Review*, 454; Jones, *Prairie Puritan*,
67.)

Monday 19th

Morning Stormy and exceeding Cold. It was very warm and pleasant during the Night till about 2 Hours before day light, when it burned windy and blew up a <u>Snow Storm</u> which continued till 12 O'Clock; when it cleared off a little for an hour, but again clouded over and grew very Cold indeed. The wind Still high from the North wet till 10 O'Clock at Night. This was truly a winter day, and by far the Coldest Since the last winter.

Tuesday 20th November 1810

Morning clear and excessively cold. It froze <u>very</u> hard last Night. <u>Ice Running very thick in the Missouri.</u> Day continued cold and fair. In the evening arrived Mr. Ira Cottle[71] from the Settlement of Quiver with 110 head of Cattle. Mr. Cottle proposes to take up his Residence at this place for a few Years, and intends to turn his attention chiefly to the raising of Cattle for the Supply of the U. S. Troops Stationed here. His Family are expected Shortly by Water, but the Running of the Ice will no doubt detain his Boat Some days. The Weather continued So Severe all day, that it was out of the question to attempt gathering Corn. I had my Beef packed in Pickle to day.[72]

Note—on the 18th, let Mrs. Lorr have <u>107</u> lbs. of Flour on Account of her husband's wages.

[71] Ira Cottle was a settler living nearby at the time; he and his family arrived in 1810 with 110 head of cattle, intending to sell beef to the garrison. He eventually became discouraged and said he was moving to the Mississippi Territory. Either he moved back to Missouri or never left, since he was living in St. Charles by 1818 and was sufficiently prominent to be elected to the last territorial General Assembly as one of six representatives from there. (Houck, *A History of Missouri from the Earliest Explorations and Settlements*, vol. 2, 8; Wolferman, *The Osage in Missouri*, 82.)

[72] Pickling is a method of preserving meat in brine.

Wednesday 21st November 1810

Morning clear and cold. Ice running very thick in the Missouri. day continued cold and at times Cloudy.

Thursday 22nd

Morning cold and fair. Ice Still very thick in the River. Day Somewhat cloudy. Quite unwell to day.

Friday 23rd

Morning fair and cool. River blocked up with ice opposite the Factory, and continued So all day. Gathered in <u>29 1/2</u> Barrels of Corn in the ear to day and had it hucked and housed.

Saturday 24th

Morning cool and Rainy, and Sleety till after dinner, when it began to Snow briskly and continued till Night.

Sunday 25th

Snow 5 Inches deep cloudy all day and cold.

Monday November 26th, 1810

Morning Clear and Cold. Continued fair all day, but it did not thaw much.

Tuesday 27th

Fair and Cold.

Wednesday 28th

Cold and Cloudy. A little Sleet just after dark.

Thursday 29th

The Morning Cool and fair day tolerable pleasant.

Friday 30th

Morning cold and fair. Several men came up from the Boats (Mr. Cottle's & the Contractor's) which are Stopped by the Ice below here about 30 Miles near the Sacque Prairie. Received a Letter from Mr. R. H. Price and a package of News Papers from Washington.[73]

> [73] Newspapers were rare and valued at the time, especially so far west. When Sibley wrote this entry there were some 366 newspapers published in the United States—about double the number in 1800. When the first issue of the *Missouri Gazette* came out in June 1808, it was the first newspaper in was is present-day Missouri. Even though the papers were weeks or months old when they arrived at Fort Osage, they would still have been a welcome arrival.

Saturday December 1st, 1810

Morning cold and Rather Cloudy. Wrote to Mr. Risdon H. Price to day on the Subject of his Hogs &c. See copy filed. Day continued Cloudy. Put up 4 Hogs to fatten to day.

Sunday 2nd
Morning cool and Rather cloudy began to Snow about 12 O'Clock and continued to Snow moderately for an hour.

Monday 3rd
Fair and Cold.

Tuesday 4th
Morning fair and pleasant. Day pleasant enough.

Wednesday 5th
Fair and pleasant. To day I gathered and housed __28__ Barrels of Corn in the ear for Mr. Price.

5th December
This evening a party of Osages consisting of Men and Women Returned from a hunt which they have been engaged in for about 16 days past, down on a branch of the La Mine River. On the 3rd Inst. they were Surprised by a large party of Sacques and Ioways (in the number about 200) who killed and took prisoners __5__ Men and __1__ Boy of their party, and plundered them of Several Horses and all their Peltry Provisions &c. This War Party told the Osages they were going in pursuit of the Big Osages.[74]

[74] Both the Sauks and the Ioways were traditional adversaries of the Osage, but expansion by the Osage put them into greater contact (and therefore conflict) with these and other neighbors.

Thursday 6th
Morning Cold and fair. At about 12 it Snowed a little and turned very cold. Wind high all day. Got in __16__ Barrels of Mr. Price's Corn to day, which completes one Field.

Friday December 7th, 1810
Morning fair and Cold. Day very cold and windy, but fair.

Saturday 8th
Morning Cold and Somewhat Cloudy. Day turned out tolerably pleasant.

Sunday 9th
Morning fair and pleasant. Day very pleasant.

Monday 10th
Morning __exceeding cold__, and clear. Day cold and fair.

Tuesday 11th

Morning cold and fair. Last Night at about half past Ten O'Clock. After I was a bed and asleep, Pierre Lorr my Interpreter arrived from St. Louis, whither I had Sent him on the 1st of November. Lorr met with a very unfortunate accident within about 16 miles of this place on his Return. His gun burst in his hands and very much hurt him, he will lose one Finger from his left hand, and be Sometime in the Doctor's hands before he Recovers from the wounds he has Received.

Letters Received by Lorr Vizt.

1 From General Clark dated 14th November, 1810
1 From J. G. Comegys & Co., dated 11th November 1810
1 From R. H. Price dated 12th November 1810
1 From S. H. Sibley dated 1st October 1810
1 From J. G. Comegys 11th & 14th of November

See Files

Wednesday 12th

Morning cold and clear. Day pleasant and fair.

Thursday 13th

The day very pleasant and fair. Finished gathering in Mr. Price's crop this day, off of about 14 1/2 acres of Ground I got 800 bushels housed. About 100 bushels were destroyed by Hogs &c. before it could be gathered. Paid Jo. La Revey $9.50 in full.

Friday December 14th, 1810

A very pleasant day.

Saturday 15th

Morning Cold and Somewhat Cloudy. About 12 it began to Snow and continued for 2 Hours. Snow very light. Cold and Raw all day.

Sunday 16th

Morning excessively Cold, and clear. Clear and cold all day. At Night it Snowed a little.

Monday 17th

Morning cloudy and excessively cold. Snow 1 1/2 Inch deep. Very cold day.

Tuesday 18th

Morning pretty fair and more moderate than yesterday. Day moderate. Paid William Wells $24 in Corn, in full to the 1st day of November.[75]

[75] Hard money was often in short supply in frontier settings such as territorial Missouri; the first Bank of St. Louis opened three years later but still lacked sufficient assets to support all the economic growth of the period. Payment in food might have been part of the original agreement.

Wednesday December 19th, 1810

Morning fair and moderate. Day Somewhat Cloudy and quite Cold.

Thursday 20th

Morning Cold and a little cloudy. A pleasant day. A number of Indians came in to day from their Hunting ground, of the Kansas and Missouri Tribes. Their view is to Trade at the Public Store. Mr. Cottle arrived in the evening with his Family (Wife & 2 Children) from the Boats about 2 days Journey below here, where they have been detained by the Ice near a Month. I gave Mr. Cottle leave to occupy the House that I got from Doctor Robinson until he can provide himself with one of his own.

Friday December 21st, 1810

Morning moderate and cloudy. Day unpleasant.

Saturday 22nd

Morning cool and clear. Day pleasant and fair. Killed 4 Hogs for Pork and had them packed away in Salt.[76] Weight 552 lbs. net Pork.

[76] Salt was always a valuable commodity, but it would have been more readily available for Sibley, since the Boone Salt Works was just east of him on the Salt River.

Sunday 23rd

Morning fair and cool, day pleasant

.
Monday 24th

Morning fair and pleasant, a pleasant day.

Tuesday 25th

Morning fair and very pleasant. A very pleasant Christmas day. This is the 3rd Christmas that I have passed at Fort Osage.

Wednesday December 26th, 1810
Morning cloudy and moderate, a very pleasant day.

Thursday 27th
Morning cloudy and warm. Mr. Ira Cottle and his Family moved this Morning into one of the Rooms occupied by my Interpreter.[77] I have permitted him to make use of that Room and my Kitchen until the 1st of April Next. Mrs. Cottle is to attend to my cooking[78] &c. and will be principally engaged make Candles and Soap for the Factory, for which her compensation will be fixed after She has made a trial and ascertained what She can afford to make them for per Hundred weight. The day continued Remarkably warm & pleasant. I lay very comfortably under one Blanket this Night, though I usually find 4 None too many.

[77] Lorr.

[78] Apparently the "serious talk" with Lorr's wife didn't work out the way Sibley had hoped; clearly, Mrs. Cottle is taking up her old job.

Friday 28th December 1810
Morning warm and Cloudy. For the first time Since 23rd Utlo. The Ice was this morning dispersed in part, in the Missouri opposite the Factory and a clear passage made by the channel on the other Side. Several Indians crossed the River on the Ice late yesterday evening. It turned cool at about 3 O'Clock P.M. Had all my Cattle driven up to day.

Saturday 29th
Morning cold and Somewhat cloudy. River clear of Ice opposite the Factory.

Sunday 30th
Day fair and cold. Unwell.

Monday 31st
Morning cold and fair. The day moderate and tolerably Pleasant.

Fort Osage Tuesday January 1st, 1811
Morning clear and pleasant. About 10 it turned cold and continued So all day. The Night excessively Cold, by far the coldest we have had this winter.

Wednesday 2nd
Morning clear and most bitter cold. My Ink was froze in the Stand, which

has never happened before Since I have occupied the new Factory House. Very cold day.

Thursday 3rd
Morning very cold and Somewhat cloudy. Missouri closed in the bend above the Factory. Day moderate by continued Rather cloudy.

Friday 4th
Morning moderate and Cloudy. Day Same.

Saturday 5th
Day warm and cloudy <u>very</u> thick mist at night.

Sunday 6th
Morning very foggy and quite warm. The day Remarkably warm and pleasant. <u>River open again</u>. Loose Ice Running.

Monday January 7th, 1811
Morning cloudy and moderate. Day cloudy and a little Rain. A little Snow at Night.

Tuesday 8th
Morning cold and cloudy. At about 11 O'Clock A.M. Mr. Wilson P. Hunt arrived on foot with <u>6</u> Men from his winter Camps about 150 Miles above hereon his way to St. Louis. He States that the Band of <u>Sioux </u>Robbed Capt. R. McClelland's Stores near the mouth of the Platt[e] last fall of about $2000 worth of Property. Mr. Hunt will proceed to St. Louis in a few days with <u>2</u> Men, the other <u>4</u> will Return to the Camp.

Wednesday 9th
Morning cold and fair. The day disagreeable. Mr. & Mrs. Cottle and 4 Osage Women commenced to make dipt [dipped] candles[79] to day for the Factory at 3 1/2 cents per pound.

[79] Since one of the objectives of the factory system was to transform hunter-and-gatherer Native Americans into self-sufficient and productive members of American society, the Office of Indian Trade encouraged factors to find ancillary industries and skills for the Indians. Sibley did so over the 1810-1811 winter, starting a candle-making operation. These women made the candles from buffalo tallow to sell—initially to the settlers in the region and, a bit later, for a more widespread commercial market. Sibley sent a sampling to John Mason, Superintendent of Indian Trade, who offered a mixed reaction. Mason commended Sibley's innovation and initiative, and agreed to expanding the

operation at government expense: "I am much pleased to see that you are likely to encrease [sic] the making of candles and thereby give to the Indian much employment and of course the means of subsistence and comfort—your plan of putting up a slight building for that purpose is approved and I beg you will give the subject every attention." But then Mason added that he had tried the samples, and "they were no great proofs of skill—but your red women it is to be hoped will become more neat in execution. They sold pretty well as a matter of curiosity but they will not bear the carriage to this place your principal market must be St. Louis for them as I presume." (Jones, *Prairie Puritan*, 60-61; John Mason to George Sibley, July 2, 1811, *Territorial Papers* 14, 458.)

Trade posts such as the one depicted here tried to compete with the factory system. By the late 1810s, such trade posts conducted more business with Native Americans than did the factors. (Used by permission, State Historical Society of Missouri, Columbia)

Thursday January 10th, 1811

To day I had the Public Buildings valued by Mr. Hunt and Mr. Audrain.[80]

[80] Placing a value on the buildings, along with the furs and merchandise on hand, was part of the annual report all factors were to submit to the Office of Indian Trade.

Friday 11th

Mr. Hunt departed for St. Louis, at about 11 O'Clock. He is to Return early in the Spring. By Mr. Hunt I Sent to Risdon H. Price a Bay Horse[81] belonging to him; and I lent Mr. H. a Saddle to be Returned in the Spring. I wrote the following Letters and Sent them by Mr. Hunt, copies of which are in my Letter Book.

1 to Risdon H. Price, St. Louis dated 8th January 1811
1 to John G. Comegys St. Louis dated 8th January 1811

a very pleasant day.

[81] Most likely he is referring to the color—reddish-brown—rather than the breed, which was originally bred in England. The Cleveland Bays, for example, did not arrive in the United States until early in the nineteenth century.

Fort Osage January 8th.1811.

Mr. Risdon H. Price, St. Louis

My dear Sir,

I wrote you on or about the 1st Ulto. and Sent the Letter about 30 Miles (to where the Contractor's and Mr. Cottle's Boats are froze up) by Mr. Cottle, who forwarded it to you by Jo. Morary,[82] and I do not but you have dully Received it.

Mr. Hunt[83] has just arrived here on his way to St. Louis and affords me and opportunity (though I am just now very much engaged in public business) to Say a few words to you Respecting your Hogs Corn &c. at this place. The harvesting of your Crop was completed on the 15th of December the following is transcribed from my diary.[84]

"Thursday December 13th. The day pleasant and fair. Finished gathering Mr. Price's corn to day, off of about 14 Acres of ground I got Somewhere about 800 Bushels of Corn housed. About 100 Bushels were destroyed though the Summer and fall by the Pigs &c." Out of these 800 Bushels I have paid myself 200 Bushels that were due to me by Dr. Robinson[85] and excepted in his power of Attorney to you, and I have let Mr. Audrain have 28 Bushels at $1, which he says he will pay you as soon as the Troops are paid off.[86] Wells has fed away Several Bushels to your Hogs, how much I do not know, though I do not believe more than necessary. I have been at

Osage leaders with whom Sibley dealt routinely probably looked similar to Tallee, depicted here by George Catlin. (Used by permission, State Historical Society of Missouri, Columbia)

Some considerable pains to collect all of your Hogs together and Succeeded in getting about <u>150</u> into an enclosure, where they were kept for about a fortnight and fed a little with corn. They are now Running out, but come up pretty Regularly to be fed, they are tame and gentle enough, and would no doubt do well to let alone.[87] The wild gang of Hogs above the Garrison have not been brought up yet, they are frequently Seen, and look extremely fat and well. I do not by any means despair of getting them up yet before the winter is over. I am only waiting for a Snow to fall, when I shall Send Wells and a party of Active Indians to chase and tire them down, and then they can easily be driven home. I was advised to defer chasing or disturbing them until it can be done effectively, and this it Seems may be done very easily when there is a crust of snow on the ground. Many of the old Sows have had Pigs, but very few of them have been Saved, owing in the cold weather and a variety of her causes that could not be easily guarded against.

It was out of our power to have them penned up Separately, near enough to my House to answer any good purpose. I would Require one Man's whole time to attend properly to the Sows, and after all it would only be raising Roasting Pigs for the (two legged) Wolves.

We declined having any of the Sows put up to be fatten 'till I hear from you again on the subject, for it might happen that after they had been fed awhile at a considerable expense of Corn &c. you would be obliged to turn them out again for want of a purchaser. I am sorry to say that I do not believe it will be easy, if at all possible to prevent many of your Hogs from being destroyed. Wells has frequently Reported to me latterly, that they come up crippled, and lately has found 2 grown Sows killed lying near the Garrison Somewhere about Mr. Audrain's Store. Wells attributes these things to the Soldiers and he is very probably not far from the truth. It is impossible to prove the thing against them, and until that can be done, it would only be making bad worse to make any fuss about it. In confidence though I will observe to you, that I have become convinced myself of the great Risk there is in having property of Citizens as we are contemptuously called by them, that it is absolutely alarming to those what are interested or who are obliged to look on Such irregularities without the power to prevent them. The Villains take care to keep their acts hidden from the view of others, and thereby Screen themselves from the proof. But it is clear enough to all from whence these outrages proceed. The unfortunate coolness that exists between myself and the Gentlemen of the Garrison, among whom I include the Suttlers prevents my making as Strict enquiry into these matters as I Should perhaps otherwise do; and it is possible then that this coolness (which will probably ever continue, at least as far as it depends on me) may operate in Sole degree to stimulate the Soldiers to do towards me many things for which they have no other motive than to gratify or ingratiate themselves with their Masters.[88] I would however be very loathe to believe that they are at all encouraged to do these things; on the contrary I think they are not, and I only Suggest the idea for _your_ benefit as a you will very clearly perceive. I Should certainly though pass Some pretty candid censure on this Gentleman or Some of them if this coolness did not exist, but under the present circumstances candor _might_ be mistaken for ill nature, & I should then get no credit for my pains.

Upon the whole my dear Price, after turning and twisting the thing in all manner of Shapes, and viewing it in lost all possible positions; I am constrained by the Sincere good will I feel for you, and the wish to Serve you all in my power, to offer it as my decided opinion, that you had better dispose of your Hogs &c. here as quickly as possible; and in the meantime give them in charge to some person whose intimacy or good understanding with the officer commanding the Soldiers, may in Some measure intimidate those fellows from their outrages. Such a person if he had an interest in the Hogs might prevent their being destroyed, and probably turn them to a good account. In giving you this advice I run the Risk of depriving myself of the pleasure of Serving you, but what do I Say? I forget that my circumstances, my unavoidable misunderstandings with the Garrison, and above all that my official duties absolutely deprived me of the pleasure to Serve you. Therefore I can only expect to derive that pleasure from advising you to place your affairs in Some other person's hands, whose situation a promise more Success to you than mine. It was a duty which I owed to myself and to your Sir; to have given you this candid exposition of your affairs here. I have no fear that you will mistake my motive, or that you will depreciate it. It has arisen from circumstances which we had no Right to expect when you were here. You may Rely on it, that whatever Service I _can_ Render you here I will most certainly do it. I require almost the whole time of Man Wells, but Still I make him attend more or less to your Hogs everyday; and in Reality they would all do very well if they were not disturbed by our Neighbors. Wells has lately had a dispute with Lt. Brownson for confining him in the Guardhouse, and has told him he would thrash him if he ever caught him out Side of his Centinels; this has caused Some irritation among Some of the most abandoned of the Soldiers, and it is Since this affair that the 2 Hogs were killed. I mentioned this, that you may be able to Judge of the propriety of Sending up a Man to take care of the Hogs, but take notice; if you do Send one, let him be an easy kind of body who can occasionally Submit to be cast into prison and yet be honest and careful of his trust, for it is easier for a Camel to go through the eye of a needle, than for an Independent American to live near an outpost like this, and keep on good terms with those who command the Garrison. This I lay down as one of my indisputable facts. Have I said enough or have I Said too much to you on these Matters? I had an hour to devote to you, and I determined to use it most for your profit, even though I should disclose Some things that I am by no means over Solicitous to have known too publicly, do not Suppose though that we have had any difficulties here lately more than common, except a most mortal and invincible coolness, we go on pretty well considering all things. Each one attends <u>chiefly</u> to his own concerns I believe, and does not meddle any more in his neighbor's affairs than may perhaps be consistent with the true Spirit of Gossiping. Cottle will not give me a bid for the hogs. I talked with him about them this very day and pressed him to write to you on the subject. He says he "will buy them if you will make the payment easy, and let him have them on Such terms as that he can make Something on them." These are his very words I believe. I also proposed to him to take the management of them on Shares, but this he appears to decline. You had better make up your mind what you will take for them and make an offer of them to him and Audrain. I Suspect Audrain would buy Some of them and perhaps the whole, though I have never Spoken to him on the Subject. I wish you to come to one conclusion about these things as quick as possible and let me hear from you. In the meantime I Shall pay as much attention to your affairs as I can properly do. Nothing Shall be Sacrificed to my knowledge without an effort to save it. If my ability half equaled my disposition to render you service, I should not now have troubled you with So lengthy an Epistle about Hogs, Pigs, Sows, Soldiers &c. I have not been able yet to Sell the House and fields. Cottle will not buy them; nor do I expect any body ever will. I wish I could meet with Some fool who would give me <u>$350</u> for them.[89] I should think myself well out of the Scrape I assure you. I am sometimes tempted to Set fire to the whole lot, and Rid myself of the plague. I Suspect I feel nearly the Same uneasiness about my valuable possession at this most delectable and promising of all possible places; that a certain tall, handsome, blue-devilish, lady-loving friend and acquaintance of mine does about <u>180</u> Swine, 2 Bulls and an

old Horse that he has (God Help them) the said delectable and
most promising of all possible places. I like to Joke about Such
Serious matters, it does no manner of harm, but lightens my
cares and Raises my Spirits amazingly. I Shall Send the Glass
down by the first boat, the pipes I have given you credit for, in
our private account. Mr. Hunt will deliver you a Bay Horse of
yours, I thought it would be best to Send him down to you by
So good an opportunity.

> *Yours &c.*
> *G. C. Sibley*
> *Mr. John G. Comegys*
> *St. Louis*
> *Pr. Mr. Hunt*[90]

[82] Mail was routinely delivered in this fashion—hand-carried by someone who was traveling to another city or region. For someone like Sibley living at Fort Osage which had no post office (and won't for several years yet), this was the only method of communication with the outside world.

[83] Wilson Price Hunt (see above).

[84] Sibley and Price were partners in a business to raise hogs and corn to sell to the military garrison at Fort Osage.

[85] Dr. John Robinson.

[86] Troops used their own pay for a variety of goods and products, only some of which were available from the factor—and besides, it was questionable if policy allowed the factor to sell goods and incidentals to the troops. Audrain probably made a good profit off the troops, especially in those goods Sibley could not or would not sell them in unlimited quantities, such as whiskey.

[87] It was not entirely uncommon to let farm animals forage, a practice dating to the early seventeenth century. Cows tended to stay near by, and hogs reverted to a wild state fairly quickly and had no natural enemies—except humans. The primary reason to keep them penned in was to avoid theft or poaching by either troops or Indians—both of which were ongoing problems. Price and Sibley lost about half the hogs to running away, freezing, or poaching.

[88] Relations between the military and civilian sides of trade factories and forts were generally tenuous at best, and worse at some than others. Sibley's relationship with the commanders at Fort Osage was never very good. Part of the problem was that Sibley needed the troops for a number of jobs that

involved fairly hard physical labor—helping construct buildings, felling huge trees, pressing and packing furs, loading and unloading boats and carrying goods from the river up to the fort on a bluff. Enlisted men weren't paid well to begin with, and their "fatigue pay" wasn't much. Sibley and fort commander Capt. Eli Clemson had a particularly sticky relationship that clearly went beyond the usual problems, though, which confirms Sibley's tendency to be rigid and uncompromising. His penchant for taking his problems with Clemson to higher-ups in the territorial government or military did nothing to ameliorate the problem, either.

[89] He didn't. Two horses he figured to be worth about $120 was all he could get from James Audrain the following month. Before Dr. John Robinson arrived at Fort Osage, he and St. Louis merchant Risdon Price had formed a partnership for raising hogs and corn to sell to the garrison and, presumably, trade to the Osage living around it. When Robinson left government service in 1810, Sibley apparently bought Robinson's interest in the venture. He exerted a great deal of time and energy on the project against a number of challenges including hogs being stolen or butchered, escaping or being released, and dying from natural causes. When he added up all the expenses and revenues from the venture, Sibley figured he made a profit of about ninety cents. In his February 24, 1811 journal entry (below) Sibley provided the details. (Jones, *Prairie Puritan*, 67.)

[90] Wilson Price Hunt had just arrived from upriver problems and was on his way to St. Louis.

Fort Osage January 8th.1811.

John G. Comegys
My Dear Sir,

I do most Sincerely and ardently hope that this may find you perfectly Recovered from the Severe illness which your esteemed favors of the 11th of November describes to be So truly painful and distressing. When a Man is fairly laid on his beam's ends (no matter how he came there) it is not the part of good fellowship to Roast him with trite witticism or to make market for Sarcastic innuendos and censorious morality at the expense of the unfortunate wight who lies, as it were, at his mercy – for I lay it down "as an indisputable fact" that pain is – pain - and whatever occasions it. Still it is pain and demands our commiseration.

Lorr met with a terrible accident on his way home – about 16 miles from here his Gun burst in his hand and wounded him very badly. But he got home, and delivered every thing (but himself) Safe and Sound on the 10th of December.

In looking over the account you Sent me, I find the following errors and omissions, which I attribute altogether to your Sickness, which prevents your attending very particularly to business. I find a note at the foot of the account, which tells me indeed that have merely Sent a Memo of my Account. The errors are

Ten dollars in the Tobacco Say 12 cents. instead 10 cents per lb.
Fifty cents for drayage of Tobacco
Nine dollars & half for Burns[91] the Tailor's Bill
Four Dollars omitted which I paid to Morin. These are all against me. I may be mistaken, as to [the] Burns Bill, but I am under the Impression that it was to have been paid by you.

These things happening to occur to me at this moment, I deemed it proper to mention them to you; leaving them however for future adjustment. I wrote you by Mr. Zadock Woods on the 8th, of November last, advising you of Sundry Drafts that I had drawn on you amounting to $139.13 The Draft 1 in favor of James H. Audrain or Order for $16.13, I have Since cancelled and stopped, So that you need not expect it ever to appear. I hope you will not fail to cause to be procured and Sent up to me by the first Boat in the Spring, the Articles I requested per letter of 9th October; and by all means two Barrels of good Flour, unless you Send me the Flour I apprehend I shall be put to hard Shifts for Bread, which is pretty near the case already, I assure you.

Being to take a pretty Serious jaunt next Spring through the Indian Country; I shall want a good Pocket compass. and I will thank you to Send me one by Mr. Hunt, also a pair of plain Strong Gold Ear rings of this size for my own use. You must know that my Eyes are growing very weak, and I am advised to wear Gold Rings in my Ears to prevent their growing worse. I don't pretend to know why in the name of all that's pretty I Should wear Gold Ear Rings because I have weak Eyes, unless it is, that Suppuration about the ears is useful. However, this is none of my business, if Gold Rings will cure weak eyes I am willing to try their effect, or Iron ones either. In Haste,

Yours ever and truly
G.C. Sibley

---

[91] Calvin Burns, a St. Louis tailor. Burns was apparently quite successful, since he advertised that he needed two or three journeymen "immediately; good wages." And Sibley would have known the tailors, since he apparently wore fine tailored clothes even on the frontier; he paid similar bills to tailors

in Georgetown in 1817 from journeys to the District of Columbia as well. (*Missouri Gazette*, August 24, 1808; Jones, *Prairie Puritan*, 117.)

Saturday 12th
Morning Raw and Somewhat cloudy. A pleasant day.

Sunday January 13th, 1811
Morning cold and a little cloudy. Day tolerable pleasant.

Monday 14th
Morning cool and cloudy and very likely for Snow. A <u>little</u> Snow at Sunrise. Day moderate and Rather Cloudy.

Tuesday 15th
A <u>little Snow</u> again this morning. Somewhat cloudy.

Wednesday 16th
About 1/8 inch of <u>Snow </u>fell this morning.

Thursday 17th
Day fair and moderate. Late last night or Rather very early this morning, <u>Mr. Audrain's</u> kitchen was burned to the ground with all its contents, consisting of Corn, Meat, Flour, Furniture and nearly the whole of his and his Family's wearing apparel which had been just given out to be washed his loss is pretty considerable, and is attended with great inconvenience in many Respects.

Friday January 18th, 1811
The day fair and very pleasant. Sent my Man Wells with my Oxen, to assist Mr. Audrain to day. A number of Soldiers were at work to day for Mr. Audrain under the direction of Lt. Brownson; it is to be hoped that the losses Mr. A. has Sustained, may be in Some measure Relieved by the Kind offices of those who have it in their power to assist him, at least so far as to Rebuild his House, and make him and his Family as comfortable as the nature of the case will admit.

Saturday 19th
A very pleasant day.

Sunday 20th
A very pleasant day. Rode out into the River bottom. 7 Osages arrived from the <u>Verdigris</u>,[92] where Ne zu mo ne[93] the Chief of the Little Osages is encamped with the greater part of his Tribe.

[92] The Verdigris River is in present-day east-central Kansas.

[93] Sibley identified Nee-zu-mo-nee in 1813 as "head Chief Little Osages" when he met with them in November to solicit their thoughts on relocating the fort during the War of 1812. He was one of the Osage leaders for whom Sibley seems to have genuine respect. (George Sibley to William Clark, November 30, 1813, *Territorial Papers* 14, 712.)

Monday January 21st
The day very fair and very pleasant.

Tuesday 22nd
Day very pleasant and fair.

Wednesday 23rd
Pleasant day

Thursday 24th
Pleasant day

Friday 25th
Pleasant day

Saturday 26th
Pleasant day

Sunday 27th
Morning cloudy and cool. Story day Sleet Snow and Hail. High wind at night. To day wrote to the <u>Secretary of War</u>[94] and <u>Superintendent of Indian Trade</u>.[95] See Letter Book.

[94] William Eustis.

[95] John Mason.

Monday 28th
Rainy day. Wrote the following Letters to day See Letter Book. General Wm. Clark. John H. Comegys and Joseph Gales, Jr. Wrote also a few lines to R. H. Price about his Hogs &c.

Fort Osage January 21st.1811

William Clark
Dear Sir,

I have your letter of the 14th November now before me. From the manner in which you Speak of the Houses and Improvement[86] made at this place by Dr. Robinson, I am fearful that I have not had the good fortune to make myself properly understood, by you in my Letter by Lorr of the 31st of October wherein I informed you of the circumstances which brought these houses and improvement into my hands, and used the freedom to request the favor of you to enquire of His Excellency Governor Howard at Some convenient opportunity how the Osage Treaty[87] will effect those Houses &c. and what control the Government would think fit to exercise over them? I have no idea that the <u>ground</u> was transferable by Dr. Robinson or any other individual. All that the Doctor has transferred to me is the Horse and fences, and that is all I pretend to claim under him. The <u>10</u> Acre field adjoining and enclosing the Houses, I <u>think</u> I have Some claim to the <u>use</u> of while I Reside here in a public capacity, to Raise corn vegetables &c. for domestic purposes. but however reasonable Such a claim may be, I Shall certainly never press it as a Right, though I shall expect it to be allowed me as an indulgence that I am as much entitled to at least as <u>private</u> Individuals who occupy land at this place. As to the Houses, fences &c. they were made by Dr. Robinson at his own expense, by Special permission of the Governor, under Such circumstances to as gave him a peculiar claim to all the advantages to be derived from them. And if he was not entitled to Sell them when and to whom he thought proper, I am much in error. If not too near the Garrison, I think this Improvement would be useful to the Indian Dept. for the accommodation of blacksmith, Miller[88] &c. if Such persons are necessary for these purposes or for any other, I presume there can be no objection to my Cultivating the ground. Having accidentally and much against my inclination acquired an interest in these Buildings, &c. (to the tune of $500 which they intrinsically worth) I hope you will have the goodness to excuse my making Some enquiry of you hope Respecting the interference and control which the Government may think proper to exercise over them under the provisions of the Osage treaty. Not wishing though by any means to give you the least trouble in this matter.

Provided unforeseen occurrences intervene to prevent it, I Shall take a little excursion in the Spring to the Kansas,

Pawnees, Arkansaw Osages and Great Osages, and probably to the Ottos and Missouri. The principal object of this excursion will be to form Some commercial arrangement with those Tribes and to extend to them if possible Some of the advantages designed for them by the Government in this establishment. This being the object, I can with much confidence Request your assistance to effect it provided the thing has your approbation. I am led to believe that Some Such Step is necessary to remove the jealousies and Suspicions excited among these Indians by a few interested and unprincipled Traders;[99] and that by a personal interview with them attended with Such ceremonies as are customary among Indians on Such occasions, with a few trifling presents &c. a more frequent intercourse may be effected which would be mutually beneficial to them and our Government. To them it would afford Regular Supplies of Merchandise, and to us it would afford the best opportunities of becoming well aquatinted with their habits, dispositions &c. and present the best means of collecting their friendship and good will towards the U. States.[100] As it will be necessary to procure and preserve Such an understanding among the different Tribes, especially the Kansas, Pawnees & Ottos, as will prevent their interrupting each other when on their way here to trade, your influence will be the more necessary.[101] Therefore if you think fit to promote this object, I will with the utmost cheerfulness make Such communications to the Kansas, Pawnees, Ottos and Missouris as you may be pleased to direct; and any other aid you may think proper to give, will be gladly Received I should be glad if you would furnish me with an American flag to be left at each of the Towns of the Kansas, Pawnees, Ottos, and Missouris, in the hands of the principal Chiefs, which ought to be delivered in your Name as tokens of the genuineness of your Messages.[102] I propose to Set out on this jaunt early in April, and Shall be extremely glad to hear from you on the subject as Soon as possible Say by the Return of Mr. Hunt Audrain.

I have some Reasons to believe that the Kansas and Missouris will Remove their villages and Settle near this place with the Little Osages if they Revive any encouragement from this quarter. I have been Several times consulted about it, but have declined giving them any positive encouragement, not knowing if it would be proper, though I am very clearly of opinion that they ought to be encouraged and invited. Will you be good enough to inform me if there is any objection to their being encouraged to come here to Reside that I any act accordingly. It *is my interest as Agent of Indian Trade to bring as many Indians to this neighborhood as I can Supply with goods – but I wish to be very cautious how I interfere in other people's concerns. I am persuaded that with proper exertions this Factory may be made a place of great Resort for the Indians, and I am determined to moat no exertions on my part to promote its Success.*

I will thank you to forward the enclosed dispatches by the very first mail, and if you have any Commands for me, please Send them by the bearer, who promises to call on you before he starts. Please tender my most Respectful Compliments to Mrs. C.[103] and believe me,

Sir to be very truly yours
G. C. Sibley

[96] Apparently Clark had the impression that Sibley was claiming ownership of the property itself which was inside the Osage lands as defined by the treaty, and thus unavailable for private ownership.

[97] The treaty with the Osage was signed by the United States, represented by Pierre Chouteau, and the Osage in November 1808, but not ratified by Congress until two years later.

[98] Both a blacksmith operation and a mill for processing grain were included in the original treaty with the Osages Clark negotiated in September, 1808; it remained in the one negotiated with Pierre Chouteau in November. At the time of this letter, Congress had only ratified the treaty recently—some two years after Chouteau and the Osage tribes agreed to it. The blacksmith shop and mill were supposed to help "civilize" the Native Americans there. Since one of the objectives of the factory system was to help the tribes settle into agriculture with private land ownership, services such as those to repair farm tools and process farm products were seen as facilitators in the process.

[99] Free-lance traders were particularly problematic for factors like Sibley, and the Office of Indian Trade implemented regulations to limit their impact. Since a key objective of the factory system was to use trade and goods to "civilize" the Indians, the factors had regulations regarding what they could and could not sell to anyone other than the Indians themselves. Small-time traders were also the ones most likely to provide alcohol to the tribes.

[100] This "collecting their friendship and good will" was particularly acute at this time. Tension between the United States and western tribes was rising in the west. The Shawnee brothers Tecumseh and Tenskwatawa were organizing a broad confederation of Indian tribes west of the Appalachians to oppose

further American encroachment on their territories, and were already talking to some of the tribes in this region. By early 1811, when Sibley wrote this letter, he no doubt understood that strengthening friendships between himself and the tribes under his domain would make it harder for either the British or the Shawnees to bring them into their fold. William Clark, who was Indian Agent in St. Louis and Sibley's boss, was in regular contact with territorial governors Ninian Edwards of Illinois and William Henry Harrison of Indiana, monitored the situation east of St. Louis, and continued to provide intelligence about such activity in Upper Louisiana. (*American State Papers, Indian Affairs*, 1, 797-801.)

[101] Clark was Indian Agent, so carried particular influence with these tribes.

[102] Flags were a typical gift to cement loyalty, much as were medals. It would not be unusual to swap an American flag for a foreign one to give tangible evidence that loyalty had changed to another government.

[103] Clark first met young Julia Hancock (1791-1820) in Fincastle, Virginia, before leaving on his expedition to the Pacific. When he returned, he began courtship in earnest, and married her in 1808. By this time, the Clarks' first child, Meriwether Lewis Clark (1809-1881) was a toddler; their second child, a son named William Preston Clark (1811-1840), was born in October. Julia was always close to her in-laws, and had an especially close relationship with Sarah Clark (d. 1819) and her husband Jonathan (1750-1816), the oldest of William's brothers. (Holmberg, *Dear Brother: Letters of William Clark to Jonathan Clark*, 6).

January 28th. 1811

> *Mr. Joseph Gales Jr.*[104]
> *Editor of the National Intelligencer*
> *Washington City*
> *Postage Paid*

> *Fort Osage 350 Miles up the MissouriSir,*

> *The difficulty of procuring Notes at this Remote Station has prevented my discharging my Subscription arrears for your paper before now. Herein you will find a Post note on the Kentucky Bank for Five Dollars,* [105] *which I know to be genuine and have no doubt will very Readily pass off to Some of the Kentucky Representatives in Congress. Please to address the Intelligencer to me at "St. Louis Territory of Louisiana" as usual.*
> *Will you do me the favor to tender my most Respectful Compliments to your Father's family, and believe me to be Sir*

Yours With esteem and Respect
G. C. Sibley

Post Note Bank of Kentucky, Sept. 10th.1810.
Payable 40 days after date to A. Whitlock or order (and endorsed by
Whitlock) for Five Dollars – <u>No. 1047</u> Will S. Waller Cashier Robert
Alexander President

[104] Joseph Gales (1786-1860) published the *National Intelligencer* in
Washington, D.C. The *National Intelligencer* started as a Jeffersonian paper
in 1800 (the same year the federal government moved to Washington) under
Samuel Harrison Smith. Gales, his assistant, took over the publication in
1810, and took on William Winston Seaton as his partner two years later. The
Intelligencer was the paper of record for Congress, publishing speeches and
proceedings (the *Congressional Record* started publication in 1873). Since
Gales and Seaton allowed senators and representatives to edit their remarks
before they were published, the two had privileges and access envied by
other editors and publishers; Gales, who covered the Senate, sat next to the
President of the Senate during its deliberations (Seaton had similar privileges
next to the Speaker of the House of Representatives). Sibley subscribed to
the *National Intelligencer* almost his entire adult life. ("Reporters of Debate
and the Congressional Record," United States Senate, http://www.senate.gov.)

[105] It was not unusual for a bank to issue its own currency which was,
presumably, backed by specie in the vault. People honored the notes so
long as they retained confidence in the bank's stability. Of course, not all
banks were stable, and not all banks had much to back their currencies. A
bank might print more paper currency than perhaps it should to respond to
a "capital shortage" in the area. In growing towns and regions where there
was a need for more money, banks issued notes to fund growth, construction,
transportation, infrastructure ("internal improvements" at the time), or
manufacturing. On one hand, these notes often weren't honored in distant
places; on the other, someone like Sibley or a businessman in St. Louis might
have acquired bank notes from a number of far-off banks, since they dealt
with merchants, shippers, and manufacturers in other places. Here, Sibley is
hoping that Gales accepts what might have been dubious money.

Fort Osage January 28th 1811

Mr. J. G. Comegys
St. Louis
My dear Sir,

Our friend Hunt will no doubt have handed you my letter of
the 8th Inst. Long ago.

I flatter myself that you are now Restored to the Blessing of Health again. I pray you let me hear from you Soon. Just as Mr. Hunt was Setting off, it occurred to me to Request of him to hire for me a Good Servant for the term of one year and bring him up with him in the Spring, which he was good enough to Say he would do if he could; but Suggested the idea of getting your assistance in the matter, as from his long absence from St. Louis he was fearful he was not well enough acquainted with the <u>Market</u> at present to enable him to find a proper person.

Now I am absolutely ashamed to be So often troubling you with Such unprofitable and out of the way commissions, but when I weigh all things maturely and justly, and consult my own wants without deciding on the willingness or unwillingness of my friends to relieve them, I then divest myself of a certain peculiar delicacy, which too frequently comes athwart the path of my interest; and fly off to the other extreme, when I find myself free from all embarrassments and can beg Request nay Sometimes even <u>demand</u> the good offices of others without any Squeamishness or hesitation at all.

Thus having Settled the premises (to my own Satisfaction) we will proceed to discuss the merits & demerits of the Said Servant in demand.

I want a Sober, industrious, good natured but where's the use of description, when everything is embraced in the words "Good Servant"? I want to hire a good Servant then, for a year and am willing to give Such wages as are customary or a <u>Little</u> more Rather than let an extraordinary good one Slip by me. If I could meet with a Negro lad Say from 16 to 20 years of age to my liking, I would purchase him if I could, in preference to hiring one; Perhaps it may come in the way to procure me Such a one or hire for a Short time by way of trial, and if I liked him and the price would buy him. At all events I must beg of you Send me a Servant of Some kind either Black or White;[106] provided it will not cost you too much trouble to find one. Please to get the best you can, and make the best <u>terms</u> you can.

Mr. Audrain, the bearer, promises to call on you just before he Sets out on his Return, by whom you will be good enough to Send all my Letters and Papers. There is a Letter enclosed for the Post Office which I will thank you to pay the postage of.

Yrs. Truly &c.
G. C. S.

Here, he suggests that either a slave or someone he might hire under a sort of indenture was acceptable.

Independent trappers were also part of the West, and sometimes went to work for a period of time for one of the larger fur companies. (Used by permission, State Historical Society of Missouri, Columbia)

Tuesday January 20th, 1811
Day cloudy and cold. 1/4 Inch of <u>Snow</u> fell an hour after dark. Swettled in full with Mr. Rawlings up to 31st Dec.

Wednesday 30th
Cloudy till 11 O'Clock, and then cleared off and turned pleasant.

Thursday 31st
Morning cloudy and cool. Mr. Isaac Cottle Started this morning for the Settlements on the Quiver in company with three other Men.

Sent my public dispatches by Mr. Cottle under cover to General Clark, Securely wrapped in Buckskin; also a Small Packet to Mr. Comegys enclosing a Letter to him and one for J. Gales Jr., Washington City for him to forward by Mail. Mr. Cottle Says he will deliver these packets as Soon as possible and take Special care of them while in his hands.

Friday 1st February, 1811
Pleasant day

Saturday 2nd
Pleasant day

Sunday February 3rd, 1811
Day warm and pleasant though Somewhat cloudy. Rode out to the Osage Town after Dinner.

Monday 4th
Morning fair and very pleasant.

This day I hired a young Man named <u>Augustus Legare</u> (a Relation of Lorr's) for the term of Three Months commencing this day at $13 1/3 per month and find him provisions. William Wells will be hereafter employed entirely about Mr. Price's affairs. Heavy Rain at Night.

Pleasant day

Tuesday 5th
Day warm and pleasant. Missouri clear of Ice except a little drifted ashore.

Wednesday 6th
Morning fair and pleasant. 2 young Men of the Missouri Tribe arrived here to day from their hunting camp a few miles above the Kansas River. They Say they were Sent by their Chiefs to know if they could be permitted to Reside near this place. I Referred them to the Little Osages at the Same time hinting the advantages of their Removing if no objections are made by the proper authority which I did not believe would be the case. There

are about _20_ lodges of them near the Kansas and _8_ or _10_ more are up the Platt[e] with Mr. Airde a Trader.[107] They Say that Mr. A. will not take anything but _Furs_ for his Goods, at the Rate of 8 Beaver Skins for a 3 Pt. Blanket, which at the rate Beaver is taken at the Factory would buy 3 Blankets.[108] They Say also, that the whole of their tribe will certainly be here in the Spring and probably the Ottos too.

[107] James Aird (see above).

[108] A "3 point blanket" meant something very specific in the Native American trade, which was valuable information for a factor since blankets were always highly coveted; the most desirable ones were modeled after the Northwest blankets, sold by the Northwest Company. A 3 point blanket was 6' X 5' 2", weighing 4 pounds (by contrast, a 2 1/2 point blanket was about a foot smaller on both dimensions) and, according to Indian Trade specifications, was to "be woven twilled all white except two cross stripes of very dark blue placed two inches distant from each end of the Blanket, and each stripe should not be less than three nor more than four inches wide; near one of the stripes should be placed the points also of dark blue, extending inwardly from the selvage to shew [sic] on the right side of the Blanket . . . . The Blanket after milling should be dressed so as to raise a long shag as per samples." The specifications became important because the Native Americans were especially fussy consumers when it came to blankets—they only purchased twill so it would shed rain better; if it was twilled on both sides they figured it was a cheap one. They refused any with red or black stripes. Factors sold some 20,000 blankets annually, all of which were manufactured in England. (Peake, *A History of the United States Indian Factory System*, 53-54.)

Thursday 7th

Pleasant day. To day the 2 young Missouris came to me and expressed a desire to See the Store, Goods, &c., which I very willingly Showed them, and took a good deal of pains to explain to them the Regular and fixed mode of trading at the Factory. They were a good deal Surprised at the cheapness of the Goods and appeared Rather to Suspect that I was joking with them.[109] I Referred them to the Osages however who confirmed what I had told them, and advised them to prove the thing and Satisfy themselves by bringing their Furs.

[109] If the Missouri had only dealt with independent traders, the Factory's prices would have seemed incredibly reasonable. However, this changed by the end of the decade. As the Senate considered disbanding the factory system in 1822, it solicited testimony from a number of experts, including William Clark, who commented on the higher prices, inconvenient locations and loss of business at the trade factories. Clark, among others, testified that private trading companies could perform this function better and provide

better products at lower prices than the federal government. (William Clark to Thomas Hart Benton, January 23, 1822, *American State Papers, Indian Affairs*, 2, 329-331.)

Friday February 8th, 1811

Snow. 3 Men of the Ottos [Otoes] came here this morning, they were discovered by the Osages just before they got here, and a number of the foolish young Men went out armed to kill them, but were prevented with much ado by a few old Men, who extended to them the Rights of hospitality by instantly Smoking and eating with them with the usual ceremony on Such occasions, and thus put a Stop to all hostilities on the part of the Osages. These 3 Ottos came here they Say to Reclaim 5 Horses lately Stolen from them by the Osages, which Horses are now here. I Sent for them to my House and they came with Several of the Osages, when I apologized in behalf of the Osages for the treatment they Received on their first arrival, and told them it would not have happened if any of the Chiefs or principal warriors were here. I desired the Osages to feed them and treat them well at all events, let their business be what it may, and they all went off together apparently Satisfied.

Snow about an Inch deep at Tattoo. I discharged William Wells from my Service to day, for irregularity and drunkenness.

Saturday February 9th, 1811

Morning cloudy and cold likely for Snow.

Sunday 10th

Day tolerably pleasant. Ice Running pretty thick in the Missouri. Settled accounts in full to day with William Wells and paid him $44.80 in Cash being in full. Note—Wells has been in my employ Since the 21st of September last and has Received from me $78.00 in full compensation for his Services. $27 of this I charge to Mr. R. H. Price for the time Wells has been engaged about his Crops Hogs &c. and $15 I Shall charge to the Factory for time taken by Wells to get Fire Wood &c. leaving $36 for my private expence of which, I paid $24 in Corn at $1 per bushel. It has cost me about 15 to 20 Dollars to Subsist Wells the whole time he has been with me, Say 20 dollars. Went to an Indian dance at night but was not much amused.

Monday February 11th, 1811

The day cold and Snowy.

Tuesday 12th

Snow about an Inch deep this morning, very cold day.

Wednesday 13th
Day cold and fair.

Thursday 14th
Day exceeding cold. Arrived Mr. Peter Pepenoe, and 2 Frenchmen from the Contractor's Boat. Popenoe delivered me 2 Packages containing Letters & Papers and Some Silver ware, which were forwarded from St. Louis by General Clark by the hands of Mr. Morin and by him to this place from the boat by Popenoe. Letters Received Vizt.
1 from Supt. of Indian Trade 28th Nov. 1810
1 from General Clark 23rd Jan. 1811
John C. Comegys 23 Jan. 1811
R. H. Price 24 Jan. 1811
Washington Papers up to 18th Dec. 1810.
General Clark Sends me 600 pr. Silver Ear bobs and 20 Silver Hair Plates, but no Invoice of them. John G. Comegys Sends me a pair of Gold Ear Rings Price 3 Dollars.

Friday 15th
Day Snowy and most bitter Cold.

Saturday 16th
Day excessively cold. A large Party of the Little Osages came in to day from the Swan Pond with their Families.

Sunday 17th
Last night was most insupportably cold the day exceedingly cold.

Monday 18th
Morning very cold. The Missouri completely closed and block up with Ice as far as we can See up and down from the Factory Piazza. The Chief and a number of the Warriors of the Little Osages arrived this evening almost froze. Their families and the whole Nation will be here in a few days.

Tuesday 19th February, 1811
The weather a good deal moderated. Pleasant day.

Wednesday 20th
Pleasant day.

Thursday 21st
Day fair and pleasant. Ice in the River Separated about 2 O'Clock, but

Stopped again, leaving many vacancies between the large Cakes. Several Soldiers happened to be crossing just as the Ice gave way, but were fortunate enough to get off without injury. Sold a Stock of Hogs belonging to Mr. R. H. Price, to Mr. Ira Cottle for $550.

Fort Osage Feb. 21 1811

> *General Wm. Clark*
> *St. Louis, p. Mr. F. Audrain*

> *Dr. Sir,*
> *I have been importuned not a little of late, by the Osages on the Subject of their treatment for the last two or three years from the other tribes, particularly the Ioways, Potowatomies & Ottos and although I have repeatedly Referred them to the Agent Mr. Chouteau,[110] and told them (till I am tired that I have no official Right of interference in Such matters), yet they will continue to burden me with their complaints and Representations and I am absolutely obliged either to listen or by Refusing, give them great offence. They address themselves to me as an agent of the U. S. there being no one else here [who] will take any part in Indian Affairs of any kind; and no one appointed to attend to them here, and it being very inconvenient they Say to wait upon their Agent in St. Louis and in a very Serious and impressive manner have Related their grievances and desired me to Represent them to the Authority most likely to afford Redress; at the Same time expressing their wish that I Should make them known to you, in the hope that although your agency does not extend over them, yet it may not be looked upon as improper to expect your interferences in their behalf with those Tribes which the President has placed under your control. They complain (and I believe justly) that while they have for the last two or three years faithfully observed the counsel they have Received from the U.S. and Strictly Refrained from making war on the neighboring Tribes; that while they have considered themselves under the Care and Protection of the U.S. and treated our Citizens as brothers;[111] they have Successively and heretofore without Redress been Subjected to the unprovoked attacks of the Ioways, Ottos, Sioux, and Potowatomies, who have Robbed them of their Horses, and murdered their people insulted the benevolent and just policy of the U.S. and have nearly, if not quite compelled them (the Osages) to the last Resort, the Tomahawk and Scalping Knife. In the month of November 1809 four of their people were murdered almost within Sight of the Garrison by a party of Sioux and Ioways (as they are well*

informed) who Surprised them in their hunting Camp in the following Spring, a number of Horses were Stolen from them, within a few Miles of the Garrison by the Ottos, as they have Reasons to believe.

In July following, two of their Men were wantonly killed as they were peaceably traveling to their village in this vicinity, as they very much Suspect by the Ottos. And in December last, five of their People were killed and made prisoners by a war party of the Potowatomies. Several other affairs of less consequences have taken place, which though too trivial to need a particular detail after the above, are nevertheless Sufficient to alarm their fears. These unprovoked attacks have very much alarmed this Tribe of Osages, and have tended very much to lessen their confidence in the protection that has been promised them by the U.S. and if not Redressed and prevented from Reoccurring in future, will compel them to Seek Revenge themselves contrary to the advise and disinterested counsels of the President. "If", Say They, "the U.S. will not Redress our Wrongs, which are So manifest and great, Suffer us at least to Redress them ourselves, and not keep our hands tied (while those our enemies are left untied) till we are all cut off by piece meal."

Thus much I have been induced to Say on the Subject, by the earnest desire of the Chief[12] and leading warriors of this people; and let me add, partly from a conviction on my mind of the propriety and justice of the appeal. I have neither time nor inclination to enter more minutely into the subject, or to make any comments on the matters complained of nor do I Suppose it at all necessary.

The Chief and leading Men of the Little Osages are very much inclined to encourage the Kansas and Missouris to join them in their Settlement nears this place, and I Suspect Some negotiations are going on among them to that effect. The Missouris have Sent two Men here to Sound the Osages on the Subject, one of whom has Returned to bring the whole Tribe here (as I am informed) who are daily expected. There are also Three of the Ottos here on business with the Osages. It is Rumored that the Ottos will also Remove to this neighborhood, if the Missouris leave them. (You know the Missouris and Ottos live within Sight of Each Other and are as one Nation in case of War)

That Osages have an influential Man at this time among the Kansas, probably his business may be to effect an alliance between the two Tribes. It is well understood that about half of the Kansas are Ready now to Remove here. Although I do not *by any means calculate on all their movements taking place (for I know well enough how little Reliance is to be put in Indian projects which a Storm of Snow may defeat or postpone, and a thousand trivial accidents may overturn) yet I could wish to encourage them if it can be done with effect and propriety. If it were a thing to be desired, I have no doubt but the Big Osages would be glad to Return here, at least Report Seems to justify the belief, But I am by no means Solicitous for them to Return, unless indeed they will Reform a little.*

March 5th. I expected to have Sent this off long ago, but Mr. Audrain waited for the Contractor's Boat, which is expected to day.

Agreeably to your request I have presented the Note you sent me to Mr. Audrain for payment, and have Received $37 on it which I enclose you herein together with the Note, and Refer your for further information Respecting it to young Mr. Audrain who will hand you this, and will call on you when he is Ready to Set out on his Return for Ft. Osage, for any commands you may have for me, which please to put in his care.

Some of the Ottos have been here lately on business with Osages, they have partially Settled the disputes between the 2 Tribes but have not been able to Remove entirely the Suspicions of the Osages Relative to the Murders committed in July last. They promise to Satisfy you on this Subject through the medium of Mr. Airde their Trader[113] when he Returns to St. Louis. I have Reasons to believe that the Osages are preparing to set off in a few days to war against the Ioways.

They consulted me (as usual) on this matter but I could only Say to them, that if they went to war, I did not believe you would interfere with the Ioways to obtain Redress for the injuries they have done to them (the Osages). Sans Oreille and the Big Soldier[114] appear to be inclined to Stop the war, but Say it will be very difficult to appease those whose Relatives have been killed and who are numerous and influential.

I am Sir very Respectfully
Your Most Obedient Servant
G. C. Sibley

---

[110] Pierre Chouteau was the Indian Agent for the Osage, someone Sibley was not particularly fond of. The relationships within the factory system were complicated as they involved the military, civilian factors who were full-time government employees, and civilian appointees. An Indian Agent was appointed to be the primary contact between the government and the tribe, whereas the factor oversaw trade between the government trading operation and the Native Americans. This was all complicated when tense working

relationships existed, as was the case between Sibley and both Chouteau and garrison commander Eli Clemson.

[111] By the time the Osage signed their first treaty with the United States in 1808, the tribe had already been sufficiently expansionist to have tense relations with several of its neighbors. The government offered security and protection, but the quid pro quo was that the Osage weren't to attack another tribe without government approval. The incident Sibley refers to here appears in his journal entry for December 5. The Osage returned from a hunting trip, and reported that a war party of Ioway and Sacs (who often hunted and raided on Osage territory) attacked them, killed some of the party and took others prisoner, and stole their provisions and furs. (Rollings, *The Osage*, 181.)

[112] Most likely Neezamone, or Walking Rain, who was a Little Osage leader. Both he and Clark knew Neezamone, since he was part of the treaty council in 1808 that Clark conducted.

[113] James Aird (see above).

[114] Both Sans Oreille and Big Soldier were generally favorable to open and friendly relations with the United States.

Friday 22nd
A fine day.

Saturday 23rd
A fine day. Fire quite unnecessary.

Sunday 24th
Sold all my Stock of Hogs and 20 Bushels of Corn to Mr. Audrain (Say about 30 Hogs) for one Bay Horse and one Gray Mare worth about 120 Dollars. Say the Horse $70, the Mare $50. Rain in the Morning.

Hog Account

Dr.		Cr.	
February 21st, 1810 Cash paid Mr. Zadock Woods for 15 Breeding Sows	$120	May 1st, 1810 Sold 411 lbs Pork Say 3 wild Sows, for	$30.82 1/2
February 24th, 1811 Expence of feeding and attending to Hogs one year, Say at most	45	May 19th '10 Sold 2 Sows for	25.00
	$165		

Interest on $165 for one Year at 6 pct.	9.90	December 22nd, 1810 Killed 4 Sows for my own use weighed 352 lbs. Net worth at least 6 cts. per pound	33.12
20 Bushels Corn given as food for Horses p. Contract at 75 Cts.	15.00	February 24th, 1811 Sold the whole Stock to J. H. Audrain for a Bay Horse and Gray Mare giving also 20 Bushels of Corn. The Horses Stand me in	100.95 1/2
	$189.90		189.00

Monday 25th
Morning warm and fair. Fine day.

Tuesday 26th
Fine day. All the Little Osages have now assembled at this place from their winter hunt.

February Wednesday 27th, 1811
Pleasant day. Rather warm. About 12 O'Clock a Trading Boat arrived here from the Kansas on its way to St. Louis. Five Men from Mr. Hunt's Camp are with this Boat on their way down, having declined going any farther with the party.[115] They Represent that the Sioux are assembled in great numbers on the Missouri Banks not far above the Mahas, and that they are hostile to the Whites.

[115]The party commanded by Wilson Price Hunt (see above). Crew members in this trade were more willing to take their pay to date and leave the group if a better offer came along or the going got too rough as civilians. Since this was a commercial venture, Hunt had little recourse but to leave them behind. One of the striking features of river commerce was the frequency with which people got a ride with a boat or group, so this would not have been atypical. This is why Sibley comments on it in such a matter-of-fact fashion. The fact of their having been through the Fort recently with Hunt's expedition is noteworthy to him, not their mode of transportation.

Thursday 28th
Day fair but Rather cooler than Yesterday.

Friday March 1st 1811
Morning fair and cool. Pleasant day.

Saturday 2nd
Fair and windy.

Sunday 3rd
Pleasant day.

Monday 4th
Fair and cool.

Tuesday 5th
Cloudy morning. Contractor's Boat arrived in the evening. A Number of the Big Osages arrived with <u>Sans Nerf</u>.[116]

> [116] Sans Nerf was a chief of the Great Osage. When Sibley was trying to determine a location for a temporary trade factory after Governor Benjamin Howard closed Fort Osage in 1813, Sans Nerf told Sibley that he didn't like the old location because it was too far from their village, and Native American highwaymen robbed and killed his people. (Rollings, *The Osage*, 231.)

Wednesday March 6th, 1811
Day warm. Ice running in the River very thick, occasioned by the Rising of the River over large Drifts of Ice.

Thursday 7th
Contractor's Boat Started (the Ice having ceased Running) about 3 O'Clock. Young Mr. Audrain went to St. Louis in her. Sent the following Letters by Mr. Audrain. See Letter Books.
1 S. H. Sibley dated Feb. 12th, 14th, 15th
4 General Clark dated Feb. 21st, March 5th & 7th
1 J. G. Comegys dated March 1st & 5th
1 James Callaway dated March 1st
1 R. H. Price dated March 6th
1 Supt. of Indian Trade (duplicates) Feb.
1 Same, Mar. 7th
Mr. James Callaway
Care of M. Wherry Esq.[117]
St. Charles

> [117] Sibley had known Capt. Mackay Wherry (1766-1828) for at least three years at this point. Sibley accompanied the merchandise for the factory and the army regulars under Eli Clemson to the fort site by river in 1808, while William Clark traveled overland with a contingent of St. Charles Dragoons. This group included Nathan Boone, who was a scout for the expedition. The Dragoons were originally organized, trained, and now commanded by

Capt. Mackay Wherry. He had arrived in St. Charles from his home state of Pennsylvania by way of New Orleans, where he met and befriended fur trader Manuel Lisa. Wherry moved to St. Louis in 1798, married two years later, then moved to St. Charles by 1804 where he became a tanner. Wherry was also the first sheriff for the St. Charles district, which originally included all of upper Louisiana west of the Missouri River. (Clark, *Westward with Dragoons*, 61-62; "Mackey Wherry by his Grandchildren," *Bulletin of the Missouri Historical Society*, 264-266; Billon, *Annals of St. Louis in its Territorial Days*, 223.)

Fort Osage March 4th 1811

Mr. James Callaway Jr.
Care of Mr. Wherry Esq.
St. Charles

     Sir,

     I wrote you on the 1st of March last advising you of my having directed J. G. Comegys & Co. to pay you Seventy five dollars for me on account of the hire of your Negro Boy Book, which you have no doubt Received ere this. I now enclose you my Draft on General Clark for Thirty Seven Dollars, which is in full for the hire of your Boy up to and including the 15th of this month, about which time you will probably Receive the Boy. I Shall leave here in a few days to be absent 2 months if the Contractor's Boat Should not arrive before I Start (by which I Shall Send your Boy Down) I Shall leave directions for him to be Sent down in her and left at Capt. Wherry's at St. Charles. Any errors in the amount between us can be adjusted when I See you again.
     Please to tender my Compliments. To Mrs. C. and believe me to be Sir

     Your very obedient Servant
     G.C. Sibley

Fort Osage March 1st 1811

     Mr. R. H. Price [Risdon H. Price]
     St. Louis

     Sir,

     I have this day Requested Mr. John G. Comegys of St. Louis to pay you on demand the Sum of _Seventy-five Dollars_ Cash

on account of the hire of your Negro boy Boch, which Sum
you will call for when you think proper, & Receipt to him for
it. I Should have Sent you this money Sooner, but could find
no conveyance to you direct that I approved of. Your boy is in
good health, conducts himself pretty well, and you will think
him much improved when you See him.

Having been disappointed in getting another Servant from
St. Louis, I am induced to keep Boch a few months longer;
probably I Shall Send him home in May or perhaps Sooner.
Whenever I Send him you will at the Same time Receive
payment in full for his hire. Please to make my Compliments
acceptable to Mrs. C. & believe me to be Sir.

Your very obedient Servant
G. C. Sibley

Fort Osage March 6th 1811

Dear Sir,

I have Received your Letter of the 24th January and
agreeably to your desire (and as I conceive your interest) I have
conditionally Sold all your Hogs and one Hundred Bushels
of Corn to Mr. Cottle. Wells is now collecting the Hogs as fast
as possible (which are very much Scattered Since the Indians
arrived from their hunt) and as Soon as he has got them together
I Shall conclude with Cottle, and inform you fully on the
Subject. There will Remain about 200 bushels of Corn (more or
less) which I fear cannot be Sold to advantage, as Lt. Brownson
is to Send a Boat down for what Corn he wants, and at the
Same time I expect to be able to Send you a full account of all
your affairs here closed except as to the Corn.

At present in haste,
Yours truly
G. C. Sibley

Friday 8th

Head ache all day.

Saturday 9th

Unwell to day. By my Request, the Chief of the Little Osages, Neezamone,
brought me the copy of the Treaty entered into between the U. S. and
the Osages, at this place in November 1808; furnished him by Governor
Lewis, which I have hastily Copied in the following pages. It has been
Said on good authority that this Treaty has been duly confirmed by our

government[118] *(though it has never yet been officially communicated to the Osages) which made me desirous of having a copy of it. It is certainly a very imperfect and irregular Instrument, and withal very unfair (in my opinion) in its present State, and I cannot yet believe that the Government of the U. S. can have Sanctioned it without many exceptions and alterations in favor of the Osages, particularly when it is understood the manner in which it was executed. See a note of mine on this Subject on page 44.*[119]

[118] The Senate confirmed the treaty in 1810.

[119] He means on page 44 of his hand-written journal.

Articles of a Treaty made and concluded at Fort Clark on the Right bank of the Missouri about five miles above the Fire Prairie, in the Territory of Louisiana, the Tenth day of November in the year of our Lord one thousand eight hundred and eight, between Peter Chouteau esquire Agent for the Osages and Specially commissioned and Instructed to enter into the Same by His Excellency Meriwether Lewis Governor and Superintendent of Indian Affairs for the Territory aforesaid, in behalf of The United States of America of the one part, and the Chiefs and Warriors of the Great and Little Osage for themselves and their Nations Respectively on the other part.

ART. 1.
The United States being anxious to promote peace, friendship and intercourse with the Osage tribes, to afford them every assistance in their power, and to protect them from the insults and injuries of other tribes of Indians, situated near the settlements of the white people, have thought proper to build a fort on the right bank of the Missouri, a few miles above the Fire Prairie, and do agree to garrison the same with as many regular troops as the President of the United States may, from time to time, deem necessary for the protection of all orderly, friendly and well disposed Indians of the Great and Little Osage nations, who reside at this place, and who do strictly conform to, and pursue the counsels or admonitions of the President of the United States through his subordinate officers.

ART. 2.
The United States being also anxious that the Great and Little Osage, resident as aforesaid, should be regularly supplied with every species of merchandise, which their comfort may hereafter require, do engage to establish at this place, and permanently to continue at all seasons of the year, a well assorted store of goods, for the purpose of bartering with them on moderate terms for their peltries and furs.

ART. 3.

The United States agree to furnish at this place, for the use of the Osage nations, a black-smith, and tools to mend their arms and utensils of husbandry, and engage to build them a horse mill, or water mill; also to furnish them with ploughs, and to build for the great chief of the Great Osage, and for the great chief of the Little Osage, a strong block house in each of their towns, which are to be established near this fort.

ART. 4.
With a view to quiet the animosities which at present exist between the inhabitants of the territory of Louisiana, and the Osage nations, in consequence of the lawless depredations of the latter, the United States do further agree to pay to their own citizens, the full value of such property as they can legally prove to have been stolen or destroyed by the said Osage, since the acquisition of Louisiana by the United States, provided the same does not exceed the sum of five thousand dollars.

ART. 5.
In consideration of the lands relinquished by the Great and Little Osage to the United States as stipulated in the sixth article of this treaty, the United States promise to deliver at Fire Prairie, or at St. Louis, yearly, to the Great Osage nation, merchandise to the amount or value of one thousand dollars, and to the Little Osage nation, merchandise to the amount or value of five hundred dollars, reckoning the value of said merchandise at the first cost thereof, in the city or place in the United States, where the same shall have been procured.
And in addition to the merchandise aforesaid, the United States have, at the date before the signature of these articles, paid to the Great Osage nation, the sum of one thousand dollars, and to the Little Osage nation, the sum of five hundred dollars.

ART. 6.
And in consideration of the advantages which we derive from the stipulations contained in the foregoing articles, we, the chiefs and warriors of the Great and Little Osage, for ourselves and our nations respectively, covenant and agree with the United States, that the boundary line between our nations and the United States shall be as follows, to wit: beginning at fort Clark, on the Missouri, five miles above Fire Prairie, and running thence a due south course to the river Arkansas, and down the same to the Mississippi; hereby ceding and relinquishing forever to the United States, all the lands which lie east of the said line, and north of the southwardly bank of the said river Arkansas, and all lands situated northwardly of the river Missouri. And we do further cede and relinquish to the United States forever, a tract of two leagues square, to embrace fort Clark, and to be laid off in such manner as the President of the United States shall think proper.

ART. 7.

And it is mutually agreed by the contracting parties, that the boundary lines hereby established, shall be run and marked at the expense of the United States, as soon as circumstances or their convenience will permit; and the Great and Little Osage promise to depute two chiefs from each of their respective nations, to accompany the commissioner, or commissioners who may be appointed on the part of the United States, to settle and adjust the said boundary line.

ART. 8.

And the United States agree that such of the Great and Little Osage Indians, as may think proper to put themselves under the protection of fort Clark, and who observe the stipulations of this treaty with good faith, shall be permitted to live and to hunt, without molestation, on all that tract of country, west of the north and south boundary line, on which they, the said Great and Little Osage, have usually hunted or resided: Provided, The same be not the hunting grounds of any nation or tribe of Indians in amity with the United States; and on any other lands within the territory of Louisiana, without the limits of the white settlements, until the United States may think proper to assign the same as hunting grounds to other friendly Indians.

ART. 9.

Lest the friendship which is now established between the United States and the said Indian nations should be interrupted by the misconduct of individuals, it is hereby agreed that for injuries done by individuals, no private revenge or retaliation shall take place, but instead thereof complaints shall be made by the party injured to the other, by the said nations or either of them, to the superintendent or other person appointed by the President to the chiefs of the said nation; and it shall be the duty of the said chiefs, upon complaints being made as aforesaid, to deliver up the person or persons against whom the complaint is made, to the end that he or they may be punished agreeably to the laws of the state or territory, where the offence may have been committed; and in like manner, if any robbery, violence or murder shall be committed on any Indian or Indians belonging to either of said nations, the person or persons so offending shall be tried, and if found guilty, shall be punished in like manner as if the injury had been done to a white man. And it is agreed that the chiefs of the Great and Little Osage, shall to the utmost of their power exert themselves to recover horses or other property which may be stolen from any citizen or citizens of the United States, by any individual or individuals of either of their nations; and the property so recovered shall be forthwith delivered to the superintendent or other person authorized to receive it, that it may be restored to the proper owner; and in cases where the exertions of the chiefs shall be ineffectual in recovering the property stolen as aforesaid, *if sufficient proof can be adduced that such property was actually stolen by any Indian or Indians belonging to the said nations, or either of them, the superintendent, or other proper officer, may deduct from the annuity of the said nations respectively a sum equal to the value of the property which has been stolen. And the United States hereby guarantee to any Indian or Indians of the said nations respectively, a full indemnification for any horses or other property which may be stolen from them by any of their citizens: Provided, That the property so stolen cannot be recovered, and that sufficient proof is produced that it was actually stolen by a citizen of the United States. And the said nations of the Great and Little Osage engage, on the requisition or demand of the President of the United States, or of the superintendent, to deliver up any white man resident among them.*

ART. 10.
The United States receive the Great and Little Osage nations into their friendship and under their protection; and the said nations, on their part, declare that they will consider themselves under the protection of no other power whatsoever; disclaiming all right to cede, sell or in any manner transfer their lands to any foreign power, or to citizens of the United States or inhabitants of Louisiana, unless duly authorized by the President of the United States to make the said purchase or accept the said cession on behalf of the government.

ART. 11.
And if any person or persons, for hunting or other purpose, shall pass over the boundary lines, as established by this treaty, into the country reserved for the Great and Little Osage nations, without the license of the superintendent or other proper officer, they, the said Great and Little Osage, or either of them, shall be at liberty to apprehend such unlicensed hunters or other persons, and surrender them together with their property, but without other injury, insult or molestation, to the superintendent of Indian affairs, or to the agent nearest the place of arrest, to be dealt with according to law.

ART. 12.
And the chiefs and warriors as aforesaid, promise and engage that neither the Great nor Little Osage nation will ever, by sale, exchange or as presents, supply any nation or tribe of Indians, not in amity with the United States, with guns, ammunitions or other implements of war.

ART. 13.
This treaty shall take effect and be obligatory on the contracting parties, as soon as the same shall have been ratified by the President, by and with the advice and consent of the Senate of the United States.

In testimony whereof, the said Peter Chouteau, commissioned and instructed as aforesaid, and the chiefs and warriors of the Great and Little Osage nation of Indians, have hereunto set their hands and affixed their seals.

Done at fort Clark, the day above mentioned.

We, the undersigned chiefs and warriors of the band of Osages, residing on the river Arkansas, being a part of the Great Osage nation, having this day had the foregoing treaty read and explained to us, by his Excellency Meriwether Lewis, esquire, do hereby acknowledge, consent to, and confirm all the stipulations therein contained, as fully and as completely as though we had been personally present at the signing, sealing, and delivering the same on the 10th day of November, 1808, the same being the day on which the said treaty was signed, sealed, and delivered, as will appear by a reference thereto.

In witness whereof, we have, for ourselves and our band of the Great Osage nation residing on the river Arkansas, hereunto set our hands and affixed our seals.

Done at St. Louis, in the territory of Louisiana, this thirty-first day of August, in the year of our Lord one thousand eight hundred and nine, and of the independence of the United States the thirty-fourth.

Sunday March 10, 1811

Morning Rainy. Missouri Rising very fast. Mr. Auguste Chouteau, Jr.,[120] arrived this Morning from the Osage River; his business as appeared before Night is to persuade the Little Osages to accompany him to the Osage River and carry with them their Peltries to trade with him. The Chief of the Little Osages,[121] and the Tattoo Back informed me that they were Solicited by him to that effect, but they will pay no attention to him.

After dinner I rode out about 8 miles into the Prairie and Returned at Sun down.

[120] Pierre Chouteau (1786-1838); see the longer biography of the Chouteaus in the "Biographies" chapter of this volume.

[121] Probably Nee-zu-mo-nee (see above).

Monday 11th

Foggy Morning. A little after Sunrise a Party of Osages to the number of _100_ Men Set off in a body to War against the Ioways, they have _3_ Leaders neither of whom are distinguished Warriors and the party altogether consists of Young Men with Some few exceptions. Lieut. Brownson[122] Sent a party of Soldiers to Set them across the River in the Public Boat.[123] They appeared to be pretty well armed and equipped, and may probably Strike a Sore blow on their enemies <u>Should they find them unapprised of their approach.</u>

After Breakfast I Rode out about 10 or 12 Miles with 2 Men and Some Indian Boys in pursuit of Mr. Price's Hogs, but found none. Returned about 3 O'Clock in the afternoon.

[122] Lt. John Brownson was stationed at Fort Osage from 1810 to 1812. After the War of 1812, he apparently started distilling whiskey and selling liquor. (Hempstead, "I at Home: Part VII," *Bulletin of the Missouri Historical Society*, 70.)

[123] Meaning government-owned.

Tuesday 12th

Morning fair and pleasant. Abut Sunrise another War Party set off from the Osage Village against the Ioways of about <u>45</u> Men consisting of about an equal number of Osages & Missouri, led by a distinguished Warrior of the Missouris named <u>Che-o-ho-ge</u> or Hole in my House. Their plan is to attack the enemy by Surprise after the party which Went yesterday have Struck a blow. Lieut. Brownson Set them across the River, and they immediately Set out on their March. We Shall probably hear how these War Parties <u>Succeed</u> in less than Ten days from now, it being understood that the Ioways are at no great distance from the Missouri.

Mr. Chouteau handed me 3 Letters this evening, which he Received in St. Louis last fall and has had ever Since in his hands, one of them is from Mrs. Mary Sibley, another from Robert H. Sibley, both under one cover and dated F. Ville 19th September '10. Postage 50c. The other is from Samuel H. Sibley, dated Wilmington 11th October '10 Postage 25c.

Wednesday 13th, & Thursday 14th

Two Rainy days.

Friday 15th

Cloudy and Some Rain.

Saturday 16th

A fair and pleasant day.

Sunday 17th

Fair and pleasant. Mr. Thomas Hemstead[124] arrived this evening in 12 days from St. Louis brought me the following Letters Vizt.

1 from General Clark dated 5th March
1 from R. H. Price dated 5th March
1 from J. G. Comegys dated 4th March
and Washington Papers up to 12th January.

[124] Thomas Hempstead was a merchant and store operator in St. Louis; he operated a store at Fort Belle Fontaine after the factory closed and sold merchandise to Sibley and the garrison periodically. (Hempstead, "I at Home," *Bulletin of the Missouri Historical Society*, 36, 46.)

Monday 18th

Sold off all Mr. Price's Hogs, Corn &c. &c. to Mr. Cottle and Mr. Audrain and Settled his business finally which I have informed him fully of by Letter of this date. See Letter Book.

Fort Osage March 18th.1811.

Mr. R. H. Price

St. Louis

> *My dear Sir,*
> *Your letter of the 5th. Inst. by the hand of Mr. Hempstead found me yesterday in the very act of complying with its contents by anticipation, that is, I was just concluding the Sale and delivery of all your Hogs, Corn, Potatoes &c. to Mr. Cottle and Mr. Audrain. I was Strongly inclined to hasten the disposal of these things by the variety of causes. The Indians were assembled here in considerable numbers and Seemed more than usually inclined to be mischievous. In Spite of my Repeated efforts to prevent it, I Saw with Regret and Mortification, that your property was daily destroyed in the most Shameful manner. Indeed there has been a most dreadful and affirming destruction of Individual property here, and yours has Sustained its full Share, as you will find from the enclosed papers which contain a full Statement and Settlement of your business here as far as I have any knowledge of it,[125] and is the Result of my Very best endeavors to turn your property here to the best account for you.[126]*
> *About a month ago, I bargained with Mr. Cottle to deliver him your whole Stock of Hogs and 100 Bushels of Corn for*

$550 payable in 12 months, and engaged that the manner
Should be at least 180. all over that number were to be paid for
in addition, at the rate of *180* for *$550* and all under were to be
deducted at the Same Rate. Not long before this arrangement
was made, I had myself Seen and counted upwards of *150* and
Wells assured me that there could be no doubt that there would
be more than *180* when all were collected. Cottle was So
Remarkably prudent that he would not agree to take the Hogs
as they Run for *$180* which I pressed him to do, and he was
advised by others to do it. He would have them delivered and
exactly counted for my own part, I had the Smallest doubt but
there were at least *200* of them. I immediately employed Wells
for a Month (I discharged him from my Service early in February
having nothing for him to do) and Set him to collecting the
Hogs. In the meantime the Indians arrived, and necessary
Required all my time and attention, and of course proved a
Serious detriment to Wells in his pursuit of the Hogs. I Several
times Sent out parties of young Indians to assist Wells, and out
with them once or twice myself. After a constant and I believe
a faithful Search for near a month; will you believe will(?) only
96 Hogs can be got up, and no more are to be found (Save
the Skeletons and bones) except a Small gang of very wild
ones that cannot be caught, and which no one here will offer
even one Dollar for. If I had not myself Rode all through the
country about here I could possibly believe that in So Short a
time, So many Hogs could have been destroyed, but I really
am compelled to Submit to the truth however unpleasant. I will
not attempt to investigate the causes of this destruction, it lays
at the doors of the wolves, the Indian Dogs, the Indian and the
Soldiers, but they Shift it from one to the other, and all deny it
except the Wolves and Dogs, who are the most honorable of
them all in this matter, and I Suspect the least culpable.[127] As to
the Corn, it has fallen Short of my estimate a great deal of it was
fed away to your Hogs and a great deal of it was latterly Stolen
by Osages, who broke the Houses Repeatedly at Night, Spoiled
the Locks &c. and induced me to offer it all to Mr. Audrain at
75 cents per Bushel Rather than keep it a trouble on my hands
for the Indians to prey on. The Potatoes had not escaped the
Indians either, and many of them were Rotten. The Bulls, the
plow and old Oxcart have sold for their full value.

I had borrowed *10* Bushels of your Corn (the Indians having
Spoiled the Lock of my Corn House So that I Could not use it)
which I have given you Credit for at 75 Cents. I cannot express
to you how much I am chagrined and disappointed at the Result
of this business which I promised so fairly Six months ago, and

which I so confidently hoped and believed would in 12 months net you a handsome profit but time and chance happened to all things and we must not wonder if Speculations go backwards at this <u>Savage place</u>, when we find it So frequently the case among Civilized Christians, in a land of liberty and Laws.

I have sold off the Remnant of my Stock of Hogs for old Horses, which of the two I thought would be the Safest and least troublesome. In proportion to the number I have Sustained about as great a loss in the Hog way as you have. Enclosed I Send you <u>Twenty Dollars</u> being in full of the Account between you (as Agent or Dr. R[obinson]) and myself as per Statement herewith. When you have examined and approved of this account, you will be pleased to Send me an acquittance of All accounts, in your hands between Dr. R. & I, that is, Balance on a Signed Account up to 28th Feb. last for $60 and price of a Cow and Calf $30 which you know I gave you due bills for, and which you will find credited in the acct. now sent.

The Sum due from Mr. Rawlings[128] to Dr. R. is about $30 I have Requested him to write you on the Subject.

Excuse haste. I am Surrounded by Indians.

Yours truly
G. C. Sibley

Papers Sent Vizt.
Acct. Current R. H. Price with G. C. S. up to this day
Note Jas. H. Audrain for ------------------------------$118.87
Note Ira Cottle for -------------------------------------303.33 1/3
Acct. against Audrain for 43 1/8 Bushels Corn at $1.
Acct. against ditto for Sund – (Settled by Note)
Acct. against Cottle for do.   ditto
Bank Notes for 20 Dollars
Sent also by the Boat a Small Box of Glass for Mr. Price

[125] A copy of the statement was not attached to the copy in the letterbook here.

[126] The hog-raising business went poorly, and Price was a partner in it; it is unclear if Sibley was a partner in operation, but he clearly had a role at least managing the affairs on site.

[127] This is still another indication of the tenuous nature of the relationship between Sibley and military personnel at the Fort.

[128] Isaac Rawlings. (See above.)

Tuesday 19th

In the evening all the Osages Returned from war, and Brought 8 Scalps and one Horse taken from the Ioways (2 Men, 5 Women, 1 Child killed).

Wednesday 20th

Wrote to Mr. Braxton Cooper (at Boone's Saline) about the Horse I bought from John Trask desiring him to do as he thinks best with him and I will Settle with him Some time when I am passing threw that Settlement. Rainy day. River Rising Rapidly.

Thursday 21st March 1811

Cloudy morning. River Rising very fast. Rainy day.

Friday 22nd

Fair day. River Rising yet. A Number of Buffalo passed, floating, which it is Supposed were drowned above attempting to cross on the ice. The Indians got Several of them ashore.

Saturday 23rd

Cloudy and Cold this morning. A little after Sunrise Ensign Bissell[129] with a command of 17 Soldiers Set out by water for St. Louis; Mr. Hempstead went down with him. Sent the following Letters Vizt.

1 to Risdon H. Price dated 18th Inst.
1 to General William Clark dated 22nd Inst.
1 Mr. Braxton Cooper (Saline) 20th

Note—I paid William Wells $21.25 in Cash, yesterday, which is in full of all accounts between us. Snowed a little in the evening.

[129] Lewis Bissell (see above).

Fort Osage March 22nd 1811

(Late at night)

General William Clark
St. Louis

> *Dr. Sir,*
> *I duly Received yours of the 5th Inst. by Mr. Hempstead. I beg leave to Refer you to mine of Sundry dates by Mr. Audrain. I am authorized to furnish you with whatever articles you need for public use, If I have them to Spare. If it is pressing, I will furnish*

*you with 25 lbs. of Vermillion. the price will be $3.50 p pound
and if you will take a quantity of Blue Beads (Say 100 lbs.) I will
furnish them at a Dollar per pound, the price Should be greater
for a less quantity, Say 125 Cents. per pound.*

*I Send you in care of Mr. Hempstead the head of a Buffalo
Bull, which I procured about an hour ago by mere accident
from an Indian for $2.50. It is fresh from the animal, and will
Reach you Safe and Sound I trust. As the Boat goes very early in
the Morning I have no time to have it cleaned.*[130]

The Osages have been Seen to war against the Ioways &c.

*We have a Report that the Big Osages have lately murdered
an American near the old Town.*

G. C. S.

[130] Perhaps for Clark's personal collection of western and Indian artifacts.
Clark had a "museum" in his home of objects from the Corps of Discovery
along with other objects from the west that others provided.

Sunday 24th
Day cool and cloudy. River Still Rising.

Monday 25th March 1811
*Fair day. About 25 Osages from the Arkansaw arrived to day. Heavy Rain
at night*

Tuesday, 26th
Cloudy morning. Rainy day. In the afternoon Mr. Crooks[131] *arrived from
the Naudoway.*[132] *River Still Rising.*

[131] Ramsay Crooks (see above).

[132] The Nodoway River flows into the Missouri just north of present-day St.
Joseph, Missouri. A small camp at the confluence was used by various
trading parties on their trips to or from the upper Missouri; for example, Wilson
Hunt of the Pacific Fur Company used it in 1811 to organize his men on his
way to the Pacific. (Oglesby, *Manuel Lisa and the Opening of the Missouri Fur
Trade*, 105.)

Wednesday 27th
*Cloudy morning. Fair day. About 12 O'Clock 9 Horses were discovered
crossing the Missouri just above the Factory driven over it was a Supposed
by Some Hostile Indians whose design appears to have been to take them
off. About 100 Osages immediately crossed, and in a Short time Returned*

to the bank opposite here with all the Horses, (4 of which were mine) they found them in the water under the bank, utterly unable to get out, and if not So Seasonably Relived by the Indians (who had to dig a Road to them with their knives and tomahawks) would all have perished inevitably. I distributed 2d. Vermillion[133] a Barrel of Flour to the Indians for their activity in bringing back my Horses, with which they were well Satisfied. A Perogue arrived from the Mahas just at dark owned by Rudedoux.[134]

[133] Vermilion was a red paint that was a standard gift from whites to Indians. Originally made from the mineral cinnabar (the main ore in mercury), artists made a synthetic vermilion starting in the thirteenth century from mercury and sulphur. In 1805, Meriwether Lewis used vermilion to win the trust of a group of Shoshone women and, through them, Chief Cameahwait. (*The Definitive Journals of Lewis and Clark*, vol. 5, August 13, 1805, 78-79.)

[134] Joseph Robidoux (1783-1868), like his namesake father, was active in the fur trade. As early as age seventeen, Robidoux first traversed the Missouri River looking for a site for a trading post; originally he stopped near present-day St. Joseph, Missouri, where he eventually founded the town, but then moved on upriver to Council Bluffs. Robidoux was prominent in the fur trade, a dogged competitor with Manuel Lisa, and became a rigorous contender for the trade out of Council Bluffs in the 1810s. Trader Rudolf Kurz recounts one incident that illustrates the nature of both the personal competition between them and the nature of the fur business along the early nineteenth-century Missouri River:

> "Each of them tried to acquire by trade as many pelts as possible for himself without being at all squeamish as to the means employed, and, for that reason, they often quarreled. In order to prevent such wrangles and under the conviction that neither had the power to ruin the other, they pledged reciprocally to be 'loyal,' i.e., if a band of Indians arrived at their trading posts for the purpose of exchange and barter, neither would attempt to take advantage of the other. Manuel Lisa, however, had no intention of trading on honorable terms for any length of time; accordingly, upon occasion when both of them expected a band of Pawnee he tried to circumvent Robidoux. While he ordered his post supplied in secret with commodities to barter with the Pawnee, he went over to see Robidoux by way of putting him off his guard, by his own presence there to hinder operations, and to see what was really going on in the other storehouse. Robidoux played the part of unsuspecting host just as well as his opponent played his role; acted just as though he had allowed himself to be really duped. He invited Lisa to drink a glass of champagne to the success of the prospective trade; but regretted that on account of his gout he was not able to stoop down, and therefore would have to ask Lisa to fetch the flask from the cellar

himself. The latter obligingly raised the trapdoor in the room and went down the steps. Joe let fall the door, rolled a cask upon it, and with mocking words left his opponent imprisoned, in order that he might trade alone with the Pawnees."

Robidoux was among the first to enter the Santa Fe trade after Mexico gained independence from Spain in 1821. When the fur trade in the Council Bluffs area declined, he made a lucrative career of selling town lots in his newly founded St. Joseph, Missouri. (Houck, *A History of Missouri from the Earliest Explorations and Settlements*, vol. 2, 3; Hyde and Conard, *An Encyclopedia of Early Missouri*, vol. 4, 1930; Rudolf Kurz, Journal, quoted in Oglesby, *Manuel Lisa and the Opening of the Missouri Fur Trade*, 19-20; Thorne, "Joseph Robidoux III," in *Dictionary of Missouri Biography*, 653-654.)

Thursday 28th March 1811

Day very changeable, Sometimes fair, Sometimes Rainy, at Sundown a tremendous Storm of Rain and Hail with thunder and Lightning. I never Saw it Rain harder than it did for about <u>10</u> Minutes; and for about one Minute the <u>Hail Stones</u> fell very thick, the Size of Pigeon's eggs. The Storm continued, with frequent intermissions until 8 O'Clock, when it cleared off and continued warm.

Friday 29th

The day fair and pleasant. Began to Trade to day with the Osages, they having paid nearly all their credits.[135]

[135] On the one hand, credit was a necessary part of the trade; Indians needed supplies and equipment for upcoming hunts, but couldn't pay for the goods until they returned with furs. However, the United States government used credit in order to gain more land; when treaties were renegotiated during this period, they often included statements that cleared all debts in exchange for large parcels of land.

Saturday 30th

Day fair and pleasant.

Sunday 31st

A violent hail Storm about 11 O'Clock, after which it cleared off but continued windy. Day quite cool.

Monday April 1st, 1811

Day disagreeably cool.

Tuesday 2nd
Fine day.

Wednesday 3rd
To day Lieut. Brownson very unadvisedly and very improperly had one of the Warriors of the Little Osage punished by 10 or 12 lashes on his bare back in the Garrison, for infringing Some petty Regulation or other, which has very much irritated and offended the whole tribe.

Thursday 4th
To day Some of the young men of the Osages Shot Some Cattle (belonging to Mr. Audrain it is Supposed) in Revenge for the indignity offered their Tribe yesterday by punishing one of their Warriors. This affair Seems to have caused much alarm and irritation among the Indians and in the Garrison, and a Report is in circulation that the Osages design to attack the Garrison to night which has caused unusual vigilance. I have not learned the grounds of the Report nor can I find any cause of alarm. The Osages are certainly greatly offenced with Lt. Brownson for his harsh and improper conduct towards them; but are firm in their attachment to the U. States I believe.[136] Lt. B. does well however, I think to Show <u>alertness</u>, on the occasion. It is making Sure of tranquility at all events.

[136] Motivation for loyalty is difficult to discern, but that of the Osage may have been out of necessity as much as any genuine affection. The Osage were fast becoming completely dependent on the United States for goods, supplies, and defense against hostile neighbors.

Friday 5th
There was no alarm last night, nor any unusual Stir among the Osages except what was occasioned by their own apprehensions of an attack from the Ioway, founded on Some Suspicious noise heard over the River by one of the Sentries.

Saturday 6th
The Osages have agreed to pay for the damage done to Mr. Audrain & Lt. Brownson (by killing Hogs, Shooting Cattle, &c.) in Horses.

Sunday 7th
Fine day. The Osages danced to day before the Factory House.

Monday April 8th, 1811
Day cool and changeable. Mr. Wilson P. Hunt arrived by water from St. Louis which place he left on the 5th of March, by him I Received 2 Letters

from John C. Comegys, and Sundry Articles as Flour, Medicine, &c. also a few newspapers up to 23rd January.

Tuesday 9th
Some of the Kansas Arrived yesterday to Trade. Some of the Big Osages arrived to day (Sans Nerf and Jo Ma Lambero are along) <u>they</u> have come to eat. Pretty good day.

Wednesday 10th
Rainy day. This Morning Mr. Hunt and party pursued their voyage. There are two Gentlemen Naturalists with Mr. Hunt, Mr. Bradbury[137] from Liverpool who is making Researches under the patronage of Sir Joseph Banks.[138] And Mr. Nuttle[139] from Philadelphia, Sent out by Doctor Barton.[140] The former is an elderly Gentleman, and latter quite a young man; both men of Science and indefatigable in their Researches. Mr. N. will probably go to the Pacific. Mr. B. no farther than the Mandanes.[141]

[137] John Bradbury (1768-1823), like Thomas Nuttall (see below) was an English botanist who traveled from St. Louis to the upper Missouri in 1811 with Wilson Price Hunt. Bradbury and Nuttall met in St. Louis and decided to journey together, mostly on foot. At the Great Bend of the Missouri, Bradbury went overland to the Mandan villages, so he collected plant specimens from the plains that Nuttall didn't find. Since he had a friend in Henry Marie Brackenridge who was traveling with Manuel Lisa's party, Bradbury often joined them as well. He returned to St. Louis later in the summer when Hunt's group went farther upriver; Nuttall stayed, returning in the fall. Given news of the impending war with Great Britain, both Bradbury and Nuttall decided to return to England. Bradbury stayed in New Orleans longer before booking trans-Atlantic passage, and was unable to return to England because of the war, delaying his publication of his findings. He and Nuttall were among the first to collect and document the flora of the Missouri.

[138] Sir Joseph Banks (1743-1820) was an English naturalist. He accompanied Capt. James Cook on his circumnavigation of the world aboard the Endeavor and later became a guiding force in the development of Kew Gardens as its unpaid director. Banks sent a number of botanists to other parts of the world to collect plant specimens for Kew, including Bradbury.

[139] Thomas Nuttall (1786-1859) was an English-born printer-turned-botanist who met Dr. Benjamin Smith Barton (see below) soon after he arrived in Philadelphia in 1808. After expeditions to the Chesapeake and the Great Lakes collecting botanical specimens for Barton, he traveled to Mackinac Island on Lake Huron in 1810, where he found out about a trip up the Missouri River planned for the following year. He traveled with the party to

St. Louis, where he took a temporary job with the *Missouri Gazette*, using his printing skills. He met another naturalist planning to travel the Missouri, John Bradbury, and the two ended up joining Wilson Price Hunt's party heading to the Pacific as part of John Jacob Astor's efforts to gain control of the fur trade in the Northwest. Nuttall traveled at least as far as the Mandan villages on the Missouri in North Dakota before returning to St. Louis in October 1811 with Manuel Lisa and others from the Missouri Fur Company. Nuttall left St. Louis for New Orleans, from which he embarked for England; when heard that war between the United States and Great Britain was imminent, he gave up his plan to go to Philadelphia. Nuttall had the good fortune of making the journey at the height of the growing season, so he had an especially profitable collecting season. Lewis and Clark collected plants along the same stretch of the river, but they lost most of the specimens from the spring of 1805 in a flood. The Corps of Discovery findings weren't published yet, so all the plants collected were new to Nuttall.

[140] Dr. Benjamin Smith Barton (1766-1815), perhaps the most preeminent botanist of the new republic. Before embarking on the voyage to the Pacific, Meriwether Lewis went to Philadelphia to study a number of scientific subjects under the leading minds of the age, such as Barton and physician Benjamin Rush. Barton published *Elements of Botany,* the first textbook on the subject published in the United States.

[141] The Mandans had lived in close proximity to the Hidatsas since a smallpox epidemic ravished both populations in the early 1780s. Lewis and Clark spent the winter of 1804-5 with the Mandans. Both tribes lived just downriver from the point where the Missouri turns west, just north of present-day Bismarck, North Dakota.

Thursday 11th April
Day cool and changeable.

Friday 12th
Rainy day.

Saturday 13th
A fair day but very windy.

Sunday 14th
Late last night Mr. F. Audrain arrived from St. Louis which place he left the 3rd Inst. Letters Received by him.
2 from General Clark dated 1st and 2nd Inst.
2 from R. H. Price April 2nd & March 24th
1 from John Sibley dated 1st February

and 3 Washington papers up to 19 February also Received from General Clark per Mr. Audrain 8 Indian Medals 5 Small and 3 Middle Size.[142]

[142] For details on medals and their production, see above.

Monday 15th April 1811

About half of the Little Osage Village Set out for the Osage River to day with the Chief. Some disputes of an unimportant nature with the Garrison and Some pretended fears of their enemies, have occasioned this Sudden change in the plans of this people, for but a few days ago they were unanimous in their determination to stay here and the Chief Seemed to be the most determined of any.

The Rest of the Tribe (about 60 families) have Resolved to Stay here till Sansoreille[143] *and the Big Soldier*[144] *arrive, who are now out hunting.*

[143] Sans Oreille was a chief of the Little Osage, and considered by Sibley to be a primary leader of the tribe—someone who Sibley clearly held in great respect. Sans Oreille was one of two chiefs who readily signed the treaty with William Clark in 1808; in return, Clark gave each of the chiefs a rifle, gunpowder and an assortment of gifts worth more than $300. Sans Oreille was sufficiently touched to dub Clark his white brother, telling him that his "friendship goes to our hearts," then offered to adopt Clark through an adoption ceremony. Normally something of a test of strength and courage, Clark apparently balked since he was running a bit short on both because of his usual problems with dysentery on such trips. Sans Oreille suggested that Clark had already proven worthy on both counts already, was let off easy, and dubbed the "Red-Haired Chief," a moniker that was used by several tribal leaders when visiting him as Indian Agent, Territorial Governor, or Indian Commissioner in St. Louis. Sans Oreille and other Osage leaders were less impressed by the treaty that Pierre Chouteau brought them two months later; it called for a marked increase in the land they had to cede to the Americans, although they eventually agreed to it. (Rollings, *The Osage*, 258; Wolferman, *The Osage in Missouri*, 68-70.)

[144] Big Soldier (c. 1773-1844) was a Little Osage war leader who was already well known to Spanish officials such as Lieut. Governor Zenon Trudeau by the mid-1790s. He was part of a delegation of Osage and Pawnee who traveled to Washington, D.C., in 1805, then returned to the Osage villages with Zebulon Pike the following year. At this stage—spring 1811—Sibley considered Big Soldier and Sans Oreille, along with Chief Ne-zu-mo-nee, to be the most influential and prominent Osage leaders. He fell from favor with Sibley temporarily when his primary competitor Sans Oreille convinced the factor that Big Soldier was behind the attempts to stop and molest trader

Joseph Robidoux (see above). He generally favored cooperative relations with the United States, although he told Sibley at least once that the federal government was "afraid of [Pierre] Chouteau and dare not oppose his Measures." Big Soldier had an interesting life after the factory closed. St. Louis promoter (and former fur trader) David Delaunay and some others convinced him and five other Osage to be part of a traveling show in Europe exhibiting the "wild Indians." They were quite popular when they first arrived in Paris in the summer of 1827; once the novelty wore off and Parisians were no longer willing to pay to see them, Delaunay found himself in prison over debts, and the Osage began wandering around Europe. After roaming through Italy, Switzerland, and Belgium, a group of French (including the Marquis de Lafayette) took pity on them and raised enough money for their return in 1830. For the rest of his life, Big Soldier wore the medal Lafayette had presented to him at all public occasions. (Rowe, "Big Soldier," in *Dictionary of Missouri Biography*, 67-68.)

19th

Sansoreille arrived and has advised his people not to think of moving and they will most likely follow his advice. The weather changeable; a good deal of rain. River Rising Note: Gagare lost 3 days in March by Sickness.

Thursday 25th April 1811

Nothing Strange has occurred Since the 19th, the Weather has been very Changeable. Mr. Manuel[145] arrived in 21 days from St. Charles, on his way up to the heads of the Missouri. A Mr. Brackenridge[146] is a passenger with mr. Manuel and intends going as far as the Mandanes from whence he will Return (in September) with Mr. Bradbury, who has gone on with Mr. Hunt. Mr. B's object appears to be chiefly to indulge his curiosity in a view of the country, its productions and Curiosities &c. an account of which is Said he intends to publish.[147] He is Said to be a young Gentleman of handsome acquirements and to possess a happy facility in writing. By Mr. Manuel I Received 1000 lbs. of Bar Lead, 1 Tea Canister and 3 Flags Sent me by General Clark, with a Letter from the General dated 1st Inst. He has Send me no Invoice of the Lead.[148]

[145] Referring to Manuel Lisa; for a detailed biographical sketch, see "Biographies" chapter in this volume.

[146] Henry Marie Brackenridge (1786-1871) moved to St. Louis in 1806 from Pittsburgh, initially practicing law. He was a friend of botanist John Bradbury (see above), both of whom were traveling to the Mandan villages in 1811. Expeditions led by Manuel Lisa for the Missouri Fur Company and Wilson Price Hunt of Astor's Pacific Fur Company were racing up the Missouri to gain an edge in the fur trade.

[147] Brackenridge's *Views of Louisiana together with a Journal of a Voyage up the Missouri River in 1811* was published in 1814; it was one of the sources used by Washington Irving in his Astoria.

[148] Lead was used for making ammunition; since it was going to Sibley rather than Capt. Eli Clemson, it was probably for the Indians.

Friday 26th April 1811

It Rained hard all night and had not done till 10:00 O'Clock. To day Mr Manuel pursued his voyage this morning.

Saturday 27th

The Big Soldier arrived to day from his Beaver Hunt, owing to the wet weather his party were only able to take about 40 Beavers.[149] The Big Soldier pretends to be very much dissatisfied with his Town for leaving this place, and Says positively he will not go.

[149] These were undoubtedly hunted for their pelts, which were among the most coveted and valuable of the furs purchased from Indians. As a consequence, beaver were over-hunted by the Indians until they were extinct in many regions.

Sunday 29th

Had a long conversation with the Big Soldier to day. He is certainly a man of good Sense, but is not as decided and firm in his measures as many others. He appears to have Suffered his confidence in our Government to be in Some degree impaired, by Some of the measures taken by Governor Lewis to assemble all the Osages near this place having either failed, or been changed in favor of Mr. Chouteau's plan of Recollecting them at the Osage River. And hinted more than once that the Americans are afraid of Chouteau and dare not oppose his measures, and offers this as a Reason why the Osage affairs are in Such confusion.

Tuesday May 1st 1811

To day I bartered with Mr. Audrain (or Rather exchanged) Horses as follows

Dr.
1 Sorrel Horse which I bought in St. Louis February 1810 from Mr. John G. Comegys for $90.00

1 Bay Horse which I bought from Mr. Audrain 24th last February (See page 97)[150] Stands me in 60.00 - - - - - - - - - $150.00

Note—the Sorrell is Rather a delicate animal and fit only for light Service. The Bay has a fistula[151] coming, which may be troublesome.

Cr.
1 Bay Horse (nicknamed Paddy) worth fully $35.00

1 Bay Horse (late F. Audrain's)—better worth 35.00

1 Mouse Colored Dun Horse 30.00

1 Calico Stallion (Indian) 30.00

1 Black Stallion 20.00

This is what the 5 actually Stand me in $150.00

My motive for making this exchange, is to procure a number of hardy tackies for an excursion I am preparing to commence in a few days into the Indian Country.[152] Neither of my two Horses will answer, besides I Require four or five. Four of the above are proved to be very hardy.

[The subsequent four pages are missing from the original journal. The following entries for May 4, 5, 6, and 7 appear elsewhere on torn leaves from the diary.]

[150] Page 97 of his written manuscript.

[151] An abscess often caused by an ill-fitting saddle or harness; at that time it was most common on draft horses.

[152] This is the first mention of his plans to travel to the "Salines" in northern Oklahoma.

Friday May 4, 1811
A number of Horses were Stolen to day from the Osages and they are hurrying to plant their corn &c. and to be off to the Buffalo Ranges. They greatly fear an Attack from the Ioways or Ottoes.

Saturday 5th
The Osages have lost twenty horses, Stolen by Indians.

Sunday 6th May
The Osages are encamped within 100 yards of the Stockade, and are much

alarmed this evening. I directed them to post Sentinels and keep a good watch, and be Sure to hail before firing.

Monday 7th

Last night at about 11 O'Clock, there was an alarm among the Osages. One of their Sentries discovered _3_ Strange Indians Stealthily approaching the Camp, and within _300_ yards. After hailing 3 times with no effect, he fired his Rifle at the foremost one, who fell badly wounded. The others Ran off to the woods. The report of the Rifle and yells of the guard Roused, not only the Osage Camp, but the Garrison; and in a twinkling all was bustle and confusion among the Indians. Many ran to the place where the wounded Man lay; and Shocking to Relate, instantly fell upon him with tomahawks and knives, and in two minutes time cut the poor creature into _50_ to _100_ pieces. Men, women, and boys engaged in this horrid butchery; and so quickly was it done, that the victim must have _felt_ every blow and cut. His head, arms, hands, legs, feet, fingers, toes, ears, &c. were severed from the body, and the entrails let out. It was after the Osages had Returned to their camp from this butchery, that the Garrison was aroused by the unusual Noise. My own _arousing_ was Rather Startling; Sans Oreille had made his way into my Sleeping Room, and Stood at my bedside holding the head of the Slain Indian in one hand, and a blazing torch in the other, and calling my Name in a voice of the most Savage excitement. I had faintly heard the gun, but not Regarding it, fell asleep again and was in a Sound Sleep when thus aroused by my unwelcome visitor. I was quickly dressed and over at the camp; and there found the Osages in a temper far more Savage than I had ever before believed them capable. Here one Showed me a leg, one a hand, another a finger – foot – Strips of Skin - the Scalp – the mutilated head had been Seized by boys and Rolled about as a foot ball; every one aimed to get a piece. All this was accompanied by yelling and howling, enough to distract one. As Soon as I was able to quiet the tumult, and make them listen to Reason, I hastened back to my quarters, but not to bed. I was under Serious apprehension for the Safety of Mr. Cottle and family, who were living alone in an open log cabin 3/4 of a Mile from the Garrison, in the direction whence the Strange Indians came, and without doubt from a large party, now exasperated by the loss of their Chief, for Such was the man Slain. I asked the officer then commanding the Garrison, Lt. Brownson, to Send a Corporal and file of Men to bring Cottle & family in, and to fire a cannon two or three times, but he Refused to do either. I then took a party of Osages, and went and brought the family to my house in Safety. On the Road Side leading to Cottle's, a Short distance from his cabin, lay the Remains of the body of the poor wretch So Recently killed, which the hungry Indian dogs were Ravenously devouring with the far Stretched entrails and what else Remained. The Slain Man was Recognized as a distinguished Ioway war chief. Sans Oreille apologized for his Rude intrusion, as well as he could; he Said he very Seldom allowed himself to become So excited. His Son had Shot and Scalped the Ioway chief, and that had no doubt Roused his feeling to So high a pitch.

[start of next available entry]

frequent intercourse between them and this place. General Clark has furnished me with three Flags and Eight Medals to be distributed at the Several Nations in his Agency that I may visit in Such manner as I may think best, and he has Requested me to Speak to them in his name, in a Style Suitable to the principles and policy of the Government of the U. S.

Having seen these Nations, I propose to visit and examine the celebrated Salines beyond the River Arkansaw, to visit the Several Tribes and bands of Osages at their Hunting Camps, and if not too inconvenient, to Return home, by way of the Towns of the Chaniers[153] and Big Osage.[154]

I Shall note whatever Remarkable may fall within our view, make Some enquiries concerning distant objects of curiosity, and inform myself generally as to the country, its inhabitants, productions, and Resources. I take with me Pawnee & Osage Interpreters, also a few active Osages as Hunters and Scouts, and Shall carry a few articles of Merchandise, as Calico, Paint, Scarlet cloth &c. as presents, Should I find it fit to make any.

An express is to Set out from the Garrison Tomorrow for St. Louis, by whom I Shall forward to General Clark, my public Accounts, for the last quarter (for him to forward by mail)[155] also some private letters which I have written.

To The Supt. of Indian Trade (under cover with Accounts &c.)
To John Sibley
To General Clark
To James Callaway
To John G. Comegys and
To Risdon H. Price, for copies of all which (except the 2nd) See Letter Book Pages 38-46-48-54 and 58.

[153] Another common name at the time for the Arkansas Osage.

[154] Part of effort to unite the three Osage groups, which was U. S. policy and preferred by the Chouteaus. It is unclear if the idea of this expedition was Sibley's or ordered from either St. Louis or Washington.

Starting in 1806, all factors were required to submit quarterly reports instead of semiannual ones to the Treasury Department. (Peake, *A History of the United States Indian Factory System*, 2.)

Fort Osage May 4th.1811.

Mr. John G. Comegys
St. Louis

> My dear Sir,
> I have the pleasure to acknowledge Receipt of your two favors of 5th and 6th, March by Mr. Hunt (who passed this way place on the 10th, Ulto.) with Sundry Articles Amount as per bill <u>$52.12.</u>
> Enclosed I send you my Draft on General Clark for <u>Fifty Dollars</u>, which you will please to Receive and give me Credit for. I am at this moment in haste, preparing to Set out for a distance part of the country in the Interior, whence I hope to Return by the 1st of July, next. Being So much busied among the Indians who are to accompany me, and having Such a variety of necessary trifles to call off an engage my attention I must needs beg your indulgence till my Return, for a particular notice of your lengthy and friendly letter by Mr. Hunt; which I can at present only thank you for. I cannot however delay to express my Sincere Regret at the prospect of your leaving St. Louis to Return no more, though I permit myself to hope that we Shall have you back again. Wherever you go Sir, you will carry with you my best wishes for your Health and Happiness, and I Shall ever Retain a grateful Sense of the numerous kind offices I have Received at your hands, which I trust I Shall yet have the satisfaction to requite.
> I Remain Dear Sir
> Truly yours
> G. C. Sibley
> Mr. R.H. Price
> St. Louis

Fort Osage May 5th.1811.

> My dear Sir,
> Your 2 Letters of 24th. March and 2d. April are before me. It were entirely needless for me to Say to you how sincerely I condole with you and Dr. Robinson on the subject of the Doctor's affairs here, which have Suffered So Seriously.[156] It is a misfortune truly to be lamented & I am Sure no one can

lament it more than I do. If it could have been foreseen or even Suspected, it might possibly have been in some degree guarded against. If my exertions could have prevented it, it would not have happened. As to the expense, it is but just to observe, that it was economized as much as possible, you only pay for the actual time Wells was employed about the Hogs Crops &c. and that at the precise Rate he was employed at by the year. I do not apprehend the least danger of Cottle's failing to discharge his note duly. He is a prudent and industrious Man and extremely punctual in all his dealings. I would as Soon trust him for the amount of his estate, as any man in Louisiana.

I have not time to Say more to you just now being busy making preparations for a long journey in the interior, which I shall commence in a few days, and hope to be back in about two months.

I am dear Sir
Yours very Sincerely
G. C. S.

[156] While Jones suggests that Sibley probably bought Robinson's share of the partnership with Risdon Price (see above), this suggests that Robinson retained some financial interest. (Jones, *Prairie Puritan*, 67.)

Fort Osage May 4th 1811

General Wm. Clark
Saint Louis

> *Dear Sir,*
> *Enclosed I have Sent you a Bill of Exchange drawn by Wilson P. Hunt April 9th 1811 on John Jacob Astor Merchant New York[157] payable at ten days Sight to my order for Four Hundred and Twenty Two Dollars Ninety eight Cents and endorsed by me. This Bill, I have to Request you to negotiate for cash and dispose of as follows.*
> *Fifty Dollars to discharge my Draft on you of this date payable on Demand to John G. Comegys or order -------$50.00*
> *Thirty Seven Dollars to discharge my Draft on you of this date payable on demand to James Callaway----------------37.00*
> *Three Hundred Dollars to be sent up to me by the Return of Mr. Audrain, or by any other Safe conveyance on or before the 30th of June if possible------------------------300.00*
> *Thirty-five Dollars and 98 Cents Retain in your hands Subject to my Drafts---------35.98*
> *----------------------422.98*

*As good Bills of Exchange are almost always in demand in St.
Louis, I do no apprehend any difficulty in procuring the cash for
this one. It was taken in payment for Merchandise Sold to Mr.
Hunt and is the property of the U.S. else I should not trouble
you with it. When you pay my Draft in favor of James Callaway,
I will thank you to take his Signature to the enclosed Receipt
and Send it to me by Some Convenient opportunity.*

*I am extremely thankful to you for the Medals and Flags
which you have Sent me. I hope to be able to make Such a
distribution of them as will be beneficial to the Service. I am
only waiting for the Contractor's Boat to arrive to Set off on my
tour. A number of the Osages are to go with me, Sans Oreille
is very keen for the expedition and will be very useful as he
is known and Respected by all other Tribes and is a firm and
Steady friend to the policy of U. States. The Kansas & Pawnees
are at war,[158] and have lately had an affair in which Several of
the former were killed. I shall make it a main point to Settle
their quarrels if possible.[159]*

[157] John Jacob Astor "Merchant" is quite the understatement. By the time
of this letter, Astor had created his Pacific Fur Company and had sent
two teams—one overland under Wilson Price Hunt and one by sea under
Jonathan Thorn—to converge at the mouth of the Columbia River; within very
few years Astor will be the dominant force in the western fur trade.

[158] The Kansas had a tense relationship with the Pawnees in part because
of their alliance with the Osage, traditionally an enemy of the Pawnees; the
Kansas were serving as a buffer between the two at the time. (Rollings, *The
Osage*, 180.)

[159] This is a typical attitude by government agents at the time in their dealings
with Native American tribes. There was a tendency to oversimplify the conflict
and assume that they could simply hold a council and settle the war. Lewis
and Clark tried on more than one occasion, but were unable to create lasting
peace arrangements.

10th

*Mr. Audrain declines going down, but an express will leave
here tomorrow, by whom I Shall Send my dispatches. I Shall
also start tomorrow for the Kansas. The Ioways or Some of the
Mississippi Indians, have lately been committing Some pretty
Serious depredations here, they have Stolen about 20 horses
from the Little Osages, 2 from me and 2 from Mr. Audrain,
and are Still lurking about here. It is Supposed there must be a*

Perhaps the greatest understatement of Sibley's journals was his description of John Jacob Astor as "merchant." Astor dominated the fur trade in North America until the 1830s. When Astor died in 1848, he was reputed to be the richest man in America. (Used by permission, State Historical Society of Missouri, Columbia)

Strong party of them. One of their Spies was caught on the night of the 5th by the Osages, within 300 yards of the Garrison, and was instantly cut into at least _50_ pieces. _They_ Suppose him to have been an Ioway. Yesterday all the Osages left here for the Buffalo hunt, they had just finished planting their Corn,[160] and were afraid to remain here any longer lest more of their Horses Should be Stolen. We learn that the Chief of the Little Osages (who was lately Removed from this place with about half his Tribe to the Osage River) has been gone

Some days with a pretty Strong party against the Ioways. He was the principal cause of the last Stroke upon that people, and it ought in justice to be represented to the Chief of the Ioways, that the few Osages who Remained here were entirely opposed to the measure, and are inclined to make a lasting peace if possible. I hope at all events there may be Some measure taken to prevent their making this vicinity the Seat of War, and that the depredations latterly committed on the property of Whites, may be atoned for. My Horses I value at 40 Dollars each, and Shall add 20 Dollars for Damage (as they were intended for my expedition & their Loss obliged me to procure others) making 100 Dollars which I Shall insist on full payment of, with legal interest till paid.[161] *Mr. Audrain's Horses are much more valuable and what makes the thing more Serious, were taken out of his enclosure near his House.*

> *Yours &c.*
>
> *G. C. S.*

---

[160] Typically, able-bodied men would leave for an extended hunt, leaving women, children, and the elderly behind at the camp. While some tend to think of the Native Americans as sorts of nomadic hunters and gatherers, many tribes had been engaged in agriculture for centuries, which was integrated into the existing environment rather than clearing everything for European-style farming. The Osage cultivated corn, but still relied on animals and wild plants to augment their diet.

[161] According to the treaty, the United States government reimbursed citizens for losses due to theft by Native Americans. Of course, the government extracted this from the tribes through subsequent treaties in which it erased the debt in exchange for ceding more land. The Osage were forced to shrink their land holdings in the 1818 treaty because of this.

Fort Osage May 10th. 1811

> *John Mason Esq.*
> *Superintendent of Indian Trade*
> *George Town*
> *District of Columbia*

> *Sir,*

> *Having devoted the last three years exclusively to the public Service, more than two of which I have passed in confined Seclusion at this place, I am now to beg of you the indulgence of a furlow for Six Months, to commence in November next*

after the Indians have gone to the Hunt, and to expire in April when they Return during which I will do myself the honor to wait upon you at the Office of Indian Trade, if you think proper to desire it.

Some family concerns of a nature very interesting to me, require my presence at Natchitoches[162] for a Short time and my health Requires Some Respite from confinement.

Although this indulgence would be particularly grateful to me, yet I would not by any means Request it unless it can be granted with perfect convenience to the Service.

I am Setting out tomorrow on an excursion for a Short time to visit our Red Neighbors the Kansas and Pawnees, to endeavor to form Some commercial arrangements to extend to those Tribes the advantages intended for them in this establishment. In this, General Clark favors me with his approbation and friendly assistance, and I am in hope I Shall be able to open a free trade with those People.

I have a quantity of Furs, Peltries &c. to the amount of about $5000 in Readiness for the market which Mr. Rawlings will dispatch to St. Louis by the first opportunity.

Except Some unimportant movements of the Osages, and Some fighting they have lately had with the Ioways, all appears to be well with our Indian concerns in this quarter.

I am very Respectfully &c.

G. C. S.

---

[162] "Family concerns" in Natchitoches would have involved his father, Dr. John Sibley (1757-1837), who was Indian Agent for the Orleans Territory from 1805 to 1814. The Sibleys moved to Fayetteville, North Carolina, where John started the *Fayetteville Gazette*. His first wife Elizabeth died in 1790; he married Mary White Winslow in November 1791.

Apparently the marriage wasn't a complete success, since Dr. Sibley moved to Natchitoches (in present-day western Louisiana) without her in 1802. His correspondence with Thomas Jefferson about the Red River and the peoples living there was among the first eyewitness accounts of the Louisiana Purchase written by Americans. He probably knew John Robinson (Deputy Indian Agent at Fort Osage) since Spanish officials delivered Zebulon Pike's party, which included Robinson, to Natchitoches in 1807 after capturing the group and marching them from Santa Fe to Chihuahua. Father and son may have run into each other again, since Dr. Sibley was part of Stephen H. Long's expedition, which stopped at Fort Osage in the summer of 1819.

Friday 11th

Rainy Morning. Mr. Audrain called to tell me that he had lost two more of his Horses, and had Reasons to Suppose they were taken by Some of the Osages who left here on the 9th. He Said he thought those people had taken the two others also and Requested me to make Some enquiry when I overtook the Osages. I cannot for a moment Suppose the Little Osages took any of those Horses. If they are Stolen, it is by Some other people.

Friday May 11th, 1811

It having cleared off a little at 2 O'Clock, we Set out from Fort Osage. Party consists of the following persons Vizt. G. C. Sibley, James Henderson Hostler and waiter, Gabriel Lorr Osage Interpreter, Sansoreille chief warrior of the Little Osages, Little Fire and Cow-tail two warriors of the L. Osage who go as Hunters and Scouts. Besides the above there are two other Osages in company who are going to join the Village. My cavalry consists of 4 Horses, one apiece for Servant, Interpreter and Self, and one to pack, all fat and in good health and Spirits. Baggage—2 Small packs of Goods for Indian presents (Amount $100) weighing each 25 lbs. and about 550 lbs. of clothing, ammunition, and Provisions. The Indians are all afoot.

July 11th

Returned to Fort Osage, having completed my tour much to my Satisfaction and without any material accident.

July 13th, 1811

Settled all accounts with James Henderson and paid him in full to this day. Hired James Henderson to cook and wait at $18 per Month to commence tomorrow.

17th

William Wells arbitrarily imprisoned by Lt. Brownson.

20th

closed my public accounts under this date.

Fort Osage July 22nd 1811

General William Clark
St. Louis

> *Dr. Sir,*
> *I Returned from my tour on the 11th Inst. having been exactly two months out, during which time I Saw all the Kansas, Pawnees, Arkansas Osages, Little Osages and nearly all the*

Big Osages. The Kansas and Pawnees I saw at their Towns, the Osages at their Several hunting Camps beyond the Arkansaw. They all Received me with great hospitality, and they all gave me assurance (the most of them honest ones I believe of their good will towards the U. States).

I succeeded in making a Peace between them the Pawnees and Kansas, which may perhaps produce some good effects. I assure you I have great hopes of the Konses[163] becoming one of the best Tribes in your Agency, they must have Reformed greatly, and are already as orderly as the Osages, much more So than the Big Osages, and by far better Indians. I left one Flag at the Konses and one flag and 6 Medals at the Pawnees. The Medals I distributed among the most influential and best disposed[164] of the Several Tribes of Pawnees. I have not time now to give you as full detail of my proceedings at the Pawnees and Konses as I intend to do. I did not See the Ottoes, they had left their Towns before I got to the Konses.

I used one of the flags you furnished me, out of your Agency, but hope to be excused when I have told the circumstances. Clermont[165] head chief of the Arkansaw Osages Received me with the utmost hospitality, and himself, Big Track and indeed the whole of his Tribe evinced Such Strong proofs of good will towards the U.S. that I could not but feel much pleased with them. Clermont apologized to me for not displaying the U.S. flag, but told me it was not his fault, for he had none;[166] I happened to have one in my baggage, and Seeing his strong desire to possess Some American badge, immediately had it hoisted on his Lodge, and then left it, and must leave it for you and Mr. Chouteau[167] to Settle.

I was long ago aware that the Big Osages had expressed Some unwillingness to abide by the Treaty, but I never doubted but it was in consequence of false Representations made to them by persons who perhaps have an interest in destroying the Treaty. I accidentally learned Some Facts while at the Arkasaw Osages, which confirmed me in this opinion—a proposal had been made to Clermont and the principal Men of his Tribe, to oppose the Treaty, but they Refused, and declared they would observe it with good faith. If I mistake not, the Big Osage are under the impression that they are to get no annuity – at all events, the U.S. must not be trifled with in this business any longer.

I embraced the opportunity while I was out, to visit and examine the famous Salines beyond the Arkansaw.

The Grand Saline is at least 30 miles in circumference, and is a perfectly level plane, covered in dry hot weather from 2 to 6 Inches deep with a beautiful clean white Salt, of a quality Rather Superior I think to the imported brown Salt.

The Rock Saline is on a Smaller Scale being not more than about <u>500</u> Acres in extent. it is also a level flat Surrounded by very high Hills formed chiefly of Gypsum of various qualities and flint and Red clay from the bases of these Hills, issue many Springs of Salt Water, which spreading Slowly over the flat is converted by the action of the Sun to hard Salt, which is more or less abundant according to the weather, a long continuance of very hot, dry weather, produces a Solid Mass of Salt from 5 to 12 inches thick covering an Hundred acres, very much Resembling a large Pond or water covered with Rough ice. There are Several Springs, which Rise within the flat, around which the Salt forms in Such Solid Masses as to defy the heaviest Storms of Rain, however often Repeated. at one of these Springs I hewed out a piece of Salt 16 inches thick, then dug about a foot below the Surface of the ground, and Still found an almost Solid Mass of Salt. An Indian Seeing me digging, laughing asked me if I expected to dig to the bottom. I am induced to believe there is a Solid Rock of Salt of Vast extent near the Surface here. At present I cannot give more Sketches of these truly great curiosities of nature when I shall have revised my notes, perhaps I may Resume the Subject in Some future letter.[168]

You will Receive this, by Mr. Rawlings who will make a Short Stay in St. Louis. I beg leave to Refer you to him for other particulars. By his Return I hope to hear from you.

I beg leave to tender my Compliments Respectfully to Mrs. C. and to assure you of my Sincere esteem.

G. C. Sibley

[163]Kansas.

[164] Typically, someone like Sibley would designate the highest chiefs, on the assumption that they knew the internal hierarchy of the tribe. These six may or may not have been particularly "influential," although they were probably the friendliest to Sibley.

[165] Clermont II (d. 1828) was son of the Great Osage peace chief of the same name. When his father died in 1796, Clermont II figured on inheriting the post. Instead the Chouteaus engineered the succession from Clermont I to their friend and cohort Pawhuska (White Hair). Clermont left the Great Osage over it and moved in with the Arkansas Osages (sometimes called the Cheniers), which had splintered and moved south and west, sharing its leadership with

Cashesegra, or Big Track. The Chouteaus wanted the Arkansas band brought back into the Osage fold, since they controlled the Great Osage through White Hair, who became something of a puppet for Chouteau interests until his death in 1810.

Clermont stood as an ardent opponent of cooperation with whites and allowing them to move into Osage territory; he dealt severely with traders, trappers, or settlers found on Osage land. It is of little wonder that the Arkansas Osage had such a confusing relationship with the United States. The Chouteaus convinced territorial governor James Wilkinson that the Arkansas Osage were renegades who had to be controlled, orchestrating a ban on trade with them starting in 1805. Meantime, the Office of Indian Trade was opening a new trade factory in the region under William Treat; when Clermont and others arrived at the factory, Treat refused to trade because of the Wilkinson ban. Soon thereafter, war secretary Henry Dearborn granted an exclusive license to Morgan and Bright of New Orleans to trade with the Arkansas band, giving the partners exclusive access to interior trade with them. When Dearborn rescinded the Wilkinson order in 1806, he opened a floodgate of traders into the region, including the Chouteaus. Governor Meriwether Lewis tried to control the group, who he considered hostile, to the point that Clermont II boycotted the 1808 treaty councils (first with William Clark in September, then with Pierre Chouteau in November), and continued to be cantankerous to work with. He agreed to an amended treaty in 1809, but never confirmed the cession of any Osage land. Clermont and Big Track maintained their village around present-day Claremore, Oklahoma (northeast of Tulsa), but found increasing problems. As more tribes moved into today's Oklahoma, competition with neighbors grew stiffer, especially with the Cherokee, who outnumbered and regularly harassed the Cheniers. (Rowe, "Clermont II," in *Dictionary of Missouri Biography*, 196-197; Rolling, *The Osage*, 196, 207-220.)

[166] Clermont tried to trade his Spanish flag, a gift from his former colonial overlord, for an American one, but federal officials declined, which did nothing to help the already difficult relationship with the Arkansas Osage.

[167] Pierre Chouteau, who was the Indian agent for the Osage.

[168] This level of detail bespeaks the value of a large salt reserve in the interior of the country. Salt was a valuable commodity that was essential as a food preservative.

Wednesday 24th
Sent Mr. Rawlings[169] *to St. Louis with public dispatches &c. Mr. Ira Cottle went with him.*

[169] Isaac Rawlings (see above).

This Osage woman and child, credited as being the wife and child of Clermont II, was portrayed by George Catlin. (Used by permission, State Historical Society of Missouri, Columbia)

Saturday 27th

Mr. Bradbury & Mr. Brackenridge arrived this Morning in 2 Barges of the St. Louis Fur Company[170] in 40 days from the Recaras[171] where they left Mr. Hunt & party preparing for an overland journey to the Columbia River, purchasing Horses from the Recaras for that purpose. Mr. Bradbury Related that Some indications had been discovered of a design of a number of Mr. Hunt's Men to desert. Mr. B. saw Mr. Reuben Lewis[172] at the Mandans in May, who was in good health & proposed to descend the River to St. Louis in September. Mr. Bradbury has been extremely diligent and active in his botanical pursuits, having collected upwards of 1500 new plants &c. more than a thousand of which he has yet in a vegetative State in Boxes &c.[173]

[170] More commonly called the Missouri Fur Company; the barges were on their

way back from the Mandan villages.

[171] Arikaras. Most recently, the tribe had caused trouble. When the United States sent a group under the command of Lieut. Nathaniel Pryor (a member of the Corps of Discovery) to return the Mandan Chief Sheheke to his home, the Arikaras refused to let them pass, attacked and killed several. George Shannon, a fellow veteran of the Corps, was wounded badly, resulting in having his leg amputated in St. Louis.

[172] See above.

[173] For more on Bradbury's botanical collecting, see above.

Wednesday 7th August

It is very Sickly at this place. I was attacked to day with ague & fever.[174]

[174] In the nineteenth and early twentieth centuries, "ague and fever" was something of a catch-all term for a variety of diseases such as malaria or leptospirosis, often marked by a fever with fits of feeling alternately hot and cold.

Thursday 8th

Took an emetic this morning. Just at Sundown the Public Boat arrived, having on board Capt. Clemson & family &c.

Friday 9th

In the evening Mr. Rawlings arrived from St. Louis. Letters Received by him

1 from S. H. Sibley dated 3rd June '11
1 from Supt. of Indian Trade dated 1st July
1 from Same dated 2nd July
1 from General Clark dated 30th July
1 from Same dated 31st July
1 from R. H. Price dated 30th July
1 from J. G. Comegys dated 31st July

and Washington papers up to 6th July.

Saturday 10th August 1811

Received a letter to day from R. H. Price dated 17th June, enclosing Sundry Accounts to collect. I had another fit of the ague yesterday.

Tuesday 13th

William Wells was Released from confinement this evening. I missed my Ague to day and hope it has entirely left me.

Sunday 18th

Sent by Mr. Z. Woods[175] to day a packet of Letters under cover to General Clark care of Col. Kibby[176] St. Charles. Letters in the packet

1 to Dr. John H. Robinson Kaskaskia
1 to General Clark
1 to Mr. R. H. Price
1 to Mr. J. G. Comegys
1 to Supt. of Indian Trade, for copies of all which See Letter Book.

[175] Zadock Woods (see above).

[176] Timothy Kibby (d. 1813) apparently moved to St. Louis some time after 1805, when he was actively recruited by James Wilkinson to participate in the Aaron Burr conspiracy. In his affidavit of July 6, 1807, Kibby tells of several very secretive meetings with Wilkinson in which the general told him of Burr's "enterprising" nature and that an attack on Spanish Mexico from New Orleans was imminent. Wilkinson was offering him officer's rank, Kibby said, under the general command of Wilkinson himself. Kibby also testified that Wilkinson told him that Zebulon Pike was, in fact, going to Santa Fe to secure it as part of this plan. Kibby reiterated several times, he said, that he was "ready to march to any place provided it was for the honor and benefit of my country. . . . at this he appeared some what surprised and from that time he appeared to be more reserved in his conversation and less desirous of seeing me."

Kibby most likely knew other leaders in St. Louis in the first decade of the nineteenth century, since a number of them (such as William Clark, Benjamin Howard, and the Wilkinsons) had also served under General Anthony Wayne in warfare against Native American tribes in the Ohio Valley. Kibby served in a group called "Kibby's Spies," named for his cousin Ephraim Kibby. His military experience came in handy in the new territory as well. Rumors circulated that Napoleon had declared war on the United States (untrue, as it turned out); Secretary of War Henry Dearborn authorized enlisting almost 400 men in the territory to defend it. When Governor Meriwether Lewis received word in late November of 1808, he ordered leaders in the six districts to organize men for companies of infantry and riflemen. Besides remaining "in readiness," Lewis instructed Kibby, Daniel Morgan Boone and James Morrison (all militia field officers) to build as many stockades and blockhouses as they thought they would need to defend the riverfront hamlet in early 1809.

When the War of 1812 started some three years later, Territorial Governor Benjamin Howard ordered Kibby to again call out and organize a group of St. Charles militia known as Col. Kibby's Rangers to patrol the area between the Missouri and Salt rivers; Nathan Boone (Daniel Morgan Boone's younger brother and partner in the Boonslick salt-making operations) served under Kibby. As a merchant, he was also a supplier for many of the men whom Howard enlisted at the start of War of 1812. Howard told Secretary of War William Eustis that the government needed to pay these men and the cost of their supplies, unlike a few years previous when he had to put up his own credit. Most of the men bought their own horses, arms and such from Colonel Kibby. (Affidavit of Timothy Kibby, July 6, 1807, *Territorial Papers* 14, 133-136; Benjamin Howard to William Eustis, June 14, 1812, *Territorial Papers* 14, 566; Billon, *Annals of St. Louis in its Territorial Days*, 137; Houck, *A History of Missouri from the Earliest Explorations and Settlements*, vol. 2, 102, 392; Hurt, *Nathan Boone and the American Frontier*, 78-79.)

In this somewhat romanticized view of Fort Osage (in the Missouri State Capitol), Sibley throws open the doors of the Fort to connect the West with the United States and the gathered Osage. (Courtesy, State Historical Society of Missouri, Columbia)

Fort Osage August 14th 1811

Dr. John H. Robinson
Kaskaskia

> *Dr. Sir,*
>
> *Being in haste and Sickness, I forbear to comment on the extraordinary character of the calumny contained in the annexed "extract of a Letter from Captain E. B. Clemson to the Secretary of War dated 20th July 1810" which I have recently*

Received from Washington in a private Letter from my friend General Mason. You can Reflect on it at your leisure. So far as I am implicated in the charges made in Capt. C's Letter, an explanation is Requested of me by General Mason, which I am preparing to lay before him, and, you will Readily conceive (much better than I can inform you) how anxious I must feel to Refute this calumny with all possible dispatch. Whatever may be the Real character of Capt. Clemson, whether good or bad, is a matter of no moment in the present case; the honorable office which he holds necessarily gives a fictitious importance to his name, & Serves to conceal from the world his foibles and his vices; and you have Seen how effectually it has been interposed to Screen him from merited punishment.

I have to Request the favor of you to State _fully_ and _formally_ in the form of a deposition what you know Relative to the arrest of the two trading Boats alluded to in Capt. C's Letter, and get the Deposition properly authenticated. Although that affair is one of the few that has occurred at this place which I assumed to myself Some credit for having taken an active part in; yet I find it Somewhat difficult (it has been So long out of my thoughts) to Recall to my memory the principal circumstances. The following I believe are the most prominent, which I merely Sketch to Serve you as a kind of glimmering light by which to aid your Recollection of the affair.

1t. I have an imperfect idea that there was Some talk about the Boats before they arrived here among the Indians, and that <u>Paul</u>[177] was implicated in Some improper expression to the Indians Respecting them, but of this I will not Say any thing positive. You were in the way to hear and know this officially.

2d. The Boats arrived here Sometime in the month of October 1809. They were owned by or in charge of Rubedoux & Dorion.[178] One of them was destined to the Kansas, the other I believe to Some tribe farther up the River. On the evening of their arrival, there was Some Stir among the Osages indicating a disposition to commit Some act of violence on them of which you were apprised I believe by the owners. Probably the Osages insisted on Seeing their licenses.

3d. I think it was after Supper (I know it was dark and Raining a little) that you and myself went down to the Boats, having heard that the Indians were crowding about the -----??----, and I believe you prevailed on them to disperse. The Chief Nezumone and the Big Soldier appeared to be the Ring-leaders.

4th. I believe it was after we Returned from the Boats that you and P. Lorr and myself were Standing on the Hill at Block-House No. 5, So called, when Sansorielle joined us in great perturbation, and lamented that his people were like to commit Some act of violence on the Boats, observing particularly that the Chief and Big Soldier were the Ringleaders.

I desired Sansorielle to exert himself to prevent his people from committing any outrage on the Boats. I told him that they were licensed by the Governor to go and trade above here, and no one here had any Right to Stop them – that they were American Citizens, and as Such looked upon them as my Brothers, and considered it my duty to prevent the Osages from molesting them or their Boats. And I told him to go down and inform his People, that if they _did_ molest the Boats, I Should Shut them out of the Factory.[179] On this Sansorielle went to the Boats and did exert himself to prevail on the Chief and Big Soldier to disperse the Indians, and give over their attempt. They Remained peaceable that night.

5th. The Boats Started the next day about ten O'Clock & a number of Indians followed on the Shore, whether the Indians were armed or not at that time I know not as I did not See them, in fact I was busy making up my public accounts and had not time to attend to the Indians or their motions.

The Boats it appears were attempting to pass a Sand bar on which they frequently grounded, the Indians Seeing this, waded to them either for the purpose of assisting or insulting them, and Some Scuffling ensued between the Boatmen and them, in which one of the Indians Received a very Severe blow from a Boatpole just as the Boat was disengaged from the Sand bar. This exasperated the Rest of the Indians to Such a degree that they drove the Boats back, and followed them Running on the Shore.

It was then that I first Saw them, being called out by the general alarm. I Saw a number of the Indians Running to their lodges for their Guns, and Return to the River. They were in great Rage. At this moment a Report was circulating that one of the Indians had been killed. Fearing for the Safety of the Boats & Crews, I went to the River, you I believe with me, the Boats had just landed when we got down & the Indians collecting in great numbers on the landing. The Scene that followed must still be fresh in your memory. It is impossible for any person who witnessed that affair to doubt that your very great exertions prevented the Indians from committing a Serious act of violence on the Boats in question, and in my opinion prevented bloodshed.

6th. After this affair, and after you had dispersed the Indians, you and I went to their camp and found the principal Men assembled at the lodge of the Big Soldier. I expressed fully my opinion of the act they had just committed, and informed them that for the present I Should Shut the factory against them. I certainly did not conceal from them my displeasure.

7th. Heretofore there had been no interference from the Garrison except to place the Boats in view & in charge of one of the Sentries. Capt. Clemson certainly knew every important circumstance of this affair. He was looking on at the time you and myself were Scuffling with the Indians. You expressed Surprise that he did not lend Some aid to Repress the Indians. Perhaps it was you, that he observed "Such affairs are common & of no consequence" or words to that effect. I remember I expressed indignation of Such a proceedings being Suffered to pass under the eye of the Garrison.

8th. The next day you and I called on Capt. Clemson to Request his interference in passing the Boats, and proposed certain Steps to that end, which Capt. Clemson agreed to adopt in Substance, and did I believe adopt this was the first of his interference except pitting the Boats under guard for a Short time as mentioned above.

After the Boats had at length passed, you were present at my Room (it was after dark) when I had Some conversation with Ne-zu-mo-me and Sansorielle, who were apologizing for what their people had done, and begging me to permit them to trade. Perhaps you may Recollect the tenor of my observations to them.

9th. On the whole, you know that So far from exciting the Osages to Stop the Boats, I zealously exerted myself to prevent them. It is probable that Rubedoux & Dorion may have expressed to you some opinion as to the primary cause of the conduct of the Osages, & the eventual cause of their passing. If So, it will occur to you perhaps. I Still have a very faint recollection that Paul was much censured for Some Report he Spread among the Osages, relative to Some Boats that were expected here. If you know of any agency Paul had in the matter in question, you will be pleased to State it. And I must *also request the favor of you to dispose of what you know and believe generally as to Paul's general character. You will serve me much Sir if you will recollect the circumstances of that transaction as you remember them and State them fully and clearly in the form of a deposition. I have also to beg of you the favor to procure the most Respectable and unquestionable testimony in your power as to your own character & reputation; I know this is a delicate Request, but it will afford me infinite pleasure to have it in my power to defeat this calumny entire both as it relates to you and myself that I have prevailed oh myself to name it to you, and I hope you will comply. It is impossible to Say what secret prejudices have been made against you at Washington. Your Silence will give a Sanction to them. I have heard you mention Mr. Meigs as your friend – you ought to Rouse yourself, and procure the testimony of your friends in your behalf, Seeing that your enemies not content with the injury they have done your fortune are attempting <u>Secretly</u> to Ruin your character, it only wants an exertion to defeat their purposes, & this you will permit me to Say you owe to yourself, your friends & your enemies.*

Should you think proper to favor me by a compliance with these Requests, be pleased to enclose the depositions, and testimonials of your own good name, to General Clark at St. Louis, addressed and under Seal to me, with a Request to General Clark to keep them 'till I call for them in person. I expect to be in St. Louis Sometime in October next on my way to the Seat of Government, having obtained a furlow from the Superintendent. I propose to lay a full & complete refutation to these charges before him, and Shall be much disappointed if you do not put it in my power to vindicate your character before him and the Secretary of War. Forward these proofs by mail to General Clark with all possible dispatch.

Very Respectfully
Your Most Obedient Servant
G. C. Sibley

[177] Paul Loise, an interpreter particularly friendly to Chouteau concerns.

[178] Joseph Robidoux and Francois Dorion.

[179] Withholding trade was one of the strongest weapons trade factors had, and

worked with some success with the Osage; Governor Meriwether Lewis used this carrot-and-stick method to successfully bring the Osage into compliance with federal wishes when he first became territorial governor.

Fort Osage August 15th 1811

General William Clark
St. Louis

Dr. Sir,
Your two favors of 30th and 31st were duly handed me by Mr. Rawlings. They found me Severely afflicted with a fever, from which I am now thank God fast recovering.

I have Received directions from General Mason[180] to furnish to your order the Goods for the Osage Annuity for the year 1810; which I Suppose you have arranged to deliver through Mr. Chouteau at the Same time he delivers that for 1811.[181]

I have heard nothing from the Osages Since I wrote you last, except that the Big Osage had all Returned to their Towns, & had Seized on a parcel of Merchandise left there by the young Mr. Chouteau.[182] Whether this Story be true or false I will not undertake to Say. I am inclined to believe that the payment of these two annuities at this time, will Silence all objections the Osages may have had against the Treaty. It will give them a very handsome Supply and will no doubt give them the utmost Satisfaction.

I hope Mr. Chouteau will not fail to meet the Osages here before the middle of September at farthest. I have particular Reasons for wishing the annuities delivered by that time, it will hasten their departures for the Hunt and operate very much in their favor, and will put an end I hope to all doubts on the Subject of the Treaty. If they are obliged to leave the Hunt to come for their annuities they cannot bring their families and many of the poorest among them will not be at all benefited by the Annuity.

The Annuity ought to be delivered to the whole Tribe Men, Women and Children, and then they will <u>all</u> be benefited. If it is delivered only to the principal men, the distribution will be partial and unsatisfactory to the bulk of the Indians. I confidently expect Mr. Chouteau here very Soon now, and am beginning to look out for the Osages.

I Shall be at St. Louis in October next if I am Spared 'till then. It will be impossible for me to go down Sooner I hear. I Shall then have the pleasure to give you a full and Satisfactory explanation of the calumnious charges alluded to in one of your Letters. Having ever felt disposed to invite a Scrutiny of my conduct as a public Agent, I rejoice at the present opportunity of proving how Zealously I have labored for the public good. I can now claim the meed of praise without the fear of being charged with vanity.

Enclosed is a Letter for Dr. Robinson, which I have to Request the favor of you to have forwarded to Kaskaskia immediately by Mail.

You will excuse me I am Sure for Referring you to the two Patrons of the Boats that were detained by the Osages. Their names are I believe Joseph Rubedoux & Francois Dorea.[183] They are now in St. Louis most probably but will have left there on Some trading expedition before I can go down, therefore I Shall lose the benefit of their testimony relative to the exertions of I made to pass them by the Osages (which it is almost impossible they can be ignorant of) unless you will have the goodness to examine them. At any Rate, I Suppose Some of their Boatmen may be found in St. Louis, whose testimony may be Relied on.

Indisposition has prevented my completing a Report (which I have commenced) of my late tour to the Indian Country. I Shall exert myself to Send it to you by Mr. Chouteau. It will embrace the best description I am able to give of the famous Salines beyond the Arkansaw and a brief account of the Indians I Saw, and probably a Rough Sketch of my Route. I Should be unwilling for the hasty and perhaps imperfect Sketch I gave you of the Grand Saline to meet the public eye. When I have revised my Journal and drawn therefrom Such an account of those Salines as will Satisfy myself, then I shall have no objection to Show it to the Public.[184]

I remain Sir with Sincere Regard
Your Obedient Humble Servant
G. C. Sibley

[180] John Mason, Superintendent of Indian Trade.

[181] The annuities were annual payments made to Indian tribes like the Osages for cession of lands in earlier treaties. According to the 1808 treaty, the Great Osages were to receive $1,000 in goods each year, and the Little Osages another $500. These annuities were paid in trade goods, not cash. See "Introduction" above. Usually, the goods were purchased by the Office of Indian Trade and shipped from a central warehouse in Georgetown, District of Columbia. There are several possible explanations for the goods coming from Chouteau instead. Fort Osage was one of the busiest trade factories in the system, ranking among the highest in fur production, so it required more goods. It was also one of the farthest from headquarters; shipping such a

quantity of goods such a distance when they were available in St. Louis was far more costly. Clark was allied with the old-line merchant class in St. Louis already, and was a partner of Chouteau's in the Missouri Fur Company, so may have played a more active part in procuring the contract. This won't be the last time the government fell behind in its annuity payments, either; the Osages received nothing during the War of 1812. After the war, the government paid its overdue annuities.

[182] Probably Auguste Pierre Chouteau (1786-1837), the son of Pierre Chouteau. A West Point graduate, Chouteau resigned from the army in 1807 to follow his father and uncle in the fur business. He was part of the ill-fated 1807 expedition up the Missouri to return Chief Sheheke to the Mandans and establish a trading operation with them. He joined his father two years later on the same errand. He represented the Missouri Fur Company on a journey to the upper Missouri River in 1810; after his return to St. Louis, he never ventured to the upper Missouri again. His father procured for him his only government appointment, as sub-Agent to the Osage, but he soon resigned since it made his lucrative trade with the tribe illegal. Chouteau had a series of financial disasters starting in 1815, when he and partner Jules DeMun traveled the Arkansas River to the Rockies to trade with new tribes, but were captured by Spanish officials who kept their goods, imprisoned them in Santa Fe for some 48 days, and sent them home penniless. The same partners started a St. Louis store on a loan from Chouteau's brother Pierre, Jr., which went bankrupt. He received a two-year license to trade with the Osage and Kickapoo on the Arkansas River in 1822; he moved there, leaving his family (including wife and children) behind, and never returned. (Lecompte, "Auguste Pierre Chouteau," in *Dictionary of Missouri Biography*, 170-172.)

[183] Joseph Robidoux and Francois Dorion.

[184] The report was never published during Sibley's life. (Jones, *Prairie Puritan*, 87.)

Fort Osage August 16th 1811

Mr. R. H. Price
St. Louis

My Dr. Sir,
Your two letters of 17th June & 30th July are before me. I have exchanged Cottle's Note for Mr. Audrain's to the Same Amount payable at the next payment of the Troops here agreeably to your desire. But I think it prudent to keep the note till another <u>better</u> opportunity offers to Send it to you. As to the papers you Sent me by Capt. Clemson, I am Sorry to Say I do not believe you will ever get a Cent on any of them except Lorr's & not on

that soon or without a good deal of disputation. Although Lorr is as honest a creature as God ever made yet he is as you know very ignorant and contentious about money matters. I have not yet mentioned Robinson's account to him but Shall know in a Short time what can be done with him. As to the others, I had as leave have the Man in the Moon's Note as theirs. None of the _Gentlemen_ are here at this time.

You have no doubt Seen and Settled with Kingsley. I hope you may not be able to get away from St. Louis before October, for I Shall then be at St. Louis, and if possible will accompany you to Baltimore.

Cottle has Sold to Audrain, he has notified to Settle up his business immediately, for that it was contemplated to order him off and he has thought it prudent to Sell all his Stock on a long Credit at a great Sacrifice. What would Such a proceeding be thought of, where justice has a temple?

In haste
yours truly & ever
G. C. Sibley

August 18th

A better copy offering I have thought it best to Send you Audrain's Note. I have broke the Seal to add this & enclose the Note. Sent by Zadock Wood to St. Charles care of Colonel Kibby. The letter under cover to General Clark St. Louis

Fort Osage August 16th 1811

Mr. John G. Comegys
St. Louis

Dr. Sir,

I have duly Received your favor of 31st. I wondered from the tenor of your letter of March 5th and from what I learned from Mr. Hunt Respecting your Motions that you would certainly be gone from St. Louis long ago. Else did you imagine I Should have let Mr. Rawlings go down without my customary tribute of a Letter for you?

I Shall be in St. Louis October next dead or alive, that is without fail and Shall be much disappointed if I do not find you there. Some official duties that I cannot possibly bend or twist in any manner whatever forbid my going down Sooner. I wish you could make it convenient to come to Ft. Osage (Mr. Rawlings tells me you Said Something about it). I would undoubtedly accompany you back in October. By Mr. Chouteau, who is Soon expected here, I hope to Receive your

*promised favor, with my account current as mentioned in your
Letter. And by Mr. Chouteau's Return, you may expect to hear
from me pretty fully. The present is a doubtful conveyance, and
I do not choose to indulge myself now in any tittle tattle with
you lest it Should get lost on the way, and never Reach you. In
my late tour through the interior I Saw all the great wonders of
the West. I employ the most of my leisure hours to Swell my
notes, and making them intelligible for the eyes of my curious
friends. "Some of these days" I have no news to write you,
unless I Should <u>bore</u> you with Ft. Osage politics, which I am
Sensible you care very little about therefore I Shall Spare you.
Nothing has yet occurred particularly interesting to me, though
Some curious Scenes have lately been acted.*

> *Yours truly and ever*
> *G. C. Sibley*

Monday 19th

*A Trading Boat passed to day for the Sioux. <u>10</u> Kansas arrived here
yesterday from their Village, to See a little Tallow for Powder &c.*

Friday 23rd August 1811

*To day <u>4</u> Osages arrived from the Little Osage Village on the Nee Osho.[185]
They Report among other things that a young Creole by name Legaire has
been killed by the Pawnee or Some other tribe living beyond the Arkansaw.
A Mr. Kyowan arrived in 7 days from St. Louis, Reports that Mr. Chouteau
is not coming here, that about <u>50</u> of the Big Osages are at St. Louis on
business with the Governor.[186] The weather has been Remarkably cool the
last 5 or 6 days.*

[185] The Neosho River is in southwestern Missouri and eastern Oklahoma.

[186] Governor Benjamin Howard (see above).

Saturday 24th

*Mr. Sanguinett[187] arrived this evening from the Mandans. He Says that
Mr. Lewis[188] was only waiting for Mr. Henry[189] who was Soon expected in,
& then they Should Set out for St. Louis. Mr. Cottle & Family are to go
down in this Boat. Mr. C. having Sold out all his Stock at this place, and
Resolved to Return to his former Residence near the Mississippi.[190] Some
personal disputes over.*

\[187] Charles Sanguinet came from a fur-trading family. Most likely this is the
one generally referred to as Charles Sanguinet, Sr., even though he shared his
father's name. After spending his early years going to school in New Orleans

and running a "grocery business" (which, given the time, may have been a sobriquet for a liquor-selling operation), Sanguinet returned to St. Louis to enter the fur trade, later becoming a merchant, real estate developer and early developer of the lead-mining industry around Galena, Illinois. (Hyde and Conard, *Encyclopedia of Early Missouri*, vol. 4, 1984-1985.)

[188] Reuben Lewis.

[189] Andrew Henry (c. 1775-1833) was a partner in the Missouri Fur Company at this stage, having gained reasonable wealth from his lead mines around Ste. Genevieve. He went on the 1809 expedition up the Missouri and stayed in the wilderness for two years, including traveling to the Three Forks area where the Blackfeet Indians offered hostile greetings (the Blackfeet were noted for trying to keep white traders from advancing upriver). After his service in the territorial militia in the War of 1812, Major Henry found himself in debt, left to try unsuccessful efforts at mining and farming. He entered the fur business again with William Henry Ashley (a former partner in lead mining), which led to his proposing key innovations to Ashley that fundamentally transformed the way the fur trade was conducted. Thanks to Henry the company focused on trapping rather than trading with Native Americans, closed fortified trading posts in the field and dealt with trappers as independent businessmen. In short, he was the architect of the rendezvous system in the fur trade. Henry left the business before Ashley and Henry could turn a profit, leaving him destitute when he died in 1833. (Foley, "Andrew Henry," in *Dictionary of Missouri Biography*, 396-397.)

[190] It is unknown whether Cottle returned to Mississippi or not; however, he was living in St. Charles, Missouri, by 1818, and was sufficiently established there to be elected to the territorial legislature.

Andrew Henry was among those who transformed the fur trade from the one Sibley knew into the rendevous system, pictured here. (Used by permission, State Historical Society of Missouri, Columbia)

Sunday August 25th

Wrote per Mr. Sanguinett to General Clark See Letter Book page 81.

> *General William Clark*
> *St. Louis*
> *Mr. Sanguinett*
> *Fort Osage August 25th.1811.*

> *Dr. Sir,*

> *I beg leave to refer to my letter of the 15th Inst. which I forwarded to St. Charles by a Safe hand & doubt not but it will reach you duly. A Boat from above arrived here last evening and is to depart this morning for St. Louis, which affords me an opportunity to drop you a line in Haste. A Mr. Kayaway alias Brazau arrived here this morning of the 23rd. in 7 days from St. Louis, who informs that he saw Mr. Chouteau just before he Started, who told him that he had declined coming to Ft. Osage. He also Says that about <u>50</u> of the Big Osage were at St. Louis. Having no reason to question the veracity of this Gentleman and fearing that Something may have occurred to postpone the delivery of the Osage annuities, I am induced to address you this Letter principally for the purpose of urging the propriety of delivering these annuities by the middle of September.*

> *I have already informed the Superintendent of Indian Trade that I can discharge the annuities for 1810 & 1811 of the Factory, <u>on the presumption that they will certainly be paid early in September.</u>[191] So as to give me time to make out & forward my order for 1812,[192] which it is obvious I cannot well do 'till those annuities are paid, not knowing what articles will be wanted for them. Now if the delivery of these annuities be delayed 'till it is too late for me to order more goods, I shall not be able to pay them without very great inconvenience and perhaps not at all, and in the case I presume no little confusion will be created. You will observe that if the annuities are not paid from this Factory, I shall not have to order more goods for the next year and the Superintendent of Indian Trade Requires that my orders Shall Reach him by the middle of October, to allow ample time for him to lay in the Goods and Send them to Pittsburgh[193] early in the Spring. The present interruption of our foreign commerce,[194] will no doubt make it unusually difficult to procure Indian Goods in our Atlantic Cities, & it will therefore Require more time than usual to furnish the orders from the different Trading Houses.*

*The Superintendent of Indian Trade has instructed me
to use my best endeavors to obviate and remove whatever
dissatisfaction the operations of the Non intercourse Law may
cause occasion among the Indians in this quarter; it being
apprehended that the usual Supply of Canada Goods will be
Short this year,[195] and that the Agents of the British Government
may use this imitation as a means to excite unfriendly
dispositions against the U.S. among the Indians.[196] I beg leave to
Suggest this is another Strong motive for hastening the delivery
of the Osage annuities, as I am convinced they will be the
means of keeping the Osages quiet and firm in their attachment
to the U.S. particularly if they Receive them in time to answer
for their fall equipment.*

*You will at once See that these Remarks are offered Solely
with the view of preventing unnecessary confusion in my
business, and not by any means to interfere with the annuities
any further that they are connected at present with my duty.*

*About Sixty families of the Little Osage will be here by the
10th of Sept. they are now about 100 miles South-Southwest
of this place on a considerable branch of the Arkansaw called
Ne,osho,[197] where they are building their Town and intend to
Reside. Fear of the Mississippi Indians has driven them from this
vicinity.*

*I will be extremely thankful to you if you will Send me
a copy of the Law passed at the last Session of Congress
Respecting Indian Trading Houses.[198] I have heard that Some
material alterations have been made in the Law, & am anxious
to know them that I may not be groping in the dark.*

*If not already forwarded, I must beg of you to hasten on the
Goods for this Factory. I shall need the powder.*

*very Respectfully Sir
Your Obedient Humble Servant
G. C. Sibley*

---

[191] Sibley is offering to pay the annuities out of the stock of merchandise
already at Fort Osage, on the assumption that the government will either pay
for or replace them. Clearly, the Osage had been pressuring Sibley about
payment of the annuities and perhaps even threatening noncompliance with
other terms.

[192] The Office of Indian Trade regulations required factors to order goods only
once year, if at all possible.

[193] The fastest and cheapest way to transport goods west was by water, which had made Pittsburgh a thriving inland port. The advent of the steamboat will fuel this status.

[194] American tensions over British and French interference in ocean trade had been on the rise. Jefferson responded to pirating and impressments of sailors with the Non-Intercourse Act of 1807, which cut off trade with both with disastrous economic impact. Macon's Bill No. 2 sought to open trade with one or the other when it agreed to honor the rights of neutral powers on the high seas. Napoleon Bonaparte made such a promise (with apparently no intent of keeping it), and the Madison administration reopened trade with France in early 1811. Great Britain, who was at war with France, responded with a blockade of the New York harbor, which made Sibley's comment about the "present interruption of our foreign commerce" seem like a gross understatement. In June, 1812, the United States declared war on Britain.

[195] St. Louis merchants routinely carried goods procured in Canada. This was especially true of those involved in the fur trade, such as the Chouteaus; they preferred sending the furs north to cooler storage climates than to New Orleans, where they were more easily damaged from mold and such caused by heat and humidity.

[196] Sibley's instincts are good here; the British were using merchandise as a means to get closer to the Indians. The War Department reported to the House of Representatives in June 1812, "the supply of Indian goods . . . distributed during the last year by the British agents, in Upper Canada, to the Indian tribes, were more abundant than usual; and it is difficult to account for this extraordinary liberality on any other ground than that of an intention to attach the Indians to the British cause, in the event of a war with the United States." The department conveyed Clark's 1809 letter with its report in which he reported that "the British, who tell them that they pity them in their situation with the Americans because the Americans had taken their lands and their game; that they must join and send them off from their lands; they told the savages that the Americans could not give them a blanket, nor any thing good for their families." (*American State Papers, Indian Affairs*, 1, 797, 799.)

[197] The region where the Neosho and Verdigris rivers converge with the Arkansas was known as the Three Forks; the Arkansas Osage had lived in the general area for some time. (Rollings, *The Osage*, 195.)

[198] The 1811 "material alteration" dealt with the way furs were sold by the government. Previously, all furs purchased at Indian factories were to be sold at public auction after a minimum of three weeks advance notice. This

turned out to be a cumbersome system, especially for the furs purchased at remote factories, since transporting them to a center where they might bring the best price consumed money and time, and sometimes resulted in furs being stolen or damaged along the way. Under the 1811 law, private sales were now permitted, although most were still sold at public auction but with a shorter public notice beforehand. This clause would have had no real impact on Sibley, since St. Louis was a fur center anyway, and there would have been no advantage for the government to sell them privately instead of at auction in St. Louis. (Peake, *A History of the United States Indian Factory System*, 144-145.)

Friday 6th September

About 30 families of the Little Osages arrived this evening with Sansoreille from the Nee-Osho the rest of his band are to be here in a few days.

Saturday 7th

This Morning Settled all accounts with James Henderson and paid him $32.40 in Cash, being in full. About half past Ten, Henderson departed for St. Louis (on his way to Pennsylvania) in a canoe with Several other persons. Letters Sent by Henderson vizt.

1 to John Sibley (7 Sheets) dated 18th August & 6th September
1 to Genl Clark, dated 4th and 7th September
1 to Risdon H. Price dated 7th September

for copies of which See Letter book pages 25, 135, 159.

Ft. Osage September 7th, 1811

Mr. R. H. Price
St. Louis
per James Henderson

I have but one minute to enclose you the accounts you sent me Some time ago for collection. Nothing can be done here with them I find. I have annexed a Memo to Some Accounts for your information. It will be utterly impossible for any one except the Doctor to adjust that account. I have taken much pains to effect & Settlement but Lorr will not allow the Account without the credits Specified in the Memo. Really I don't know what to think of the matter it is a knotty affair I shall probably write you again soon.

Yours truly
G. C. S.

Wednesday 11th

A boat owned by Sundry persons arrived to day from St. Louis, which place they left about the 1st of August. This boat is going to the Pawnees &c. & is owned by Rudedous, Papan &c.[199] they have but a Small assortment of Indian Goods.

[199] The trading party headed by Joseph Robidoux.

Thursday September 12th, 1811

To day I went down the River with two Hunters in a canoe as far as the mouth of Fire Creek (which is about 6 1/2 miles) and Returned early in the afternoon.

Friday 13th

Early arrived a Batteau from St. Louis with a Small assortment of Merchandise for the Indian Trade above here.

After Breakfast, I took another trip <u>up</u> the River about 6 Miles to the mouth of Straw Cabin Creek.

Tuesday 17th

An Eclipse of the Sun to day about Noon. Another party of the little Osages arrived to day from the Ne-osho.

Thursday 19th

To day a Soldier (By name Porter) was committed to his mother earth. He died yesterday. This is the 2nd death that has occurred here, among the whites, for 3 years. Porter was aged and infirm.

Friday 20th September 1811

Just at Sun Set arrived Mr. Auguste Chouteau from St. Louis in a Small Barge. Letters Received

1 from General Clark dated 31st August (Covering orders to pay the Osage annuities &c.)[200]
1 from Governor Howard dated 3rd September covering Osage Treaty.[201]

See files.

Also Received from General Clark per Mr. Chouteau 3 packages of Merchandise & 19 kegs Powder for the Factory, and 1 Pair of Pistols & <u>$165</u> in Cash. Mr. Chouteau reports that the Canoe which left here on the 7th containing Sundry persons, got upset about <u>20</u> miles below here and that two of the persons in her (Mr. Smith's wife and child) were drowned,

*and the baggage of the whole totally lost. Of course the letters &c. that I
Sent by James Henderson were all lost.*

*Mr. Chouteau has come here to assist in the payment and delivery of the
Osage annuities for 1810 and 1811.*

[200] The Great Osage received $1,000 a year in trade goods and the Little
Osage received $500; apparently the goods were provided several times
during the year.

[201] This would have been the 1808 treaty negotiated by Chouteau, ratified by
the Senate in 1810.

Saturday 21st September 1811
*This day I dispatched 2 Runners to the Osage River to call all the Osages
there to this place to Receive their annuities.*

Tuesday 24th
*This evening arrived the Chief and leading Men from the Osage Towns, in
compliance with my message on the 21st.*

Wednesday 25th
*After dinner I delivered in presence of Mr. Audrain & Mr. Chouteau,
Merchandise to the Amount of $1000 Cost to the Big Osages and to the
Amount of $500[202] Cost to the Little Osage, in full discharge of the annuity
due them from the U. S. for the year 1810.*

[202] The amounts set by both the Clark and Chouteau versions of the 1808
treaty.

Thursday 26th
*This day I delivered in presence of Mr. Audrain and Mr. Chouteau,
Merchandise to the Amount of $1000 Cost to the Great Osage and to the
Amount of $500 Cost to the Little Osage, in full discharge of the annuity
due them from the United States for the year 1811, agreeably to the 5th
Article of the Treaty between the U. S. and the Osages.*

*As the band of Osages Residing on the Arkansaw was not Represented, I
prevailed on the Chiefs and head Men of the Big Osages who were present
to preserve a due proportion of the two Annuities for that tribe, and they
left about half thereof (Say the value $1000 Cost for them). This they left
in my hands to be delivered on demand to the proper Representatives of
that tribe.*

Friday 27th

This morning the Chiefs and head men of the Great & Little Osages Signed Triplicate Receipts for the Merchandise delivered them yesterday & the day before. I took occasion to make Some enquiries of them by desire of Governor Howard Respecting the Mill, Block Houses,[203] &c. but could obtain from them no decisive answer to them. It appears though most probably they would generally prefer to have those things at the Osage River Rather than at this place. However they are divided on the Subject; and the wishes of the band Residing on the Arkansaw (which constitutes a full half of the Osages) is unknown. No doubt _they_ would prefer that the Mill, Smith, &c. Should be fixed in _their_ Town. Perhaps a Strict compliance with the Treaty would be best after all. For the _3_ Tribes will hardly ever agree to any one place, and it would be useless to fix those things in their Villages, where it would be impossible for them to be kept in Repair without Some person was kept there for the purpose &c. &c. &c. &c.

> [203] A mill, blockhouse and blacksmithing operation were all among the services the United States was to provide, according to the 1808 treaty. Since they still had not been constructed, the government was trying to determine the best location for them, for they would service both the Great and Little Osage.

Saturday 28th

Mr. Chouteau Started to day for St. Louis with him went Mr. Bissell[204] and Mr. F. Audrain. By Mr. Chouteau I Sent a Trunk and Package to address of General Clark. The Trunk contains Some Clothes &c. the Packet, Sundry Letters Vizt. 1 to Governor Howard, 1 to Supt. of Indian Trade, 1 to General Clark, 1 to Mr. Price, 1 to Mr. Comegys, 1 to John Sibley, which were all written in Haste and copies kept of only the one to Supt. Indian Trade.

> [204] Lewis Bissell (see above).

Sunday 29th

To day, all the Osages departed, for the Winter Hunt, leaving us at Fort Osage in peace and quiet.

Tools for Teachers:
Using This Book in the Classroom

By Jann Rudd Weitzel

The journals of George Sibley offer history teachers an extraordinary opportunity to engage students in historical thinking. Reading Sibley's words and taking into account the times, places, peoples, and events of the early 1800's allow students to ask real questions and gather evidence to answer those questions. The National Standards for History, Part One, Chapter Two states that "well-written historical narratives are interpretative, revealing conditions, changes, and consequences, and explaining why things happened as they did. Following such narratives, and analyzing the events they describe and the explanations they offer, promote important skills in historical thinking."

The National Council for Social Studies recognizes ten thematic strands in social studies. Each of the ten strands are quoted below and study options, based on the Sibley Journals, are suggested.

1) Culture
   Social Studies programs should include experiences that provide for the study of culture and cultural diversity.

   Create of list of the different Indian tribes with which Sibley made contact during his years at Fort Osage. Choose one of the tribes and through outside research, compare Sibley's encounters with that tribe with what history tell us about them. For instance, on October 10, 1808, Sibley details the need to "Shut the Store" against a tribe of Kansas Indians because of their "insolent and violent conduct." Compare his experience with the accounts of others who dealt with the Kansas Indians.

Sibley makes reference to "Smok[ing] the Pipe of Peace together" with "Chiefs & Warriors of the Big & Little Osages & the Kansas" in his Sept 27, 1808 entry. Research this practice and explain the meaning of this event.

Compare the living conditions of the Indians with that of the United States officials at Fort Osage. Conduct additional research and describe in journal form a typical month in the life of an Osage Indian man or woman. Compare that to a month from Sibley's journal.

Choose an event from Sibley's journals and write that event from the point of view of an Indian. How might the situation be the same or different through his/her eyes?

Review Sibley's letters dated January 28, March 1 and May 4, 1811. Summarize his request to purchase a "Negro boy Boch." Conceptualize this event based on historical fact.

2) Time, Continuity and Change
   Social studies programs should include experiences that provide for the study of the ways human beings view themselves in and over time.

Discuss the purpose of journaling. Why did George Sibley keep his journal? For whom and why did he write it? What do we learn about Sibley as a man, as an explorer, as a friend to the Osage Indians? Examine the use of factual account versus his own personal feelings. Explain which is more prevalent and explain why you think this is so.

Imagine that you have kept a journal for the past 3 years. What would readers of your words learn about you? If your journal was discovered two hundred years after you wrote it, what types of information might the reader learn about where and how you lived?

Review Sibley's journals and explain, either in writing or through a series of drawings, how the lives of the Indians changed from 1808 to 1811. Would these changes have happened regardless of the influences of the white man? What positive changes occurred due to the presence of the United States government in the area of Fort Osage? What negative outcomes occurred?

3) People, Places, and Environments
Social studies programs should include experiences that provide for the study of people, places, and environments.

Using Sibley's words, chart his journey from Pittsburgh to Fort Osage. Design a map that depicts the locations of land and water locations mentioned by Sibley. Identify the dates when Sibley and his party either landed or passed each site.

Create a 3-dimentional topographical map representing the travels of George Sibley to Fort Osage.

Create a 3-dimentional model of Fort Osage and the Indian villages that surrounded it.

Read the entry from Friday, July 29, 1808. Imagine that you were a newspaper reporter who witnessed this scene. Write a story for your paper.
        or

Imagine that you are an artist traveling with Sibley to record his experiences. Depict in a drawing what occurred on July 29th.

On Saturday, September 3, 1808, Sibley writes, "Capt. Clemson, Mr. Lewis & myself took two Men & a Canoe and went the River about 3 miles to a Bluff, which on examination, we all think a fine Spot for the Fort." Consider the needs of the men who were to live at Fort Osage. Explain what "a fine Spot for the Fort" might be.

Look for and identify large time gaps in the journals. For instance, Sibley does not write an entry between December 31, 1808 and March 13, 1809. What factors might account for this lack of entries during such a long period of time?

Make a list of the land and water locations mentioned by Sibley during his trip to Fort Osage. Categorize the names based on their possible derivations. Included might be "names of famous people," "physical descriptions of the locations" or "references to European locations."

Investigate the geographical locations of the various Indian tribes mentioned by Sibley. What characteristics of the land and surrounding area would the Indians have looked for when choosing a location for their villages?

4) Individual Development and Identify
   Social studies programs should include experiences that provide for the study of individual development and identity.

Throughout Sibley's journals, he references the Big Hunt which took place yearly. What was this? Who participated? Who did not participate and why? How did this event provide for the basic needs of the Osage Indians during the rest of the year?

Reread the account of May 6, 1811. Describe in your own words what took place and, based on the words of George Sibley concerning the events leading up to this event, theorize as to the cause of the viciousness of the attack.

Although Sibley did not specifically address the religious practices of the Indians, research the belief systems of one Indian tribe and find instances in the journals that reference those beliefs and practices.

5) Individuals, Groups, and Institutions
Social studies programs should include experiences that provide for the study of interactions among individuals, groups, and institutions.

The United States government had an effect on the lives of the Osage Indians. What types of effects, both positive and negative, did the government have on the lives and livelihoods of the Indians?

6) Power, Authority and Governance
Social studies programs should include experiences that provide for the study of how people create and change structures of power, authority, and governance.

In his September 14 and 15, 1808 entries, Sibley describes the signing of a treaty with the Osage Indians. Using both Sibley's words and information obtained through outside research, write and produce a play depicting this event.

Discuss the effect that language had on the interactions with the Indians being mindful that the treaties were written in English, a language that the Indians neither spoke nor read. Find entries from Sibley journals that concern the use of the written or spoken word and discuss whether the situation might have been different if a common language had been available. What if any advantage did the white man have over the Indians in these situations?

Examine the relationship between the officials of the United States and the Indian tribes. For what did the Indians rely on the white man? Was this a situation desired by either side? Explain the feelings and actions of the Indian nations based on the loss of land, wild life, and personal integrity. Examine Sibley's words and deeds and explain why he was viewed as a friend to the Osage Indians.

Discuss the power structure the existed at Fort Osage. Who was in power and over whom?

7) Production, Distribution, and Consumption
   Social studies programs should include experiences that provide for the study of how people organize for the production, distribution, and consumption of goods and services.

Create a list of the food products mentioned by Sibley in his journals and research the food preservation techniques used in the early 1800's. Create a "how-to" manual for both the preservation and preparation of foods common to this time and location.

Throughout his journals, Sibley mentions the types of items he traded to the Indians. Discuss the items and why the Indians wanted those items. Consider items in various categories, such as weapons; farming equipment; food, tobacco, and alcohol; and personal items such as blankets and cloth.

Create a list of the types of pelts traded by the Indians to Sibley. Research the use and importance of these pelts. Compare the items that the Indians received in trade for the different types of pelts and develop a theory as to the relative importance of each variety of animal.

8) Science, Technology, and Society
Social studies programs should include experiences that provide for the study of relationships among science, technology, and society.

After creating a map of Sibley's travels from Pittsburgh to Fort Osage and identifying the date on which he arrived at each location, determine that rate at which he was able to travel, whether by land or water. Approximately how many miles per day did he travel from May 26, 1808, until September 2, 1808?

List the various types of boats discussed in Sibley's journals. Research the vessels and describe the appearance and use of each in written form and then create a scale drawing comparing and contrasting the boats. Among the types of water vessels might be canoes, keel boats, and barges.

Research the weather patterns during the years Sibley lived at Fort Osage. Take into consideration the population of the area and the physical characteristics of the land. Also consider the lack of modern conveniences such as electricity, running water, and heat. Describe what it might have been like to live in this environment.

Find examples of journal entries that state specific dates, times, and locations, such as Saturday, June 11, 1808. Using the information given, determine Sibley's rate of travel. Compare that to a man traveling the same distance today.

Examine the entry from Tuesday, June 28. Sibley describes Cincinnati as a "flourishing town contain[ing] about 400 Houses besides Several elegant Public Buildings." Using historical data concerned with average family size in 1808, compute the size of Cincinnati when Sibley visited to the city of Cincinnati today. Propose theories as to the successful growth of the city.

Discuss the various measurements used during the early 1800's. For instance, consider a pack of deerskins, a carrot of tobacco, the distance referred to as within gunshot of a location, a barrel and a bushel of corn, a head of cattle, a stock of hogs. What do these measurements mean? What other types of measurements were common in the early 1800's?

Research medical practices mentioned by Sibley in his journal. Describe those practices and others common at that time. Include the use of a "powerful dose of salts" (November 10, 1810), how a gunshot wound might have been treated (December 11, 1810), the account of taking an emetic as a remedy for "ague and fever" (August 8, 1811), and Sibley's request for "Gold Rings" for his ears to prevent his eyesight from failing (Letter to Comegys dated January 8, 1811).

9) Global Connections
   Social studies programs should include experiences that provide for the study of global connections and interdependence.

Discuss the interdependence between the United States and the Indians. On what did each depend on the other? Find examples from Sibley's journals to support your assertions.

10) Civic Ideals and Practices
Social studies programs should include experiences that provide for the study of the ideals, principles, and practices of citizenship in a democratic republic.

Describe the rights and responsibilities of both the Indians and the United States government in their relationship at Fort Osage.

Give specific examples of the ways in which George Sibley attempted to help the Osage Indians. Were his efforts successful?

Works Consulted

American State Papers, Indian Affairs. 2 vols. Washington, D.C.: Gales and Seaton, 1834.

Anderson, James. "Fort Osage: An Incident of Territorial Missouri." *Bulletin of the Missouri Historical Society* 4 (April, 1948): 174-176.

Billon, Frederic. *Annals of St. Louis in its Territorial Days, from 1804 to 1821.* St. Louis: Frederic L. Billon, 1888.

Brackenridge, Henry Marie. *Brackenridge's Journal up the Missouri, 1811.* Early Western Travels, 1748-1846, ed. Reuben Gold Thwaites, vol. 6. Cleveland: Arthur H. Clark Company, 1904.

Chittenden, Hiram Martin. *The American Fur Trade of the Far West.* 2 vols. New York: The Press of the Pioneers, Inc., 1935.

Clark, William. *Dear Brother: Letters of William Clark to Jonathan Clark.* Edited with Introduction by James J. Holmberg. New Haven: Yale University Press, 2002.

-----. *Westward with Dragoons: The Journal of William Clark.* Introduction by Kate L. Gregg. Fulton, Missouri: Ovid Bell Press, 1937.

Cullum, George W. *Notices of the Biographical Register of Officers and Graduates of the U. S. Military Academy at West Point, from its establishment, March 16, 1802, to the Army reorganization of 1866-67.* New York: D. Van Nostrand, 1868.

Dictionary of Missouri Biography. Edited by Lawrence O. Christensen, William E. Foley, Gary R. Kremer, and Kenneth H. Winn. Columbia: University of Missouri Press, 1999.

Douglas, Walter. "Manuel Lisa." *Missouri Historical Society Collections* 3 (1911): 233-268.

-----. "Manuel Lisa." *Missouri Historical Society Collections* 3 (1911): 367-406.

"Earliest Picture of St. Louis." *Glimpses of the Past* 8 (June-September, 1941): 71-98.

Early History of Greater Kansas City: The Prophetic City at the Mouth of the Kaw. Vol. 1. Kansas City: Charles P. Deatherage, 1927.

Foley, William E. *A History of Missouri.* Vol. 1, *1673-1820.* Columbia: University of Missouri Press, 1971.

Foley, William E. and C. David Rice. *The First Chouteaus: River Barons of Early St. Louis.* Urbana: University of Illinois Press, 1983.

Fowler, Jacob. *The Journal of Jacob Fowler, narrating the adventure from Arkansas through the Indian Territory, Oklahoma, Kansas, Colorado, and New Mexico, to the sources of the Rio Grande del Norte, 1821-22.* Edited by Elliott Coues. New York: Francis P. Harper, 1898. Reprint, Fairfield, Washington: Ye Galleon Press, 2000.

Gregg, Kate L. "Building the First Fort West of the Mississippi." *Missouri Historical Review* 30 (June, 1936): 345-364.

-----. "The Missouri Reader: Indians in the Valley, Part 1." *Missouri Historical Review* 39 (October, 1944): 75-97.

-----. "The Missouri Reader: Indians in the Valley, Part 2." *Missouri Historical Review* 39 (January, 1945): 224-245.

-----. "The War of 1812 on the Missouri Frontier, Part I." *Missouri Historical Review* 33 (October, 1938): 3-22.

-----. "A Man Named Johnson." *Missouri Historical Review* 37 (January, 1942): 150-161.

-----. "The History of Fort Osage." *Missouri Historical Review* 34 (July, 1940): 439-488.

Hempstead, Stephen. "I At Home: Part 2." *Bulletin of the Missouri Historical Society* 14 (October, 1957): 59-96.

-----. "I At Home: Part 4." *Bulletin of the Missouri Historical Society* 14 (April, 1958): 272-288.

-----. "I At Home: Part 7." *Bulletin of the Missouri Historical Society* 22 (October, 1965): 61-94.

Houck, Louis. *A History of Missouri from the Earliest Explorations until the Admission of the State into the Union.* Chicago: R. R. Donnelley, 1908.

Hurt, R. Douglas. *Nathan Boone and the American Frontier.* Missouri Biography Series, ed. William E. Foley. Columbia: University of Missouri Press, 1998.

-----. "Seeking Fortune in the Promised Land: Settling the Boon's Lick Country, 1808-1825." *Gateway Heritage* 13 (summer, 1992): 4-19.

Hyde, William and Howard L. Conard. *Encyclopedia of the History of St. Louis: A compendium of history and biography for ready reference.* New York: Southern History Company, 1899.

Indian Treaties, 1778-1883. Compiled and edited by Charles J. Kappler. New York: Interland Publishing, Inc., 1972.

Jackson, Donald. "Journey to the Mandans, 1809: The Lost Narrative of Dr. Thomas." *Bulletin of the Missouri Historical Society* 20 (April, 1964): 179-192.

-----, ed. *Letters of the Lewis and Clark Expedition with Related Documents, 1783-1854.* Urbana: University of Illinois Press, 1962.

"Jean Baptiste Roy—St. Louis Fur Trader." *Bulletin of the Missouri Historical Society* 3 (April, 1947): 85-93.

Jefferson, Thomas. *The Works of Thomas Jefferson in 12 Volumes.* Vol. 9. Edited by Paul Leiceister Ford. New York: G. P. Putnam's Sons, 1905.

Jones, Jr., Charles T. *George Champlain Sibley: The Prairie Puritan (1782-1863).* Independence, Missouri: Jackson County Historical Society, 1970.

"The Journals of Jules De Mun." Translated by Nettie H. Beauregard, edited by Thomas Maitland Marshall. *Missouri Historical Society Collections* 5 (1927-1928): 311-326.

Lavender, David. "Ramsay Crooks' Early Ventures on the Missouri River: A Series of Conjectures." *Bulletin of the Missouri Historical Society* 20 (January, 1964): 91-106.

"Letters of William Carr Lane, 1819-1831." *Glimpses of the Past* 7 (July-September, 1940): 47-114.

Lewis, Meriwether and William Clark. *The Definitive Journals of Lewis and Clark.* Vol. 8, *Over the Rockies to St. Louis.* Edited by Gary E. Moulton. Lincoln: University of Nebraska Press, 1986.

Lionberger, Isaac. "Advertisements in the Missouri Gazette, 1808-1811." *Missouri Historical Society Collections* 6 (1928-1931): 19-32.

Luttig, John C. *Journal of a Fur-Trading Expedition on the Upper Missouri, 1812-1813.* Edited by Stella M. Drumm. Preface and Notes by Abraham P. Nasatir. St. Louis: Missouri Historical Society, 1920. Reprint, Argosy-Antiquarian Ltd., 1964.

"Missouri History Not Found in Textbooks." *Missouri Historical Review* 21 (April, 1927): 501-517.

"Missouriana: Mohongo's Story." *Missouri Historical Review* 36 (October, 1941): 200-231.

Oglesby, Richard Edward. *Manuel Lisa and the Opening of the Missouri Fur Trade.* Norman: University of Oklahoma Press, 1963.

Peake, Ora Brooks. *A History of the United States Indian Factory System, 1795-1822.* Denver: Sage Books, 1954.

Peterson, Charles E. "Manuel Lisa's Works." *Bulletin of the Missouri Historical Society* 4 (January, 1948).

Potter, Tracy. *Sheheke, Mandan Indian Diplomat: The Story of White Coyote, Thomas Jefferson, and Lewis and Clark.* Washburn, North Dakota: Fort Mandan Press, 2003.

"Record of Persons Killed While Engaged in the Fur Trade and Inland Trade to Mexico." *Glimpses of the Past* 9 (January-June, 1942): 35-39.

Robertson, R. G. *Competitive Struggle: America's Western Fur Trading Posts, 1764-1865.* Boise, Idaho: Tamarack Books, 1999.

Rollings, Willard H. *The Osage: An Ethnohistorical Study of Hegemony on the Prairie-Plains.* Columbia: University of Missouri Press, 1992.

Ronda, James P. *Astoria and Empire.* Lincoln: University of Nebraska Press, 1990.

-----. *Lewis and Clark Among the Indians.* Lincoln: University of Nebraska Press, 1984.

Sheehan, Bernard W. *Seeds of Extinction: Jeffersonian Philanthropy and the American Indian.* Chapel Hill: University of North Carolina Press, 1973.

Steffen, Jerome O. *William Clark: Jeffersonian Man on the Frontier.* Norman: University of Oklahoma Press, 1977.

Stevens, Walter. "The Missouri Tavern." *Missouri Historical Review* 15 (January, 1921): 241-276.

Tabeau, Pierre Antoine. *Tabeau's Narrative of Loisel's Expedition to the Upper Missouri.* Edited by Heloise Abel, translated by Rose Abel Wright. Norman: University of Oklahoma Press, 1939.

Territorial Papers of the United States. Vol. 13, The Territory of Louisiana-Missouri, 1803-1806. Compiled and edited by Clarence Edwin Carter. Washington, D. C.: Government Printing Office, 1949.

Territorial Papers of the United States. Vol. 14, The Territory of Louisiana-Missouri, 1806-1814. Compiled and edited by Clarence Edwin Carter. Washington, D. C.: Government Printing Office, 1949.

The Lewis and Clark Journey of Discovery, www.nps/jeff/LewisClark2

Ward, Adolphus W. Ward and A. R. Waller. Vol. 16, *Cambridge History of English and American Literature.* New York: G. P. Putnam's Sons, 1907-1921. Reprint, New York: Bartleby.com, 2000.

Wherry, Maggie M., William M. Wherry, Joseph A. Wherry, and John M. Wherry. "Mackey Wherry, By His Grandchildren." *Bulletin of the Missouri Historical Society* 8 (April, 1952): 264-269.

Wishart, David J. *The Fur Trade of the American West, 1807-1840: A Geographical Synthesis.* Lincoln: University of Nebraska Press, 1979.

Wolferman, Kristie C. *The Osage in Missouri.* Columbia: University of Missouri Press, 1997.

"Zebulon Pike: Hard-Luck Explorer or Successful Spy?" National Park Service, The Lewis and Clark Journey of Discovery: http://www.nps.gov.

Index